# Involvement with Music

## ESSENTIAL SKILLS AND CONCEPTS

**ALFRED BALKIN**
Western Michigan University

**JACK A. TAYLOR**
Florida State University

Houghton Mifflin Company    Boston
Atlanta  Dallas  Geneva, Ill.  Hopewell, N.J.  Palo Alto  London

To our students — for their inquisitiveness, enthusiasm, and inspiration
To our colleagues — who believe in what we do and encourage us to do it
To music itself — for its life-enriching powers

---

Library of Congress Catalog Card Number: 73-9408     ISBN: 0-395-16989-5

# Contents

*In Chapter One you will learn to create, notate, and perform short compositions based on sounds gathered from the immediate environment. These compositions will last from fifteen to sixty seconds and will incorporate both vocal and nonvocal sounds.*

*The forming of small ensemble groups will enable you to restructure your individual compositions into group compositions, still within defined time limitations. Selection of sounds for inclusion in group compositions is accomplished through careful listening and evaluation.*

*Your increasing awareness of aesthetic principles, (for example, the necessity of silence in relation to sound, the importance of both unity and variety in a musical composition) will help guide your creative efforts. You will also learn specific musical terms in starting what will be a rapidly expanding vocabulary of musical concepts.*

*In Chapter Two you will become familiar with every facet of time (duration) and formal time notation that is likely to occur in your musical performing experience. These include note values, time signatures, tempo terms, accents, syncopation, and a variety of other musical concepts related to time. Distinctions between count, beat, and rhythm are emphasized.*

*You will create, notate, and perform a large number of rhythmic compositions. Included in the book are also many rhythmic examples—excerpts from both popular and classical music. Immediate feedback on the accuracy of much of your performing of compositions and rhythmic examples is found on the accompanying recordings.*

*At the end of Chapter Two you should be able to deal successfully with the rhythm of nearly any piece of popular music (folk, rock, show, country), children's music, and much classical music. You will be well on your way to becoming musically proficient.*

*In Chapter Three through the use of a keyboard instrument, you will begin to discover and understand such concepts as pitch, interval, melody, two-line harmony, key signature, transposition, and the pentatonic scale.*

*You will learn to identify and play all pitches from notation on the grand staff. You will compose melodies and accompaniments, write lyrics, and also devise finger patterns for playing these creations.*

*The central focus of Chapter Three is the in-depth performance of three folk songs (built on pentatonic scales and played on the black keys) which you can approach in a variety of ways to learn a variety of musical concepts.*

*Fourteen additional pentatonic songs (all on black keys) in Appendix B are available for expansion of your repertoire. At the end of Chapter Three you will be capable of playing any of the fifty-five song melodies found in Appendix C.*

## 4 Songs in Time: Melody and Harmony at the Keyboard, Ukulele, and Autoharp/Chromaharp 141

*In Chapter Four, you will learn to recognize and play all major and minor chords both from chord symbols and staff notation. The chords are first introduced in root position and then in inversions. Special emphasis is placed on the major seventh chord because of its frequent use in popular music. Diminished and augmented chords also are presented.*

*You will learn to play all of the major and minor scales, and you will develop an understanding of their relationship to chords. Specific criteria are established for the selection of certain harmonies to accompany particular melodies. The ear, however, is stressed as the final decision-maker in choosing chord patterns. Diversity of harmonic possibilities is demonstrated and encouraged.*

*You will be presented with a number of new concepts such as form, phrase, sequence, nonchord tones, arpeggio, key tone, legato, and staccato.*

*At the end of Chapter Four, you will find yourself able to play both the melody and harmony of almost any song in Appendix C.*

## 5 Sounds in Time:    Twentieth Century Contributions 229

*In Chapter Five you will become acquainted with the blues progression through analysis, playing in a variety of keys, and composing a blues song.*

*Composition and analysis, with particular emphasis on contemporary sounds and techniques, is the main thrust of Chapter Five. You will create a number of short works using such concepts as twelve-tone row, modal scale, whole-tone scale, modulation, multimetric time signatures, nontriadic harmony (chords built on intervals other than thirds), and bitonality. Musique Concrète and electronic music are also discussed because of their place in twentieth-century music. The rondo form is introduced and explored.*

*By the end of Chapter Five you will find that your creative thinking processes have been expanded, and the continuum of skills and concepts which has developed from previous chapters is now in clearer perspective. At this point* Involvement with Music *will have come full circle . . . back to environmental sounds.*

Appendix C Songs 301

# Introduction

For many people, listening to music is no longer an occasional occurrence but a major everyday pastime. The abilities to perform and create music—as well as listen to it—provide even greater incentive to incorporate music into one's life. *Involvement with Music* guides the individual in developing these abilities. From the beginning, when sounds and their durations are described as the foundations for all music, the student learns to perceive music as a unique sensory experience which grows more intelligible as a direct result of his own expanding facility with musical skills and concepts. Skills lead to concepts, and concepts pave the way for new skills. More directly stated, doing leads to knowing, and knowing leads to more doing. *In-depth understanding* is the goal.

The basic approach of *Involvement with Music* is consistent with twentieth-century music education practices and philosophies such as those developed by Carl Orff, Zoltan Kodaly, the Contemporary Music Project, R. Murray Schafer, and the Manhattanville Music Curriculum Program. These approaches also require "total immersion" into the processes of being a musician—performing music, listening to music, composing music, and evaluating music with critical perception.

*Involvement with Music* was conceived as a new way of presenting fundamentals of music to education majors and was designed to enlarge the scope of the traditional curriculum to include twentieth-century methodologies. Feedback from three years of testing in two large universities has been an indispensable aid in revising, clarifying, and refining the program. The auto-tutorial format has been enthusiastically endorsed by students and teachers because of the shift in primary responsibility for learning music from within the classroom to outside the classroom, and because students were able to set their own learning pace.

Comments from students and colleagues around the country have also resulted in a broadening of the population base of *Involvement with Music* to include:

1. Music majors or minors studying elementary music theory.
2. Non-music majors studying fundamentals of music.
3. Students of music appreciation who require a focal point for a variety of related listening experiments.

Music majors in a basic theory course will benefit from the auto-tutorial nature of both the text and the accompanying recordings.

In a combined course in music fundamentals and music for children, the book can be used for learning the fundamentals while most of the classroom time is focused on methodology. The basic methodology of the *Involvement with Music* program can be restructured and adapted for use with children. (See Appendix A for model Lesson Plans for each chapter. These lessons can be practice-taught in the college classroom and the public school classroom.)

Students may use this text as a self-instructional program in music fundamentals for a music appreciation course, thereby allowing emphasis on aesthetic and historical aspects of music during class time. In this way, music fundamentals and music appreciation can provide mutual reinforcement.

*Objectives*

**Chapter One** encourages free exploration of sounds with the purpose of a simple exposure to the basic concept of music, *sounds in time*. Using a wide spectrum of sound sources to create informal or environmental sounds, the student immediately becomes aware of sound potential, especially its relationship to organization within time.

**Chapter Two** introduces formal notation of time and presents the student with a broad and functional vocabulary of notes and durations. *Involvement with Music* shares the viewpoint of Paul Hindemith and other leading musician-educators that the durational element of music is basic, and that to conceptualize and manipulate time is the most vital aspect of learning music. Mature musical growth is highly contingent upon a secure knowledge of time. Once the student has acquired this knowledge, learning other aspects of music should prove quite successful.

**Chapter Three** introduces students to the concepts of pitch, melody, and linear harmony. The keyboard becomes a learning tool for pitches, intervals, key signatures, transposition, and the pentatonic scales. Creating simple melodies, lyrics, and accompaniment, and devising keyboard finger patterns are included in the students' experiences.

**Chapter Four** extends and further develops the melodic and harmonic skills established in Chapter Three. Through the keyboard, basic chords, including those necessary for playing today's popular music (such as the major seventh chord and the suspension), are introduced. The baritone ukelele and the Auto-harp™/Chromaharp™ are presented as instruments which provide chordal accompaniments. Major and minor scales are introduced as basic materials for the composition of melodies and harmonies. A variety of chordal accompaniments, the use of nonchord tones, and the techniques of harmonizing a melody (lacking chord symbols) are examined thoroughly. The ear is emphasized as the ultimate decision maker in selecting satisfactory harmonies. Form as an organizational device in composition is explored throughout this chapter.

You will notice in Chapter Four that chords are first introduced in root position. The authors are well aware that initially, this is not the most desirable pianistic technique. But from the standpoint of accurately conceptualizing chords, it *is* the most desirable technique. When inversions are introduced, the student can successfully relate inversions and root position without confusion.

He is also made to realize why inversions often are more desirable pianistically and musically. He learns that the use of inversions means less finger movement and therefore greater ease of playing.

**Chapter Five** deals with a number of contemporary sounds and techniques. These techniques include twelve-bar blues progression, the use of non-triadic chords (those built upon intervals other than thirds), chromatic and whole tone scales, modal scales (which are particularly common in contemporary popular and "serious" music), bitonal chords (combinations of traditional chords, one built upon the other), the twelve-tone row, musique concrete, and electronic music. Chapter Five broadens the student's creative thinking and concurrently refocuses and reinforces the continuum of skills and concepts developed in the previous chapters.

The objectives in the foregoing chapter descriptions are redefined at the beginning of each of the five chapters. These objectives are presented as summaries of musical learnings that the student can expect to achieve as a result of specific experiences in that chapter. After completing those experiences, the student may refer to the chapter's objectives and determine whether the anticipated musical learnings have been attained.

# To the Student

*Involvement with Music* is a freely structured programmed text which provides information in a logical sequence of sections called "frames." Frames are numbered consecutively throughout the book, and each one either presents concepts for the reader to learn or directs him to participate actively in the development of a musical skill.

Many frames require responses. These may take the form of written quizzes, or they may ask you to compose music. The correct responses and musical examples appear on a grey background immediately following the questions. Within other frames this symbol ◎ will direct you to listen to a section on one of the recordings accompanying this text. Unless otherwise indicated, the recording should be heard *after* the frame has been read.

The recordings provide a strong aural reinforcement to many of the experiences in the text. *In Chapter Two the recordings also provde an introduction to the sounds of orchestral instruments, heard solo and in small ensembles.* The text truly becomes self-instructional when the conscientious student listens carefully to the recordings to gain the depth of musical learning that only concentrated listening can bring.

*Involvement with Music* is rewarding for any student who carefully reads each word, follows the sequence of frames, writes all assigned compositions, and plays all musical examples. Diligent practice on the piano keyboard, Pianica™, or Melodica™ is also essential to success.

# To the Instructor

Since classroom time need not be given to excessive explanations about the fundamentals of music (the book and recordings fulfill this task), it can best be used in pleasurable group experiences which employ singing, playing, listening, rhythmic activities, and composing, thus developing skills that reinforce the concepts presented. *Involvement with Music* allows the instructor with specific skills and interests (vocal, choral, instrumental) to emphasize these strengths in class so that the student may take advantage of his or her unique contributions. *Though the primary aural feedback is from the recordings, the instructor is the primary resource in evaluating and stimulating the creative assignments.*

In any music course students will bring a variety of musical backgrounds to the group. *Involvement with Music* is designed to accommodate such individual differences and needs by posing challenging tasks to the more advanced as well as to beginning students. For this reason, the instructor is encouraged to discover the entering musical ability of each student through interviewing and testing. Having done this, the instructor is in a position to eliminate certain frames (or even chapters) for some students, and to add special assignments for others. *The program is flexible enough so that students of diverse backgrounds can fulfill diverse expectations.*

Since a knowledge of appropriate musical terminology is considered a short cut and not a detour in the learning of music, terminology is stressed in *Involvement with Music*. Musical terms are introduced *as they are needed* during the course of learning concepts, and they appear in boldface type, allowing the student to make immediate and strong connections between each concept and its name.

*Involvement with Music* is most efficiently used by assigning deadlines for the completion of a minimum number of frames. This technique allows the student to proceed at his own pace but within defined limits. As an incentive for meeting the deadlines (and also for purposes of evaluation), students should be tested in class on each deadline date with materials *similar* to those found in the frames requiring responses. *All concepts in every frame should be secure before progressing to succeeding frames.*

## Resources

We strongly recommend that the instructor have available a number of popular song anthologies published by such music corporations as Charles Hansen, Big Three (Feist, Robbins, Miller), Warner Brothers, and Screen Gems-Columbia. These contain hundreds of recent and current popular songs, many of which are considered "standards." These songs represent the catalogues of many different publishers, and for this reason they are extremely valuable. A number of individual song publishers also produce their own anthologies. All of these materials may be employed rhythmically (as in the case of the rhythmic examples in Chapter Two) or melodically and harmonically (as in Chapters Three, Four, and Five). In addition, they may be used to teach musical form.

In the field of children's musical literature there are many resources, including the music series books (K-6) of a number of publishers. The following are currently in print:

*Birchard Music Series*, Karl D. Ernst, Hartley D. Snyder, and Alex Zimmerman, Evanston, Ill.: Summy-Birchard Company.

*Discovering Music Together*, Charles Leonhard, Beatrice Perham Krone, Irving Wolfe, and Margaret Fullerton. Chicago: Follett Publishing Company.

*Exploring Music*, Eunice Boardman, and Beth Landis. New York: Holt, Rinehart & Winston, Inc.

*Growing with Music*, Harry R. Wilson, Walter Ehret, Alice M. Snyder, Edward J. Hermann, and Albert A. Renna. Englewood Cliffs, N.J.: Prentice-Hall, Inc.

*The Magic of Music*, Lorraine E. Watters, Louis G. Wersen, William C. Hartshorn, Eileen McMillan, Alice Gallup, and Frederick Beckman. Boston: Ginn and Company.

*Making Music Your Own*, Harold C. Youngberg and the Editors of Silver Burdett Company. Morristown, N.J.: Silver Burdett Company.

*Music for Living*, James Mursell, Gladys Tipton, Beatrice Landeck, Harriet Hordholm, Roy Freeburg, and Jack Watson. Morristown, N.J.: Silver Burdett Company.

*New Dimensions in Music*, Robert A. Choate, Lee Kjelson, Eugene W. Troth, Daniel S. Hooley, Josephine Wolferton, and Claudeane Burns. New York: American Book Company.

*Silver Burdett Music*, Bennett Reimer, Beth Crook, David S. Walker (1–6), Neva Aublin, and Erm Hayden (K). Morristown, N.J.: Silver Burdett Company.

*This Is Music*, William R. Sur, Robert E. Nye, and Charlotte DuBois. Boston: Allyn and Bacon, Inc.

### Use of Instruments

It is acknowledged that the piano practice facilities of most colleges and universities are not sufficient to handle large numbers of students. For this reason, the keyboard objectives can be attained most effectively if every student owns his own keyboard wind instrument, such as the Pianica™ or the Melodica.™ Because of the strong emphasis on keyboard psychomotor activity, the student must spend considerable time practicing outside the classroom.

In the testing of this program, the students used two-octave Pianicas due to their modest cost and their piano-like keyboard. (By eliminating harmonic notes which do not fit into two octaves, both bass and treble pitches of many compositions in *Involvement with Music* can be played on these instruments.) Because all students had their own instruments for use with Chapters Three, Four, and Five, they were able to play at their leisure and then transfer their accomplishments to the piano. (Note: *Although the student will gain considerable keyboard skill, the role of the keyboard in* Involvement with Music *is not to create a pianist in one semester, or quarter, but to provide the best means of extensive reinforcement of musical concepts.)*

The student need *not* wait until he studies Chapter Three to use the Pianica™/ Melodica™. It may be used effectively in Chapter Two, which deals exclusively with aspects of time notation. *Since these instruments can produce both sustained and nonsustained sounds, they are ideal for practicing rhythm.* They are also especially effective in developing sensitivity to dynamics since loudness and softness are directly contingent upon breath control. When using the Pianica™/Melodica™ in class, it is, of course, impossible to play and count aloud or play and sing at the same time. In this case, the class should be divided into players and singers. In demonstrating keyboard skills, accuracy and understanding—*not* speed—should be the criteria for success.

The use of rhythmic instruments such as bongos, conga drums, maracas, claves, cowbells, guiros, castanets, wood blocks, triangles, and tambourines is strongly recommended for motivation in Chapter Two. Also, it is suggested that the students construct some rhythm instruments. In Chapters Two through Five, the students might be given the opportunity to perform on the xylophones, metallophones, and special percussion instruments developed by Carl Orff in his approach to music for children.

The recorder is a favorite and inexpensive flute-like instrument which is also used extensively in the Orff approach to music. Since there are a number of excellent recorder methods available, *Involvement with Music* does not teach this instrument. The recorder, however, can be effectively applied in playing the rhythms in Chapter Two and the melodies contained throughout the book.

Use of the ukulele in playing chords is discussed in Chapter Four. The ukulele may be tuned to any major or minor chord rather than tuned in the usual way, allowing the student to easily perform a variety of songs *without* being concerned about fingering. The student merely covers four strings at one time with a single finger and shifts from fret to fret. Every shift will produce a major or minor (if the ukulele has been tuned to minor) chord. Many folk and folk/pop singers use this technique. Although not emphasized in *Involvement with Music*, ukulele and Autoharp™/Chromaharp™ fingering, playing position, strumming styles, picking styles, and so forth, should be explored in the classroom.

When selecting songs from any of these sources, disregard the implied grade levels (each series has a book for every "grade"), and choose songs on the basis of their musical and lyrical desirability to you, and ultimately to the needs of your students. Most truly worthwhile songs are applicable at a variety of grade levels for a variety of reasons. Your song horizons are unlimited.

In addition to these music series, these general song anthologies are helpful:

*Heritage Songster*, Leon Dallin, and Lynn Dallin. (320 songs). Dubuque, Iowa: William C. Brown Company, Publishers.
*Singing with Children*, Neva Aubin, George Kyme, Robert Nye and Vernice Nye. Belmont, Calif.: Wadsworth Publishing Company, Inc.
Both these anthologies encompass folk songs, patriotic songs, hymns, seasonal songs, nursery songs, etc.
A large variety of pocket sized song books are published by Cooperative Recreation Service, Inc. of Delaware, Ohio. These books are published for many different organizations and are very modestly priced. A listing of song book titles may be obtained by writing the publisher.

The nine elaborate Lesson Plans in Appendix A dramatically demonstrate the direct correlation between *Involvement with Music* and involvement with children. These plans, designed for use at the elementary school level, are all structured according to specific performance objectives which relate to the concepts developed in each of the five chapters.

The procedures used to develop any one performance objective can often be conceived as an entire lesson. There is no set time for completion of any group of procedures. Fulfillment of a performance objective might take one, two, or three periods. Indeed, some of these Lesson Plans might take two or three weeks of music periods to complete. It should also be emphasized that these performance objectives and procedures represent only *one* approach to the teaching of the musical concepts contained in the lessons.

All song materials needed for the lessons in Appendix A are included in the Song Appendices B and C. Additional outside materials, however, are suggested.

Fourteen pentatonic songs comprise Appendix B. They are arranged to provide easy supplementary keyboard materials for Chapter Three.

Appendix C is a varied anthology of over fifty songs including such popular selections as SCARBOROUGH FAIR, GAMES PEOPLE PLAY, MORNING HAS BROKEN, LET THERE BE PEACE ON EARTH, WINDY, AMAZING GRACE, and I LEFT MY HEART IN SAN FRANCISCO. Any of the songs in Appendix C can be used for rhythmic reinforcement in Chapter Two and as an extended song repertoire for Chapter Four.

Fourteen pentatonic songs comprise Appendix B. They are arranged to provide easy supplementary keyboard materials for Chapter Three.

Appendix C is a varied anthology of over fifty songs including such popular selections as "Scarborough Fair," "Games People Play," "Morning Has Broken," "Let There Be Peace On Earth," "Windy," "Amazing Grace," and "I Left My Heart in San Francisco." Any of the songs in Appendix C can be used for rhythmic reinforcement in Chapter Two and for providing a song repertoire as an extension of Chapter Four.

It should be clearly understood that *Involvement with Music* is not designed to develop students' singing abilities. It is assumed that all students have the potential for singing and that this potential will be explored with appropriate materials by the instructor.

## Acknowledgments

To William Allgood, for his musicianship, his music, his discerning ear, and his dedicated audio engineering.
To the Kalamazoo Symphony Orchestra, Horace T. Maddux, manager.
To Everest Records, Inc. of Los Angeles, California for their assistance in preparing the cassette.
To the many music publishers who graciously allowed the inclusion of their materials.
To the following people for their energy, their creativity, and their willingness to help: Luanne Allgood, Steve Baine, Jennifer Benner, J. B. Dyas, Mona DeQuis, Susan Haack, Rob Hayes, Kathy Kelly, Trent Kynaston, Tony Lavender, Pamela E. Lovell, Frank Merritt, Don Para, Gayle Petrick, Bill Ritchie,

Edwin P. Sabrack, Jr., Chris Schook, Mike Shannon, Patricia Ann Turner, Susan Walter, Wendy Wooley, and Chris Wormell, and also Local 228, Kalamazoo Federation of Musicians, AF of M.

# CHAPTER ONE

# Sounds in Time:

# Informal Structure and Notation

# Sounds in Time: Informal Structure and Notation

*In Chapter One you will learn to create, notate, and perform short compositions based on sounds gathered from the immediate environment. These compositions will last from fifteen to sixty seconds and incorporate both vocal and nonvocal sounds.*

*The forming of small ensemble groups will enable you to restructure your individual compositions into group compositions, still within defined time limitations. Selection of sounds for inclusion in group compositions is accomplished through careful listening and evaluation.*

*Your increasing awareness of aesthetic principles (for example, the necessity of silence in relation to sound, the importance of both unity and variety in a musical composition) will help guide your creative efforts. You will also learn specific musical terms in starting what will be a rapidly expanding vocabulary of musical concepts.*

---

**1** Music begins with sounds in time. Sounds result from vibrating materials. Silence, the absence of sound in time, is also an integral part of music. Composers organize sounds and silences to create music.

Look around the room. Do you realize that everything in sight can be a **sound source,** once activated? The interaction of two or more sound sources is a **sound-producing combination,** which functions percussively as does a drumstick striking the head of a drum. Strike your hands together (both hands are sound sources). Notice that one hand tends to be the **activating agent.** Which one?

Use your chair to create a sound-producing combination. What was the activating agent? Use a book, a glass, or other objects, to create sounds. Discover your own sound sources and create your own sound-producing combinations. Vary the loudness and softness (**dynamics**) of each combination. Your voice is a prime sound source. Use it to create different sounds at various dynamic levels.

Notice that some sound-producing combinations create **sustained sounds.** A sound is sustained when the sound source which is activated continues to vibrate after the activating agent has been removed. (Sound sources such as cymbals, chimes, tympani and tuning forks produce sustained sounds.) A sustained sound will also be produced when the initial activating agent continues to function, for example, when a finger is held on a doorbell. A **nonsustained sound** is produced when the sound source stops vibrating immediately after being activated. (Striking a table or tapping your foot will produce a nonsustained sound.) Nonsustained sounds are usually associated with solid materials (for example: book, door, table, brick).

Categorize the **environmental sounds** that you have produced as sustained or nonsustained. Develop the habit of listening consciously and perceptively to the environmental sounds around you.

All sounds (and combinations of sounds) can be used in a random way. The random use of sounds and silences is called **aleatory** or **chance** music. Many contemporary composers employ this technique when writing music for the concert hall as well as for other entertainment media.

**2**  Use the following terms to complete statements a–f:

> sound source
> sound-producing combination
> activating agent
> dynamics
> environmental sounds
> aleatory or chance music

a. The random use of sounds and silences is called _____.

b. Everything in sight can be a _____.

c. Loudness and softness are called _____.

d. The interaction of two or more sound sources is a _____ _____.

e. A drumstick that strikes the head of a drum functions as an _____ _____.

f. The sounds which you have created within your immediate environment are called _____.

Write S (sustained) or NS (nonsustained) to the left of each sound source or sound-producing combination, considering the most obvious characteristic of each sound.

| | | |
|---|---|---|
| ____ bell in tower | ____ chopping wood | ____ tapping on book |
| ____ train whistle | ____ buzz saw | ____ breaking stick |
| ____ piano | ____ doorbell | ____ whistling |
| ____ finger snapping | | ____ gunshot |

RESPONSES

a. The random use of sounds and silences is called *aleatory or chance music*.

b. Everything in sight can be a *sound source*.

c. Loudness and softness are called *dynamics*.

d. The interaction of two or more sound sources is a *sound-producing combination*.

e. A drumstick that strikes the head of a drum functions as an *activating agent*.

f. The sounds which you have created within your immediate environment are called *environmental sounds*.

| | | |
|---|---|---|
| *S* bell in tower | *NS* chopping wood | *NS* tapping on book |
| *S* train whistle | *S* buzz saw | *NS* breaking stick |
| *S* piano | *S* doorbell | *S* whistling |
| *NS* finger snapping | | *NS* gunshot |

**3** When considering the preceding list of sounds, you probably realized that many sound-producing combinations can produce *either* sustained or nonsustained sounds depending on how the particular sound sources are used. For example, striking a car horn will normally produce a nonsustained sound, but if the hand (the activating agent) continues to press (or activate) the horn, this will produce a sustained sound. Conversely, striking a chime will normally produce a sustained sound but if the chime is prevented from continuing to vibrate, a nonsustained sound can be produced.

Sing any **tone** and hold it until you run out of breath. You have created a sustained tone. Sing a tone on the word *ha*. Now sing *ha-ha-ha-ha-ha-ha-ha* in rapid succession. Now you are using a vocal tone in a nonsustained, percussive manner.

Frequently, a succession of nonsustained sounds can sound more like one sustained sound. When an activating agent is uninterruptedly operating, such as a woodpecker tapping on a piece of wood or drumsticks beating on a snare drum, the rapid series of nonsustained sounds gives a **sustained-sound impression.**

We usually think of the woodpecker's sound as continuous, because his activating agent (beak) is so industrious. A drum roll also gives a continuous impression of sound, because of the speed of the drumsticks. In both cases, the rate of motion of the activating agent produces this sustained impression.

**4** Imagine the sound of galloping horses at a race track thundering down to the finish line. Although the sound of a single hoofbeat is nonsustained, when many hoofs hit the ground in rapid succession, a sustained-sound impression is produced.

Listen, in your mind, to the sound of a large crowd applauding enthusiastically in a theater or at a sports event. When everyone applauds at his/her own rate of speed, the time between the nonsustained sounds (clapping hands) is perceived as almost nonexistent. Thus, a sustained-sound impression is created.

Can you think of similar ways in which sustained-sound impressions can be created?

Impressions of sustained sounds can also be produced by such percussion instruments as castanets, maracas, tambourine, guiro, ratchet, cowbell, and a variety of other instruments.

Now that you have imagined some sustained-sound impressions, listen to the recorded examples of galloping horses, applause, and sounds of a crowd at a sports event. Also included in the recording are sustained-sound impressions created by percussion instruments (the tambourine, guiro, and cowbell).

**5** Arrange various sound-producing combinations in three different series (**compositions**) with total durations of 30, 45, and 60 seconds. On paper, list the activating agents and the durations for each sound-producing combination. Select sound sources which are found in the home or classroom so that you will be able to perform all of the combinations.

Perform your compositions in the following ways:

a. Solo.
b. With other students:
   (1) as a series of solos, without interruption.
   (2) at the same time; for example, four students will play their 30-second compositions at the same time.
   (3) any combination of (1) and (2).

Use dynamics in your compositions. If a tape recorder is available, record your compositions and play them back at different speeds. You will be amazed at the variety of sounds you have already created.

---

**6**    Write out five sound-producing combinations, each on a separate index card. In class, all of the students' cards should be shuffled and ten cards picked at random.

Place them on a table. Play this random or aleatory composition as individuals or in groups (**ensembles**), reading the cards in any direction and performing them at any speed. Set a time limit for the entire composition.

Select ten different cards and repeat the process. Define new time limits. Repeat the entire procedure several times. Remember to vary the dynamics to create more musical interest.

---

**7**    Within a loosely-structured time limit, random sounds may be systematically arranged by the composer. This creates a sense of **unity** between the sections of a composition and thereby gives coherent form to the entire composition. One way of achieving unity is through the use of recurrent sound patterns. For example, your aleatory composition of ten sound-producing combinations would be more unified if it were played two or three times consecutively.

But, in order to establish interest *within* a unified composition, musical **variety** must be employed. For example, by changing the dynamics in the composition in frame 6, you illustrated the concept of variety within unity.

Another important method of achieving variety is the use of **contrasting sounds.** Instead of arranging your sound-producing combinations in a random order, you could have grouped them according to similar and contrasting sounds. The unique sound quality (or color) that a particular sound-producing combination or musical instrument possesses is called **timbre.** For example, the sound quality or timbre of a doorbell is different from the timbre of a train whistle.

The aesthetic foundation of all musical composition is the concept of *variety within unity.* The degree of unity and variety in any work of art is determined by the artist's technique and the mood he is trying to convey. This relationship of unity to variety applies to all art and communications media.

● Listen to the recorded aleatory composition of ten sound-producing combinations. Ask yourself these questions:

    a. How is this composition unified?
    b. How is variety created within unity?

---

**8** Write ten sound-producing combinations of five seconds each (ten cards) and separate them into two groups: (1) sustained sounds and (2) nonsustained sounds. Play the following compositions:

| | |
|---|---|
| Composition a: | Group 1, immediately followed by group 2. |
| Composition b: | Composition a twice, with no break between the first and second performance. |
| Composition c: | Group 1, group 2, group 2, group 1, with no breaks between groups. |
| Composition d: | Create your own composition, systematically arranging groups 1 and 2 or any of their individual sound-producing combinations. |

● After you have created and performed compositions a through d, listen to the recorded examples of similar compositions and try to distinguish between groups 1 and 2 in each composition.

---

**9** Complete the following statements about your compositions:

    a. You systematically arranged your sound-producing combinations to give the composition an overall sense of _____.
    b. You established musical interest by creating _____ within the overall unity.
    c. Variety in a composition can be created by changing the loudness and softness (_____) of sounds.
    d. Your use of groups 1 and 2 (composition c, frame 8) illustrated an important means of variety that utilizes _____.

RESPONSES

    a. You systematically arranged your sound-producing combinations to give the composition an overall sense of *unity*.
    b. You established musical interest by creating *variety* within the overall unity.
    c. Variety in a composition can be created by changing the loudness and softness (*dynamics*) of sounds.
    d. Your use of groups 1 and 2 (composition c, frame 8) illustrated an important means of variety that utilizes *contrasting sounds*.

7

**10** Write S (sustained), NS (nonsustained), or SI (sustained impression) to the left of each activated sound source or sound-producing combination. Consider the normal characteristics of the sound sources. If you are uncertain of any response, refer to the appropriate explanations in frames 1–4.

| | | |
|---|---|---|
| _____ firecracker | _____ foot tapping | _____ electric drill |
| _____ organ | _____ trumpet | _____ shuffling cards |
| _____ electric | _____ snapping fingers | _____ gong |
| typewriter | _____ singing | _____ teletype machine |
| _____ tin can | _____ hammering nail | _____ kettle drums |
| _____ tearing paper | _____ wind in trees | _____ harp |
| _____ chime | _____ zipper | _____ birds in flight |

RESPONSES

| | | | | | |
|---|---|---|---|---|---|
| NS | firecracker | NS | foot tapping | S | electric drill |
| S | organ | S | trumpet | SI | shuffling cards |
| SI | electric | NS | snapping fingers | S | gong |
| | typewriter | S | singing | SI | teletype machine |
| NS | tin can | NS | hammering nail | S | kettle drums |
| *S | tearing paper | *S | wind in trees | S | harp |
| S | chime | *S | zipper | SI | birds in flight |

* Possibly SI

**11** Using only your hands as a sound-producing combination, create a hand composition which uses at least twelve different sounds. Your composition should last from 30 to 45 seconds. Experiment and enjoy it.

**12** Using your body as a sound source, create and write a composition of nonsustained sounds which uses twelve different sound-producing combinations. Your composition should employ both unity and variety through the use of repetition, similar and contrasting timbres, and various dynamic levels. _Both_ your sound sources _and_ activating agents must be parts of your body (for example, you cannot stamp your foot on the floor).

Your composition should last approximately 60 seconds.

Listen to the recorded example of a 60-second composition that uses the body as a sound source. Listen for:

a. twelve different nonsustained sound-producing combinations.
b. repetition of one or more sound-producing combinations.

    c. similar and contrasting timbres.

    d. changes in dynamics.

---

**13**    Using your voice as a sound source, create and write a composition which uses twelve different sustained sounds. Words cannot be used. Your composition should employ both unity and variety through the use of repetition, similar and contrasting timbres, and varying dynamics.

    Your composition should last approximately 60 seconds.

Listen to the recorded example of a 60-second composition that uses the voice as a sound source. Listen for:

    a. twelve different sustained sounds.

    b. repetition of one or more sounds.

    c. similar and contrasting timbres.

    d. changes in dynamics.

---

**14**    Select your favorite sound-producing combinations from both frames 12 and 13, choose six which produce sustained sounds and six which produce nonsustained sounds, and restructure them to create a new composition. Your composition should employ both unity and variety through the use of repetition, similar and contrasting timbres, and dynamics.

    Your composition should last approximately 60 seconds.

Listen to the recorded example that uses sound-producing combinations from frames 12 and 13. Pay particular attention to the variety created by changes in dynamics and timbres.

---

**15**    Organize an ensemble with two other students. Arrange and perform your compositions from frame 14 together so that the twelve sections of each composition begin and end simultaneously.

Listen to the recorded compositions. Notice the intricate texture created by three different timbres sounding at the same time.

9

**16** With the two other performers, plan a new composition using the twelve favorite sound-producing combinations of the ensemble. Strive for an equal number of sustained (vocal) and nonsustained (vocal or nonvocal) sounds. Determine the order and duration of each sound and then perform this new composition as a group. Each sound should be performed simultaneously by all the members of the ensemble.

The entire composition should last about 60 seconds.

**17** Within the ensemble, each member can be a soloist, performing the same twelve sound-producing combinations:

    a. The first member of the group (member A) begins alone, performing all twelve sounds consecutively.
    b. When member A begins the fifth sound, the second member of the group (member B) enters with the first sound.
    c. When member A begins the ninth sound and member B begins the fifth sound, the third member (member C) enters with the first sound.
    d. When each member ends the series of twelve sounds, he/she should begin again at the first sound. Members A, B, and C each perform the entire composition three times. Since member A began alone, and member B entered second, member C will perform the end of the third series alone.

Listen to the recorded composition. Notice how the timbres blend to create new colors with the entrance of each member.

**18** The composition in frame 17 is called a **sound round,** similar to the familiar round "Row, Row, Row Your Boat." The difference is that your composition is not a song but a round of vocal and nonvocal, sustained and nonsustained sounds.

This diagram will clarify the structure of the sound round described in frame 17:

```
Member A   1  2  3  4  5  6  7  8  9  10  11  12
Member B               1  2  3  4  5   6   7   8  9  10  11  12
Member C                        1   2  3   4   5   6   7   8  9  10  11  12
```

The numbers represent the twelve sound-producing combinations. Any kind of round produces multiple sounds by combining and staggering single threads of sound as shown above.

**19** Perform the sound round again, but when member A begins the ninth sound and member B begins the fifth sound, let member C start with the twelfth sound and perform the entire series in backward motion three times. This technique of beginning with the last sound in a series and ending with the first sound is called **retrograde.** Notice the new effects produced by the line in retrograde and think of other ways these materials could be organized. *A skilled composer always searches for the maximum number of ways in which he can use a minimum amount of material.*

Compare this recorded sound round to the round in the recording for frame 17. The same sound-producing combinations are used by each member, but they are performed in retrograde.

Sound materials may be organized in a variety of ways. Experiment with the following:

    a. Member B starts at the second sound of member A, and member C starts at the second sound of member B.

    b. Member C starts first, then B, then A, each entering at a predetermined sound.

    c. All members begin on the seventh sound and proceed to the first sound. Each member enters at a predetermined time.

After writing and arranging several of your own compositions, you will realize that the number of ways that sounds can be organized is limited only by the imagination of the composer or performer.

Experiment further with your environmental sounds.

**20** Write true or false to the left of each of the following statements. If a statement is false, change the italicized word(s) to make the statement true.

    _____ a. Sounds that you can produce within your immediate surroundings are called *environmental sounds.*

    _____ b. Sounds result from *vibrating materials.*

    _____ c. Loudness and softness refer to *unity.*

    _____ d. Trombones are usually associated with *nonsustained* sounds.

    _____ e. Any solid object may be considered a *sound source.*

    _____ f. Any solid object may be considered an *activating agent.*

    _____ g. Aleatory music is *predictable* music.

    _____ h. The interaction of two or more sound sources is a *sound-producing combination.*

    _____ i. Coherent form is a result of *unity.*

    _____ j. An effective use of dynamics and contrasting sounds is necessary for *variety.*

    _____ k. A recurrent visual image in a film is one application of *variety.*

_____ l. The repeated use of a dance pattern in a ballet lends *unity* to the whole.

_____ m. A spiral staircase set in the middle of a square building is a stark example of *variety* within overall unity.

_____ n. A specific use of dynamics helps to produce *unity*.

_____ o. The organization of sounds and *silences* produces music.

_____ p. The unique sound quality that a particular musical instrument possesses is called *timbre*.

_____ q. A round produces multiple sounds by combining and *staggering* single threads of sounds.

RESPONSES

*true* a. Sounds that you can produce within your immediate surroundings are called *environmental sounds*.

*true* b. Sounds result from *vibrating materials*.

*false* c. Loudness and softness refer to *unity*. (*dynamics*)

*false* d. Trombones are usually associated with *nonsustained* sounds. (*sustained*)

*true* e. Any solid object may be considered a *sound source*.

*true* f. Any solid object may be considered an *activating agent*.

*false* g. Aleatory music is *predictable* music. (*unpredictable or chance*)

*true* h. The interaction of two or more sound sources is a *sound-producing combination*.

*true* i. Coherent form is a result of *unity*.

*true* j. An effective use of dynamics and contrasting sounds is necessary for *variety*.

*false* k. A recurrent visual image in a film is one application of *variety*. (*unity*)

*true* l. The repeated use of a dance pattern in a ballet lends *unity* to the whole.

*true* m. A spiral staircase set in the middle of a square building is a stark example of *variety* within overall unity.

*false* n. A specific use of dynamics helps to produce *unity*. (*variety*)

*true* o. The organization of sounds and *silences* produces music.

*true* p. The unique sound quality that a particular instrument possesses is called *timbre*.

*true* q. A round produces multiple sounds by combining and *staggering* single threads of sounds.

# Sounds in Time:

# Formal Structure and Notation

# Sounds in Time: Formal Structure and Notation

*In Chapter Two you will become familiar with every facet of time (duration) and formal time notation that is likely to occur in your musical performing experience. These include note values, time signatures, tempo terms, accents, syncopation, and a variety of other musical concepts related to time. Distinctions between count, beat, and rhythm are emphasized.*

*You will create, notate, and perform a large number of rhythmic compositions. Included in the book are also many rhythmic examples—excerpts from both popular and classical music. Immediate feedback on the accuracy of much of your performing of compositions and rhythmic examples is found on the accompanying recordings.*

*At the end of Chapter Two you should be able to deal successfully with the rhythm of nearly any piece of popular music (folk, rock, show, country), children's music, and much classical music. You will be well on your way to becoming musically proficient.*

---

**21**  In Chapter One you composed aleatory music using loose time structures and informal **notation.** Chapter Two will concentrate on formal musical notation.

---

**22**  Strike a sound four times evenly at your own speed. Use any sound-producing combination. This may include the piano, a keyboard/wind instrument, or any other classroom instrument. Repeat this process, counting 1 2 3 4 as you strike.

What you have just done may be notated in the following way:

These **notes** (♩) are called **quarter notes.** Since all of them are counted evenly, each note receives the same amount of time. Look at the quarter notes above and repeat the strike/count process.

---

**23**  What you have just done may also be notated this way, but it is found less frequently.

These notes (♩) are called **half notes.** Since all of them are counted evenly, each note receives the same amount of time. Look at the half notes above and repeat the strike/count process.

**24** What you have just done may also be notated this way, but this notation is the least frequently used.

strike: **o   o   o   o**

count:  1    2    3    4

   These notes (**o**) are called **whole notes.** Since all of them are counted evenly, each note receives the same amount of time. Look at the whole notes above and repeat the strike/count process. Notice that whole notes do *not* have **stems** (**o**, 𝅗𝅥, ♩)

**25** There are several other ways of notating the sound of even counts, but, for the moment, the focus will be mostly on the use of the quarter note (♩).

**26** You will also see quarter notes and half notes written this way (♩, ♩) with the **note heads** at the top of the stems rather than at the bottom. This, of course, does not pertain to the whole note which has a note head but no stem.

**27** Strike and count these even groups of quarter notes. Vary the sound-producing combinations. Clapping may be included. Also notice the stems in relation to the note heads.

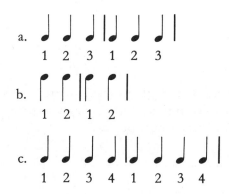

a. ♩ ♩ ♩|♩ ♩ ♩|
   1 2 3 1 2 3

b. ♩ ♩ |♩ ♩ |
   1 2 1 2

c. ♩ ♩ ♩ ♩|♩ ♩ ♩ ♩|
   1 2 3 4 1 2 3 4

Listen to the recordings of compositions a, b, and c as you follow the notes. Notice that all the quarter notes are played evenly.

**28** Notice the vertical line | between the first and second groups of quarter notes. This line is called a **bar line.** The bar line separates groups of notes into **measures.** With each new measure, the count begins anew. The bar line is a visual convenience only. It *does not* interrupt the strike/count process which should flow evenly from measure to measure.

---

**29** Strike and count the following measures, but perform each example in three different speeds: slow, medium, and fast. Be careful to strike evenly.

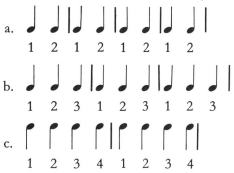

Listen to the recordings of compositions a, b, and c played in slow, medium, and fast tempos. Play along with the recording if you wish.

---

**30** The musical term for speed is **tempo.** When you changed the speed of the previous measures, you changed the tempo.

---

**31** Strike and count the following compositions in different tempos. Vary the sound-producing combinations in each example. Choose specific sound-producing combinations for measures with the same number of counts so that a measure with two counts will sound different from a measure with three or four counts (e.g., in composition a: measures, 1, 3, and 6 will employ the same sound). Be careful to maintain the even flow from measure to measure as you change sounds.

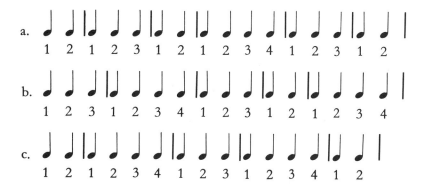

Consider what principles of composition you utilized within each example by your manipulation of sounds.

Listen to the recordings of compositions a, b, and c as you follow the music. Listen for the changes in sound-producing combinations within each composition.

RESPONSES

The principles of composition used in frame 31 are variety and unity. Each composition is unified by the use of one-count notes (quarter notes, in this instance); and variety is created within this unity by varying the sound-producing combinations.

**32**  Write a three-measure composition of quarter notes. Use a different number of quarter notes for each measure and write the counts under each note. Don't forget to add stems to each quarter note. Be certain to separate the measures with bar lines.

Varying the sound-producing combinations for each measure, strike and count your composition in three different tempos.

Be careful to strike evenly.

RESPONSE

**33**  Write a three-measure composition of whole notes, using a different number of whole notes for each measure, with the counts under each note.

Perform your composition in three different tempos as described in frame 32.

RESPONSE

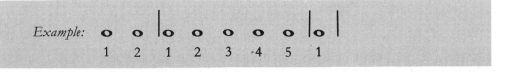

**34**  Write a three-measure composition of half notes, using a different number of half notes for each measure, with the counts under each note. Perform your composition as described in frame 32.

RESPONSE

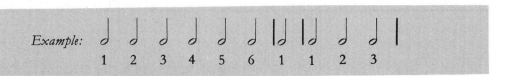

**35**  Using quarter notes, write a five-measure composition. Vary the number of notes from measure to measure and write the counts under the notes. Use the same sound-producing combination throughout the composition.

Strike and count your composition in three different tempos.

RESPONSE

*Example:*

**36**  Strike and count the following two measures of quarter notes:

Notice the $\frac{4}{4}$ to the left of the first quarter note. This is called a **time signature.** The top number **4** indicates the number of complete counts in one measure. The bottom number **4** indicates the kind of note (♩) that gets one complete count. The time signature $\frac{4}{4}$ is equivalent to $\frac{4}{♩}$ and is often written that way. Another way to write $\frac{4}{4}$ is **C**. $\frac{4}{4}$ *is perhaps the most frequently used time signature in all western music.*

**37**  Strike and count the following two measures of half notes:

The time signature $\frac{4}{2}$ or $\frac{4}{\textrm{d}}$ indicates that there are four complete counts ($\mathbf{^4}$) in one measure and that the half note ($\mathbf{_2}$ or ♩) gets one complete count.

**38**  Strike and count the following two measures of whole notes:

The time signature ($\frac{4}{1}$ or $\frac{4}{o}$) indicates that there are four complete counts ($4$) in one measure and that the whole note ($1$ or $o$) gets one complete count. Of the three time signatures presented in frames 36 to 38, $\frac{4}{1}$ is the least likely to be observed in western music. However, experience with time signatures in which the whole note receives one count ($\frac{1}{1}, \frac{2}{1}, \frac{3}{1}, \frac{4}{1}$) will help you to understand all time signatures.

---

**39** Write two measures of notes for each of the following time signatures:

a. $\frac{4}{4}$ or $\frac{4}{\text{♩}}$ or **C**      e. $\frac{3}{4}$ or $\frac{3}{\text{♩}}$

b. $\frac{3}{2}$ or $\frac{3}{\text{♩}}$

f. $\frac{2}{1}$ or $\frac{2}{o}$

c. $\frac{2}{2}$ or $\frac{2}{\text{♩}}$ or **¢** *      g. $\frac{4}{2}$ or $\frac{4}{\text{♩}}$

d. $\frac{3}{1}$ or $\frac{3}{o}$

h. $\frac{4}{1}$ or $\frac{4}{o}$

Write the counts under each note. Strike and count your compositions, using a different sound-producing combination for each composition.

* The symbol **¢**, which nearly always replaces the $\frac{2}{2}$ time signature, is extremely common in music literature.

RESPONSES

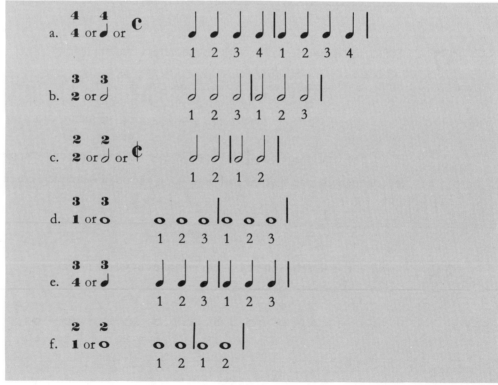

20

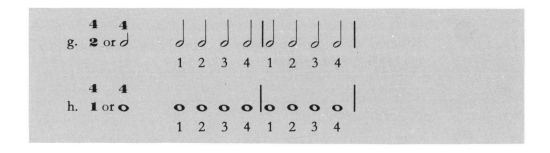

---

**40**  The bottom number (or note) of the time signature indicates what kind of note (quarter, half, or whole) gets one count, but it does *not* restrict the composer from using other kinds of notes in the same composition. If a composer used only one-count notes, his entire composition would be made up of even notes. (What effect would this have on the music?) In the composition below, there is a juxtaposition of long and short notes.

In the above example, you will notice that ♩ = 1 count; but ♩ = 2 counts and o = 4 counts when used in a composition where ♩ = 1 count (**4**/ or ♩).

*The majority of compositions have time signatures in which* ♩ *= 1 count (***2/4**, **3/4**, *or* **4/4***).*

---

**41**  All the previous compositions have been made up of even notes, and therefore your striking and counting have been simultaneous. However, when performing compositions which include different kinds of notes, your striking and counting will not always coincide. Continue to count evenly (preferably aloud), but on notes that require more than one count hold the sound for the appropriate number of counts. (S = Strike; H = Hold.)

Playing these compositions on instruments which sustain sounds, such as the piano or keyboard/wind instruments, would help you to hear the difference between the long and short notes. Or, you might sing these compositions on a single syllable, such as *la*, while counting mentally, since the human voice naturally produces sustained sounds.

Perform this composition, using the technique described above:

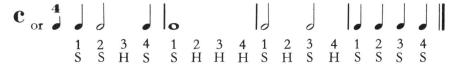

Notice the parallel bar lines at the end of the composition. This **double bar** ‖ designates the conclusion of the composition.

21

Listen to the recording of this composition as you follow the notes. Then practice this composition until you are able to coordinate your counting with the striking and holding of the notes.

**42** Here are additional compositions. Notice the juxtaposition of long and short notes. Strike (or hold) and count these compositions. Then perform them in retrograde. Whenever possible, *count out loud.*

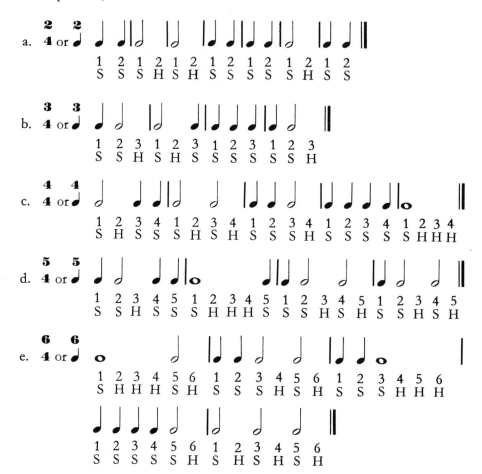

You will find this new strike/count technique useful in performing future compositions.

If you have any difficulty with this technique, strike and count along with the recordings of compositions a through e.

**43** Up to this point, you have not been required to write a note that would last for three counts. There is no way in musical notation to write a three-count note unless an extra symbol is added to another note. **Dotted notes** are most commonly used to notate three counts. A dot placed to the right of a note adds to that note one-half of its value.

a. In $\frac{3}{4}$ or $\frac{3}{2}$ time, $\textrm{♩} = 2$ counts and $\cdot = 1$ count, therefore $\textrm{♩.} = 3$ counts.

b. In $\frac{3}{2}$ or $\frac{3}{2}$ time, $\textrm{o} = 2$ counts and $\cdot = 1$ count, therefore $\textrm{o}\cdot = 3$ counts.

---

**44**     Strike and count the following compositions which use $\textrm{o}\cdot$ and $\textrm{♩..}$ Don't forget to hold the appropriate counts.

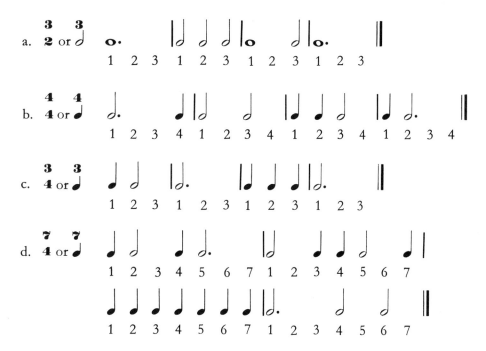

*A consistent awareness of the sound and sight of juxtapositions of long and short notes is an important step forward in the perception of time in music.*

Strike and count along with the recording of compositions a through d. Observe that a different tempo is used for each composition.

---

**45**     Repeat the compositions in frame 44, but this time perform them in retrograde.

---

**46**     You have seen that a dot receives one-half of the duration of its preceding note. (Review frame 43 if this statement is not clear.) This rule will apply to the use of a dot with *any* note.

**47**  Write your own short compositions using three of the time signatures in frame 44. Include 𝅝· and 𝅗𝅥· along with other notes which you have learned. Seek as many sustained sounds* as possible by varying the sound-producing combinations from measure to measure. Strike and count your compositions. If you arrange your sound sources in the order in which you will play them, you will be able to maintain an even count from one measure to the next. For example:

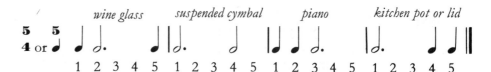

Try to achieve unity by arranging your compositions in series. For example, in frame 44 you could play composition a, then b, then a again.

* By using sustained sounds, you will be able to hold each sound for its complete number of counts.

**48**  *Any one-count note can be divided into any number of smaller notes.* For example:

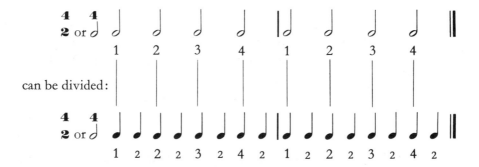

Tap your foot heavily on the large numbers (first half of the count) and raise it on the small numbers (second half of the count). At the same time, strike lightly on your desk or table on *both* the large *and* small numbers. Think of each half note as being divided into two equal parts. The large number represents the first part and the small number represents the second part. Practice the above example until your tapping and striking are perfectly coordinated.

**49**  As you tap and strike, notice that the sound of the first part of the count (large numbers) is louder than the sound of the second part of the count (small numbers). This emphasis is called an **accent.** The symbol for an accent is > and it is placed above or below the head of a note—opposite the stem ( 𝅗𝅥 or ♩ ). When you see an accent, it means that its corresponding note must be sounded louder than a note without an accent. You will notice that the first part of *any* divided count tends to be more accented (louder) than the rest of the count.

**50** Tap your foot heavily on the first part of the count (large number) and strike your desk lightly on both the first *and* second parts of the count (large and small numbers). Use a medium tempo.

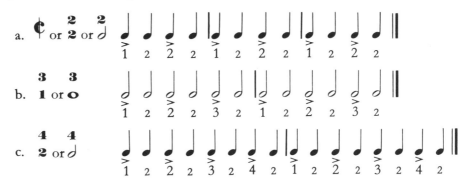

Remember, ¢ is the most common symbol used to indicate $\frac{2}{2}$ time. (It is frequently called **cut time**.) For practice, it is sometimes easier to count it in **C** ($\frac{4}{4}$), with each quarter note getting one count. Strike and tap composition a above in **C** ($\frac{4}{4}$).

Follow compositions a through c as they are being played on the recording. Practice along with this recording until you are able to coordinate foot tapping, desk striking, and counting. Then, stop the recording and perform compositions a through c on your own.

**51** Your note vocabulary thus far has been limited to o, ♩, ♪, o., and ♩. . Now it is time to increase your vocabulary so that you can explore even greater musical possibilities. Here are some additional notes:

a. ♪, called an **eighth note**. When groups of eighth notes are written, they are usually joined by a **beam** across the stems. For example:

The beam is merely a visual aid to the performer. It groups notes into even counts.

b. ♬, called a **sixteenth note**. Groups of sixteenth notes are connected with a double beam:

c.  called a **thirty-second note.** Groups of thirty-second notes are written with a triple beam:

Although notes with shorter **values** (durations) than the thirty-second note do exist, you are unlikely to encounter them in your daily musical experiences.

**52** Here is a diagram of all the notes you have learned. They are shown in descending order of values ($\mathbf{o} = \, \flat\flat = \, \flat\flat\flat\flat$ etc.).

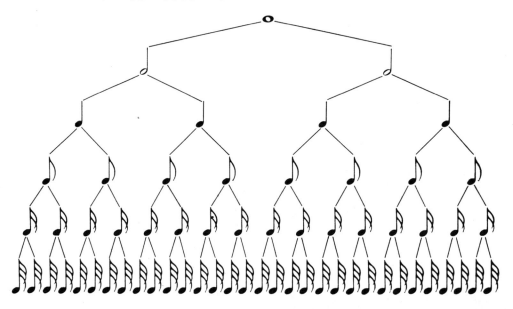

Therefore in a given time signature ($\frac{4}{4}$, $\frac{5}{4}$, $\frac{6}{4}$), if a whole note gets four counts, then a half note gets two counts, a quarter note one count, an eighth note one-half count, etc. Understanding these relationships is *essential*.

Notice that the visual appearance of a note is related to its value. The shorter the note value, the *more* there is to the note itself.

**53** You have learned (frame 48) that a one-count note can be divided into any number of parts by using shorter note values. This rule can be applied to the division of the quarter note into two equal eighth notes:

Tap your foot heavily on the large numbers only and strike your desk or table lightly on both the large and small numbers. The large number represents the first part of the count and the small number represents the second part of the count.

Follow the notes above as you play along with the recording. Practice until you can play the notes without the recording.

---

**54**  The eighth note can be divided into two equal sixteenth notes. Tap and strike the following example as described in frame 53:

Similarly, the sixteenth note can be divided into two equal thirty-second notes. Tap and strike the following example:

---

**55**  Rewrite the following examples to include (1) the division of at least two notes in every measure into two equal parts, (2) the proper placement of large and small numbers under all notes, and (3) accents on the first part of each count.

Tap your foot on the large numbers and use several sound-producing combinations for striking on the large and small numbers. Vary your own tempos.

**RESPONSES**

Here are some examples of how compositions a through h may be divided. Watch the examples and listen to the recording. Perform them if you wish.

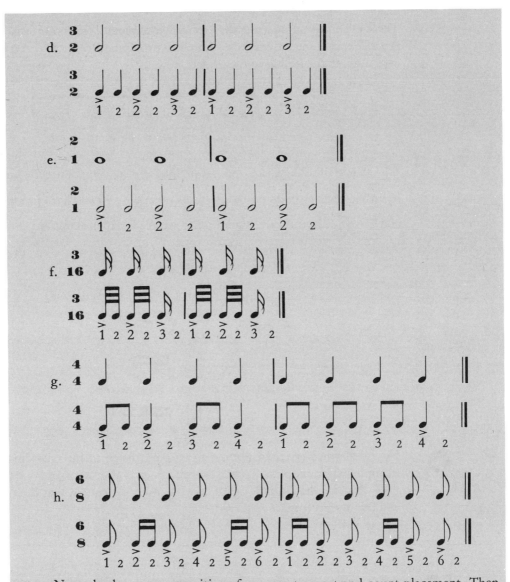

Now check your compositions for correct accent and count placement. Then play your compositions once again.

**56** All of the notes which have been considered thus far are normally divided into two equal parts. However, any one-count note can also be divided into *three equal parts*. When the number 3 is placed above a three-note grouping, the three notes are compressed into the time (one count) normally reserved for one or two notes. For example:

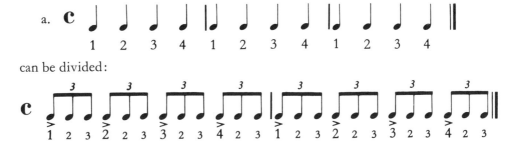

can be divided:

These even three-note groupings are called **triplets.** Triplets are very common in all types of music and are easy to count when pronounced tri-p-let. Practice the example below to get the feeling of the triplet.

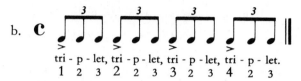

tri - p - let, tri - p - let, tri - p - let, tri - p - let.
1   2   3   2   2   3   3   2   3   4   2   3

When dividing a one-count note into triplets, always use the same note values as if you were dividing a one-count note into two equal parts. For example, ♩ = ♫ and ♩ = ♪♪♪. In this case, eighth notes are used. Other examples:

c.  𝅗𝅥 = ♩ ♩

𝅗𝅥 = ♩ ♩ ♩ (3)

and

d.  ♪ = ♬

♪ = ♬ (3)

Now that you have tried playing the triplets, listen to the recording as you follow example b in frame 56.

Practice the example again on your own. Be certain that the triplets are even and that the accents are observed.

---

**57**  For example a, tap your foot, strike, and count. For b, write and perform your own composition, using combinations of triplets and other notes.

a.  **2** / **2**
1   2   3   2   2   3   1   2   3   2   2   3

b.  **3**
   **4**

---

**58**  When a composer wants the *feeling* of triplets throughout a composition and is therefore planning to use many three-note groupings, he is more likely to use a **compound time signature** rather than write many triplets. Some examples of compound time signatures are $\frac{6}{8}, \frac{6}{16}, \frac{9}{8}, \frac{9}{16}, \frac{12}{8}, \frac{12}{16}$. Compound time signatures are related to **simple time signatures.** This relationship will be explored in depth in frame 73. By dividing the top number of a compound time signature by three, one can determine the number of three-note groupings for each measure. For example:

There are *two* three-note groupings in each of the above measures. (The 6 of $\frac{6}{8}$ is divided by three). Notice that the number 3 (triplet) is not needed above the groupings when a compound time signature is used. (The number 3 is needed only when a group of three notes must *fit in* evenly where two notes would normally sound.

For example: .)

Tap and strike the above example in a medium or fast tempo and you will feel equal accents on counts 1 and 4. In other words, there are two strong pulses or beats (on counts 1 and 4) within the six-count measure. *You feel the beat, but you see the counts.*

---

**59**   Here's another example of a compound time signature:

There are *three* three-note groupings (and three beats) in each of the above measures. Tap and strike the above example and you will feel these pulses on counts 1, 4, and 7. There are three strong beats within a nine-count measure.

A final example:

1 2 3 4 5 6 7 8 9 10 11 12  1 2 3 4 5 6 7 8 9 10 11 12

There are *four* three-note groupings (and four beats) in each of the above measures. Tap and strike the above example and you will feel these pulses on counts 1, 4, 7, and 10. Therefore, there are four strong beats within a twelve-count measure.

---

**60**   Any one-count note (or any note at all) may also be divided into four, five, and more equal parts. For example:

can be divided into four equal parts:

a.

or five equal parts:

b.

* Dividing groups of four equal parts into two equal groups of twos is also an effective counting system which you might eventually prefer.

† The number 5 is placed over the five-note grouping because five notes do not automatically fall evenly in a $\frac{2}{4}$ time signature. When dividing a one-count note into five equal notes, always use the same note values as if you were dividing a one-count note into four equal parts.

Tap and strike along with examples a and b in this recording. If you have any difficulty, keep practicing with the recording until you can play the notes evenly. Be certain your accents are on the proper notes.

**61** Perform the following example three times, keeping a steady beat with foot tapping: (1) the first time, strike all notes and say the accompanying words; (2) the second time, strike all notes and say the numbers under the words; (3) the third time, perform it in retrograde. Repeat (1), (2), and (3) until you can perform the example without any mistakes.

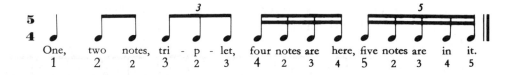

If you have any difficulty performing this example, listen to the recording. Then play the recording again and strike and count along with it.

**62** Rewrite the following measures to include (1) the division of at least one note in each measure into the designated number of equal parts, (2) the proper placement of large and small numbers under the notes, (3) accents on the first part of each count, and (4) appropriate numbers above the note groupings.

a. Two equal parts:

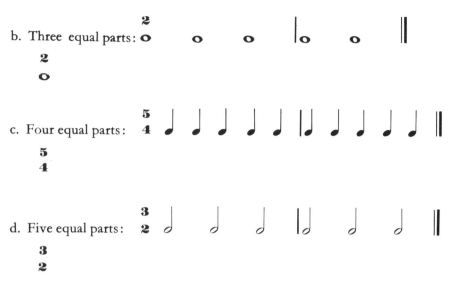

b. Three equal parts:

c. Four equal parts:

d. Five equal parts:

Tap and strike your new **arrangements** of measures a through d.

Here are some examples of how measures a through d may be divided. Follow the measures as you listen to the recording. Perform them if you wish.

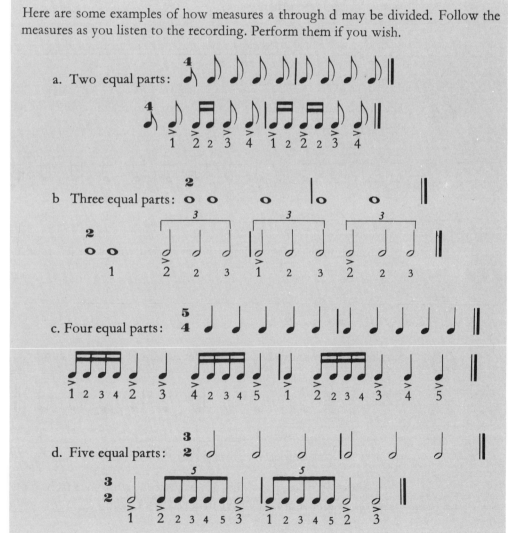

a. Two equal parts:

b Three equal parts:

c. Four equal parts:

d. Five equal parts:

**63** Unless an especially pronounced sound is desired, it is not necessary to write an accent (>) under the first count of a measure, since a **natural accent** normally falls on the first count of every measure. March in place and notice how your left foot automatically accents the first count:

count: 1  2  1  2  1  2  1  2

foot: L  R  L  R  L  R  L  R

The natural accent is a psychophysical phenomenon, and it is stronger for some people than it is for others.

**64** The composer can make the natural accent on the first count of each measure even stronger by adding an accent mark:

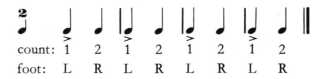

count: 1  2  1  2  1  2  1  2

foot: L  R  L  R  L  R  L  R

March in place, providing a heavy accent with your left foot (first count).

**65** Similarly an accent can be placed under *any* count in the measure:

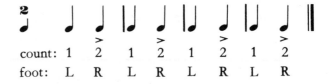

count: 1  2  1  2  1  2  1  2

foot: L  R  L  R  L  R  L  R

March in place, providing a heavy accent with your right foot (second count). Now the *second* count is stronger than the first count.

**66** By accenting counts which are not normally accented, **syncopation** is produced. Syncopation is a very characteristic sound of the twentieth century, especially of jazz and rock, where the second and fourth counts in $\frac{4}{4}$ time are most often accented:

As you count, snap your fingers on the accents. This beat has a contemporary jazz feeling.

This typical rock arrangement also accents the second and fourth counts but more motion is gained by the use of eighth notes on the second count:

As you count, clap your hands on the notes of the second and fourth counts.

Listen to the recording of the two examples above and follow the notes. Play the recording again: count and snap your fingers with the first example, and count and clap with the second example. Practice these two examples until you are able to perform them without the aid of the recording.

**67** Another way to accent counts which are not normally accented (weak counts) is through the use of a longer note value on the weak count than on the first count. (This also produces syncopation.) A longer note value automatically accents a note and produces an **agogic accent**.

Furthermore, the longer the note value, the stronger the accent:

Strike and count the following compositions:

a.

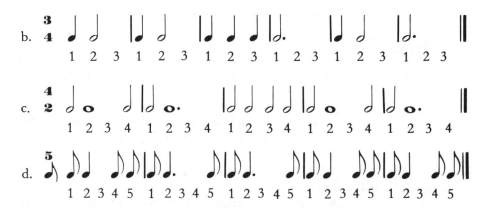

b. **3 4** ♩ ♩ | ♩ ♩ | ♩ ♩ ♩ | ♩. | ♩ ♩ | ♩. ‖

    1 2 3  1 2 3  1 2 3  1 2 3  1 2 3  1 2 3

c. **4 2** ♩ 𝅝 | ♩ ♩ ♩. | ♩ ♩ ♩ ♩ 𝅝 | ♩ ♩ ♩. ‖

    1 2 3 4  1 2 3 4  1 2 3 4  1 2 3 4  1 2 3 4

d. **5** ♪ ♪♪ | ♪♪♪| ♩. | ♪ ♩ | ♩. | ♪ ♩| ♩ | ♪♪ ♩| ♩| ♪♪ ‖

    1 2 3 4 5  1 2 3 4 5  1 2 3 4 5  1 2 3 4 5  1 2 3 4 5

*Extending the duration of a note (agogic accent) on any weak count will provide that particular note with a greater accent than a shorter note on the normally accented (first) count.*

Listen to the recording of compositions a through d. Did the longer notes sound accented? Play the compositions yourself. Be careful not to deliberately accent the longer notes, and you will notice that these notes automatically sound accented because they are longer in duration.

---

**68** Write a four-measure composition for each of the following time signatures and include in each composition (1) syncopation created by accents, (2) some divided counts, and (3) at least one agogic accent.

    Write counts under the notes, then strike and count your compositions in slow and fast tempos. Be certain to provide louder sounds for the accented counts.

a. **4** ♩

b. **2 2**

c. **3** ♩

d. **6 8**

---

**69** In frame 36 the time signature was introduced. You learned that the top number (e.g., **4**) indicates the number of counts in each measure, and the bottom number (e.g., **4**) or note (♩) indicates the kind of note that gets one complete count.

    There are three basic types of time signatures (often called **meters**): **simple, compound,** and **complex.** The *top number* (the number of counts in each measure) determines the type of time signature. Top numbers of simple time signatures are usually 2, 3, or 4, and can be referred to as **duple** (2), **triple** (3), or **quadruple** (4) meters. Top numbers of compound time signatures are usually 6, 9, or 12, and can be referred to as **compound duple** (6), **compound triple** (9), or **compound quadruple** (12) meters. They are compounds (multiples of three) of the simple time signatures. Compound time signatures were described in frame 58. Top numbers of complex time signatures are always uneven numbers greater than four: 5, 7, 11, 13, etc. They are combinations of simple time signatures. For example:

may be a combination of $\frac{3}{4}$ and $\frac{2}{4}$:

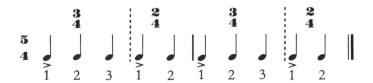

or it may be a combination of $\frac{2}{4}$ and $\frac{3}{4}$:

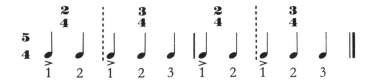

Perhaps the composer would conceive it as:

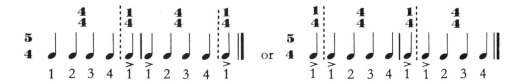

Regardless of the combination, the composer will (or should) indicate the particular combination with accents as in the preceding examples. Some contemporary composers include dotted bar lines in their music to indicate the division of the measure (as in the examples above).

Notice that there are five counts per measure in each of the above examples. *Only the accents are changed.* There is considerable use of complex time signatures in contemporary concert music, rock, modern jazz, as well as in the folk music of such Mediterranean cultures as Greece. The most frequently used complex time signature is $\frac{5}{4}$.

**70** Strike and count the following $\frac{5}{4}$ composition twice in a slow tempo and then in a fast tempo. Observe the accents. How and where have they been used to achieve unity in this composition?

Notice the symbols at the beginning ( ‖: ) and end ( :‖ ) of the composition. These symbols are **repeat signs,** and they indicate that all the measures between them are to be repeated.

Using the accent marks as guides, divide each measure into the appropriate simple time signature combinations by dotted bar lines. Write the time signatures above the notes and write counts below the notes (as in frame 69).

Unity is achieved in the first and last measures of this composition; accents have been placed on the same counts in both measures.

---

**71** Complex time signatures may include *several* combinations of simple time signatures within a single measure. Strike and count these examples:

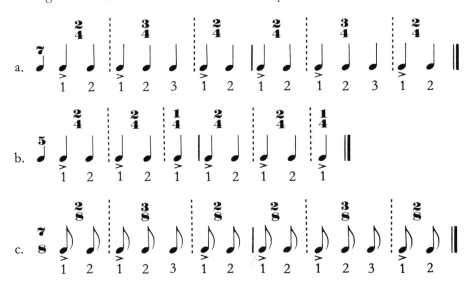

There are other combinations in both $\frac{5}{4}$ and $\frac{7}{8}$ time signatures. Can you think of any?

**72** Write a seven-measure composition, using any complex time signature. Using accent marks, change the combinations of simple time signatures from measure to measure. Include repeat signs, and write the counts below the notes and the simple time signatures above the notes (as in frame 71).

Perform your composition several times in different tempos, using different sound-producing combinations each time. Play your composition in class, then play other students' compositions.

---

**73** In frame 58 you learned that the number three is of prime importance in understanding compound time signatures. When multiplied by three, simple time signatures of 2, 3, and 4 become compound time signatures of 6, 9, and 12, respectively. These compound time signatures may be counted exactly as indicated—6, 9, or 12 counts per measure, especially in compositions of slow tempo. However, in compositions which are written in faster tempos (which are more common in compound time), the compound time signatures are *usually* counted exactly as their simple time signature counterparts:

    a. Compound 6 = 2 strong pulses/measure (counts 1 and 4).
    b. Compound 9 = 3 strong pulses/measure (counts 1, 4, and 7).
    c. Compound 12 = 4 strong pulses/measure (counts, 1, 4, 7, and 10).

This technique of counting results from considering each strong pulse or beat as *one* group of *three* equal notes. Observe the following example with the compound time signature of $\frac{6}{8}$:

In a slow tempo, this example would most likely be counted:

but in the more common faster tempo, it would be counted:

Notice that the dashes indicate the three equal counts. Strike and count examples a and b above. Be certain to play b in a faster tempo than a. Follow the same procedures with examples c–f:

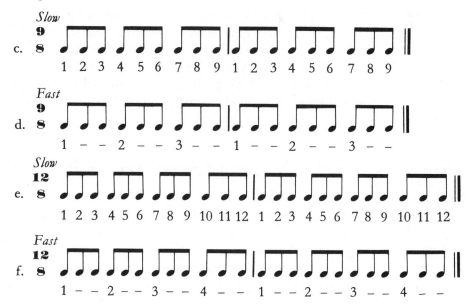

Notice the groupings of three equal notes into one pulse (fast tempos) for each of the compound time signatures.

⊙ Count and follow examples a through f as you listen to the recording.

---

**74** When one sound lasts for a complete pulse or beat in compound time (fast tempo) it is always indicated by a dotted note. (Three counts in fast compound time = one beat.)

Strike and count the above composition. Notice that the dotted note is equivalent to three eighth notes ( ♪♪♪ ). It is also equivalent to one quarter note and one eighth note ( ♩♪ ), and one eighth note and one quarter note ( ♪♩ ). To illustrate:

$$ ♩. = ♪♪♪ \text{ or } ♩♪ \text{ or } ♪♩ $$

Realizing that the internal grouping of three notes is a constant feature of compound time signatures will greatly facilitate your understanding and feeling for compound time. (Review frames 58 and 59.)

Count along with the recording of the first example above.

---

**75** The following composition illustrates the use of the dotted note and some of its *notational equivalents*. Notice that all the notes in groups of threes have been beamed so that the eye will immediately perceive them.

Strike and count the above composition. In the last measure you will feel that the accent which is normally on the first note of that measure has been shifted to the second note. This shift in accent is caused by the longer duration of the second note. This device, which occurs on the *weaker part of the first count,* is a common technique for creating syncopation. As you will recall from frame 67, extending the duration of a note (agogic accent) on any weak count provides that particular note with a greater accent. The agogic accent may also be applied to weak *parts* of counts (any part other than the first), as in the last measure of the preceding example and in measures one and two of the example below:

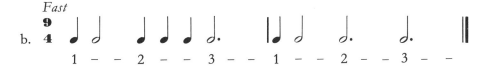

Syncopation is not limited to only the first count. It can be created on a weaker part of *any* count:

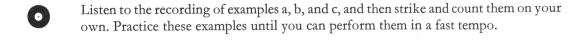

The agogic accent on a weak part of a count will shift the accent from the first part to a weaker part of the count.

 Listen to the recording of examples a, b, and c, and then strike and count them on your own. Practice these examples until you can perform them in a fast tempo.

---

**76** Write a four-measure composition in each of the following compound time signatures. Through agogic accents, create syncopation on the weaker parts of counts in at least two measures of each composition. Circle the syncopated notes and write the counts (fast tempo) under the notes. Strike and count your compositions and vary the dynamics.

a. **12**
   **8**

b. **6**
   **8**

c. **6**
   **4**

d. **9**
   **16**

Follow examples a through d as you listen to the recording. Then listen to them once again—this time playing along with recording (tap, strike, count).

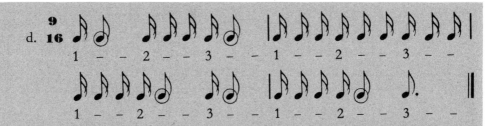

The agogic accents on weaker parts of counts are circled. Check your compositions for the correct placement of counts.

**77**  Strike and count the following compositions with different sound-producing combinations (all in fast tempos). Circle the agogic accents which occur on weak counts or weak parts of counts. Notice that this use of longer notes on weaker counts creates considerable syncopation.

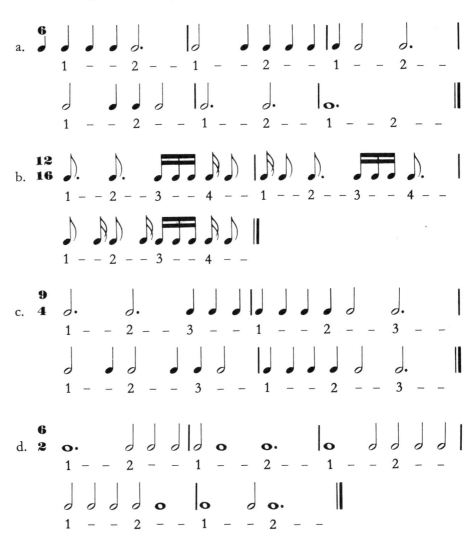

RESPONSES

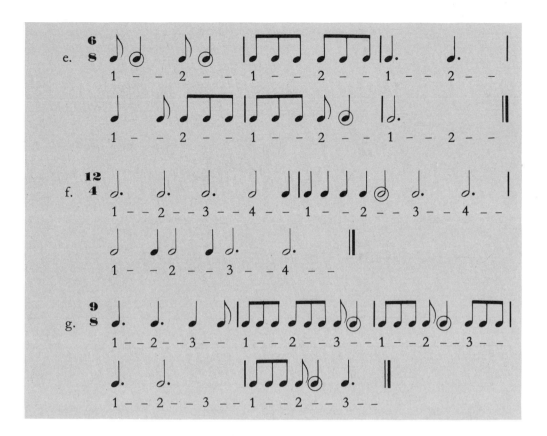

78    Write a three-measure composition in each of the following compound time signatures (all in fast tempo). Create syncopation by using agogic accents on some weak counts and weaker parts of counts. Write the counts under the notes. Then, strike and count your compositions and play them in class with various sound-producing combinations.

a.   **6**
      **8**

b.   **9**
      **4**

c.   **12**
      **8**

d. $\frac{6}{4}$

e. $\frac{9}{16}$

f. $\frac{12}{16}$

---

**79**  You have been using the dotted quarter ( ♩. ) and the dotted eighth note ( ♪. ) in compound time. Now you will learn to use and count these notes in simple and complex time signatures. You will recall from frame 43 that a dot is always equal to one-half the value of the note that precedes it:

In other words, in this example, the dot equals the time of one eighth note. Examine its use in the following measure:

1  2  2  2  3  2  4  2

Analyze the counts in the above measure. The two halves of the first count (12) fall on the first quarter note ( ♩ ); the first half of the second count (2) falls on the dot (•) after the quarter note; the second half of the second count (2) falls on the eighth note ( ♪ ). In counts 3 and 4, the situation is exactly the same as in counts 1 and 2.

Strike and count the above measure. Repeat it several times. In both simple and complex time signatures, you are very likely to see the dotted quarter note followed by an eighth note. It is one of the most common notational figures in all of music. When used, the figure gives a composition considerable momentum. It has a skipping character. The reason for this is that the ♩. ♪ is a distinctively uneven **rhythmic unit.**

After you have practiced striking and counting the measure of dotted quarter and eighth notes, listen to the recording of that measure.

If you find it difficult to count and strike at the same time, practice with the recording. But it is important that you learn to perform this measure correctly without the help of the recording.

---

**80** Somewhat less common, but still frequently encountered, is the dotted eighth note followed by the sixteenth note (♪. ♪ or ♫). Remember (frame 43) that a dot is always equal to one-half the value of the note that precedes it:

$$\text{♪.} = \text{♪} + \cdot \quad \text{or} \quad \text{♪} + \text{♪}$$

In this rhythmic unit (♪. ♪ or ♫), the dot equals one-half the time of an eighth note, that is, the value of one sixteenth note. Examine its use in the following measure:

Analyze the counts in the above measure. The two halves of the first count (12) fall on the first eighth note (♪); the first half of the second count (2) falls on the dot (·) after the eighth note; the second half of the second count (2) falls on the sixteenth note (♪). In counts 3 and 4, the situation is exactly the same as in counts 1 and 2.

Strike and count the above measure. Repeat it several times. You are very likely to see the dotted eighth note followed by a sixteenth note in both simple and complex time signatures.

---

**81** Strike and count (as indicated) the following compositions:

Once you can securely perform these compositions, dispense with the counting and vocalize them on a neutral syllable such as ta, do, mi, loo. Be sure to hold each note for the proper amount of time.

Notice that composition a begins with the third count of a measure. The first two counts are missing. Also notice, however, that those two counts are included at the end of the composition. Compositions d and e use the same device. If a composer wishes to begin a composition with notes that constitute less than a full measure, he must end the composition with the counts that were missing in the first measure. Carefully examine compositions a, d, and e to be certain that you understand this device.

When a composition begins with an incomplete measure, the note in that measure is referred to as an **anacrusis** or more commonly, a **pickup note** or **upbeat**. Often, there will be more than one pickup note, as in composition a.

As you listen to compositions a through e on this recording, carefully follow the notes.

Did you strike and count the compositions correctly? If you are uncertain, play the recording again and strike and count along with the recording.

---

**82**  Strike and count the following compositions and write the counts under the notes, as in frame 81. Check each measure to make sure that it has the complete number of counts. Some do not. When this occurs, add your own note(s) to complete the measure.

If you see pickup notes, circle them. Notice this rhythmic unit ( ) in b.

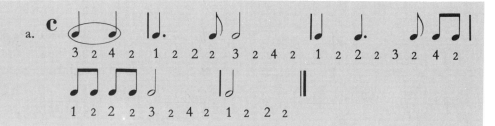

Notice that the last note in measure 2 of composition a was changed to a half note, thereby completing the number of counts in that measure.

Notice that an eighth note has been added to measure 3 of composition b to complete the counts. Also observe that a dot has been added to the last note of the composition.

In composition c, observe that the dotted half notes of measures 3 and 6 have been replaced with whole notes, thereby completing the counts in those measures.

Notice the addition of the quarter note on count 5 in measure 2 of composition d.

**83** *Silence, the absence of sound in time, is an integral part of music.* This is one of the first concepts which you learned in Chapter One. Now you will learn to notate silence. The symbols which are used to notate silence are called **rests.** For every note value there is an equivalent rest value:

| Note | Rest | Name |
|------|------|------|
| ♪ (32nd) | 𝄿 | thirty-second |
| ♪ (16th) | 𝄿 | sixteenth |
| ♪ (8th) | 𝄾 | eighth |
| ♩ | 𝄽 | quarter |
| 𝅗𝅥 | ▬ | half |
| 𝅝 | ▬ | whole* |

*A whole rest can also be used to designate one complete measure of silence, regardless of the time signature.

**84** As you know a dot may be added to a note to increase the time value of that note. Similarly, to increase the time value of a rest, a dot may be added to that rest. For example:

Note

$$\text{♩.} = \text{♩} + \text{♪}$$
$$\text{𝅗𝅥.} = \text{𝅗𝅥} + \text{♩}$$
$$\text{♪.} = \text{♪} + \text{♪}$$

Rest

$$\text{𝄽.} = \text{𝄽} + \text{𝄾}$$
$$\text{▬.} = \text{▬} + \text{𝄽}$$
$$\text{𝄾.} = \text{𝄾} + \text{𝄿}$$

Dotted rests will most frequently be seen in music with the compound time signatures of $\frac{6}{8}, \frac{9}{8}, \frac{12}{8}, \frac{6}{16}, \frac{9}{16},$ and $\frac{12}{16}$.

**85** Rests add variety to music, thereby creating more interest. Remember to count the rest(s) in the same manner as you would count the equivalent note(s). You will discover that the use of rests is one of the most common devices for achieving syncopation in a composition. Write the counts under the notes, and then strike and count the following compositions in the tempos indicated. Remember, *don't* strike on rests, but *do* continue counting.

Strike the above compositions again. But, instead of counting, vocalize each composition on a different neutral syllable (do, lee, fa, etc.).

In compositions a and d, notice the accent marks on weak *parts* of counts. Accenting weak parts of counts is another syncopation technique.

RESPONSES

Now that you have attempted to strike, count, and vocalize compositions a through e, listen to the recording as you watch the notes. It would be wise for you to practice with the recording, since the strike/count process is becoming more complicated. Be certain that you can perform these compositions correctly before going on to frame 86.

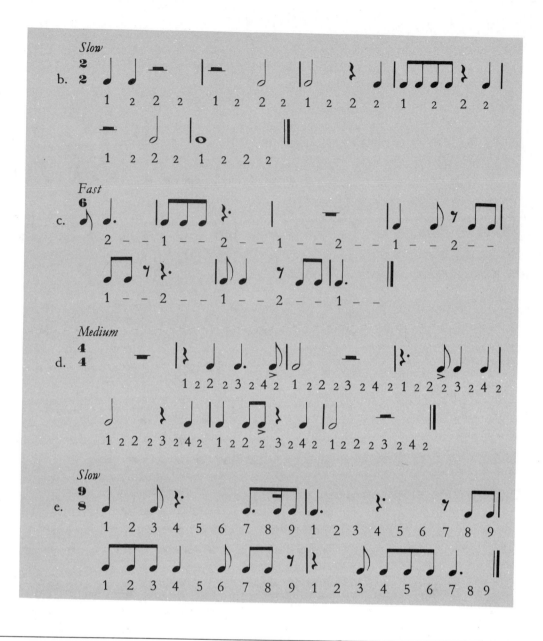

**86** Write four of your own compositions (each at least four measures long) using the time signatures indicated. Include various types of rests in each composition, and write the counts under the notes.

*Slow*
a. 4/4

*Fast*
b. $\frac{9}{8}$

*Medium*
c. $\frac{3}{2}$

*Slow*
d. $\frac{6}{8}$

Strike and count your compositions, varying the dynamics.

---

**87** Return to composition a in frame 85. Notice that, in every measure except the last measure, rests occur on the normally accented count (count one). Thus, the accent is displaced and it is shifted (as in all types of syncopation—frame 66), to the normally unaccented counts (count 2 or 3).

In other words, *the use of silence on the normally accented count causes a normally unaccented count to be stressed.*

Strike and count composition a in frame 85 again, with this new understanding in mind.

---

**88** Syncopation can also be created by the use of the **tie** (a curved line connecting two notes, such as ♩ ♩). The tie is a device which, like the dot, increases the value of a note. The second note of a tie is not played but is held from the first note and thereby adds its value to the first note. For example: ♩ ♩ = ♩..

Although the tie is most frequently used for extending a note from one measure to the next, it may occur *anywhere* within a measure. When a tie occurs within a measure, the normal accent is shifted to another count and syncopation results.

Strike and count compositions a, b, and c (S = Strike, H = Hold). *Remember that the second note of the tie is not struck.* However, it is always held and counted.

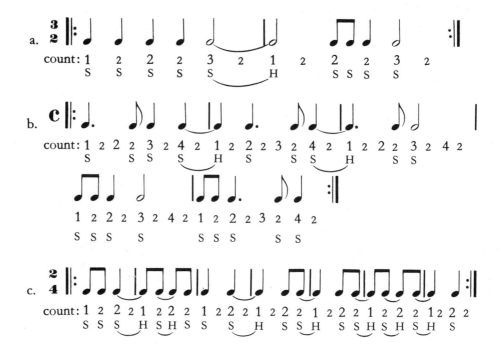

As you listen to the recording of compositions a, b, and c, follow the notes.

If you have difficulty performing the ties, strike and count along with the recording.

---

**89**  Once you understand the tie, you will have learned all of the most frequently used methods of creating syncopation. Notice that each device, the accent mark, the agogic accent, the rest, and the tie, shifts the accent from the strong beat (the beat which is normally accented) to a weaker beat and this is what produces the syncopation. Here is a summary of those methods:

a.  Accent mark on a weak count.

b.  Agogic accent on a weak count.

c.  Accent mark on a weak part of a count.

d.  Agogic accent on a weak part of a count.

e.  Rest on a strong count.

54

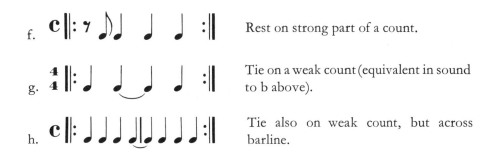

f. Rest on strong part of a count.

g. Tie on a weak count (equivalent in sound to b above).

h. Tie also on weak count, but across barline.

Strike and count the preceding measures.

---

**90** Strike and count the following compositions. Vary the dynamics, and write the counts under the notes. When you begin to feel comfortable performing the compositions throughout this text, you should gain considerable confidence in dealing with similar problems in the popular music of today.

f. *Fast*

g. *Slow*

RESPONSES

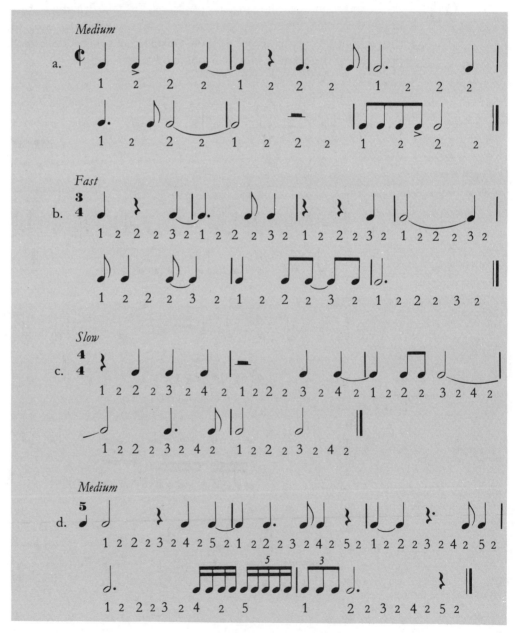

a. *Medium*

b. *Fast*

c. *Slow*

d. *Medium*

56

**91** By performing all of the preceding compositions, you have become familiar with a wide variety of note and rest values, which give interest to music. The arrangement of these values within a measure, or within many measures, is usually referred to as the **rhythm.** Do *not* confuse the rhythm of a measure (as many people do) with the basic, steady pulse or beat (review the definition of beat in frame 58) which underlies each measure. Rhythm is one of the most distinguishing characteristics of music. If the rhythmic relationships in a popular piece of music were changed, you probably would not recognize that piece of music.

Musicians generally associate the beat with the number of counts in every measure. For example, a piece written in $\frac{4}{4}$ will probably be *heard/felt* as having four beats and, likewise, a piece written in $\frac{3}{2}$ will normally be considered as having three beats. However, the tempo of the music actually determines how many beats are felt.

For instance, in a $\frac{4}{4}$ measure of medium speed, the four counts may feel like four beats. But in a fast tempo, although the time signature is notated as $\frac{4}{4}$, you may feel only *one* beat per measure. Recall from frame 73 that a slow piece in $\frac{6}{8}$ was counted in six because six beats were felt, whereas a fast piece in $\frac{6}{8}$ was counted in two (two groups of three notes) because only two beats were felt.

In a very slow tempo, in which rhythmic groupings of eighth notes are consistently used ($\frac{4}{4}$ ♫ ♫ ♫ ♫), *eight* beats may be felt. It is quite possible that the number of beats and counts will be the same, but many times they will be different. You *feel* the beat—but you *see* the counts.

When you are listening to music, try to discover the beat: let the ball of your foot fall *naturally* when it will, and try to determine on which count(s) it is falling. If you are trying to discover the beat while playing from notated music, tap the rhythm in the suggested tempo, and once again let your foot fall naturally when it will. Determine on which count(s) it is falling. If your foot doesn't naturally fall fast enough, the beat is probably on some other count. Where your foot feels *right* is most likely the true beat. Interpretations of the beat might vary from person to person, because the beat relates to feelings as well as to the intellect. However, most people respond to the same beat patterns. Attend a rock concert and you will see people agreeing on the beat: thousands of feet, hands, and bodies respond as one to the power of the beat.

---

**92**  Notice in example a that the rhythm pattern coincides with the counts. Since this example is marked for a very slow tempo, the beats will also be the same as the counts. Strike the rhythm with your right hand (RH), observing the accent marks. Strike the counts with your left hand (LH), and keep the beat with the ball of your foot (F).

In example b, since it is marked for a slow tempo, the counts and beats are the same but notice that in this example, the rhythm pattern is different from the count pattern. Be sure to observe the accents in the rhythm, following the performance procedures of example a.

In example c, the rhythm is the same as the count pattern. However, as you perform this example, you will notice that, because of the very fast tempo, the beat is only felt on the first count of every measure.

Perform example d. Did you feel the beat as often as the counts? Add the beat pattern to the diagram.

Perform example e. Did you feel as many beats as counts? In determining this, consider their relationship to the tempo. Add the count and beat patterns to the diagram.

After performing and analyzing these examples, you should have a good idea of all the things that a drummer must consider when playing a piece of music. Some drummers even use two bass drums, one for each foot. A fine drummer must be a master of every aspect of time in music and he must also have a good deal of coordination. You, too, are headed in this direction. Practice examples a–e again until you can play them without any mistakes.

RESPONSES

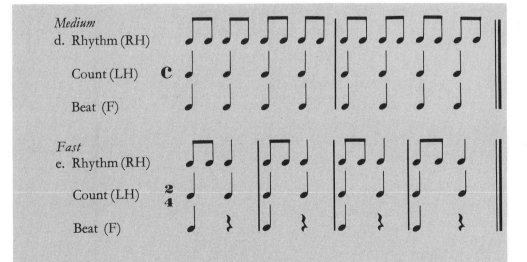

Listen to the recording of examples a through e as you follow the music.

If the distinctions between rhythm, count, and beat are still not clear to you, read frame 91 again. Then, practice examples a through e until your right hand, your left hand, and your foot are coordinated.

**93** Examine compositions a–e:

Notice that there is no repeat sign ‖: at the beginning of composition a. Since the *entire* composition is being repeated, that first repeat sign is not necessary. The composition is automatically played from the beginning. Both repeat signs are used when the measures to be repeated occur *within* the composition.

A substitute for the repeat sign is the initials **D.C.** (**Da Capo**, pronounced dä kä′ pō). *Capo* in Italian means "head," so D.C. instructs the performer to go back to the head, or beginning, of a composition. In compositions b and c, the directions, **D.C. al Fine** (pronounced äl′ fē′ nä) mean "to the end." The performer repeats the composition from the beginning and ends at the double bar with *Fine* above it. The use of the repeat signs or *D.C. al Fine* is a type of musical shorthand which allows the composer to indicate repetition without having to notate each measure again.

Another example of musical shorthand appears in compositions d and e. Here, substituting for the repeat sign, are the initials, **D.S. (Dal Segno,** pronounced däl sā′ nyȯ). *Segno* in Italian means "sign," so D.S. instructs the performer to go back to the sign (𝄋). In these compositions, **D.S. al Fine** means to go back to the sign and continue to the double bar with *Fine* above it.

Observe the double bar below the *D.C.* and *D.S. al Fine* in compositions b through e. It is a **section double bar**, and is used to indicate the end of a section but *not* the end of a composition.

Now, play compositions a–e. Strike the rhythm with your right hand (RH), the counts with your left hand (LH), and the beats with the ball of your foot (F). All these compositions are in slow or medium tempos, therefore the beats and counts will be the same.

---

**94**  Write two eight-measure compositions, using any time signatures you wish. In the first composition, use *D.S. al Fine*; in the second composition, use *D.C. al Fine*. Use section double bars where necessary.  Write the counts under the appropriate notes. Play both compositions in these four ways:

 a. Medium tempo: strike the rhythms with your right hand and the counts with your left hand.
 b. Medium tempo: strike the rhythms with your left hand and the counts with your right hand.
 c. Slow tempo: strike the rhythms with your right hand, the counts with your left hand, and the beats with your foot.
 d. Fast tempo: strike the rhythms with your right hand, the counts with your left hand, and the beats with your foot.

Practice these compositions until you can coordinate your hands and your foot. Did the beats change when you played your compositions in the fast tempo?

---

**95**  You have learned many things about time in music. You have learned that tempo refers to the speed of music, and you have performed some of your compositions in various tempos of your own choice. Obviously, the overall duration of a composition is determined by its tempo and the length of its notes.  You may have wondered if there is a precise way to indicate just how long a particular kind of note should sound. There is. It is called a **metronome marking.** A **metronome** is a mechanical or electrical machine which sounds (clicks) in a regular recurring count at whatever speed is selected. Observe the metronome pictured below.

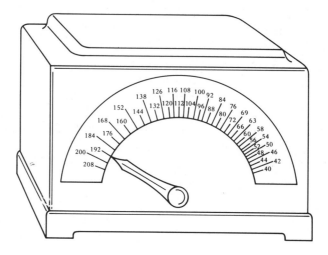

The dial is set at 192, which means that the metronome will sound at an even rate of 192 clicks per minute. If a piece has a metronome marking of ♩ = 192, this instructs the performer to set the dial at 192 and play one quarter note for each click of the metronome (192 quarter notes per minute). Similarly, for the metronome marking of ♩ = 90, the performer would set the dial at 90 and play one half note for each click of the metronome; ♪ = 120 means 120 eighth notes per minute. When a metronome marking is notated at the beginning of a composition, it is possible to estimate the approximate duration in terms of seconds, minutes, or hours of that particular composition.

---

**96**

When a metronome marking is identified with a particular note value, such as ♩ = 42 or ♪ = 60, it can also be identified by a **tempo section term** (written in Italian):

| *Metronome Marking Range* | *Tempo Section Term* |
|---|---|
| ♩ = 40-52 | Largo (lär′ gō) |
| ♩ = 54-66 | Larghetto (lär gĕt′ ō) |
| ♩ = 69-88 | Adagio (ä dä′ jō) |
| ♩ = 92-116 | Andante (än dän′ tå) |
| ♩ = 120-152 | Allegro (ä lä′ grō) |
| ♩ = 160-208 | Presto (prĕs′ tō) |

Largo is the slowest tempo section, presto is the fastest. Sometimes these tempo section terms are used in place of metronome markings, and then the composition can be performed at any speed within that particular range of metronome markings.

The performer will decide for himself. For example, if the composer indicates *Adagio* for his music, the performer may decide to play the quarter note at any rate from 69 to 88 times per minute.

In the popular music of America, you usually will not see the tempo section terms written in Italian. You will see terminology such as *fast, slowly, moderately, lively, dreamily, with a strong beat,* etc. There is no precise relationship between these terms and the Italian terms.

---

**97**   Write the appropriate tempo section terms for the following metronome markings. You may refer to frames 95 and 96.

a. ♩ = 64 _____     f. 𝅝 = 98 _____

b. ♪ = 132 _____     g. ♩ = 102 _____

c. ♩ = 200 _____     h. ♪ = 48 _____

d. ♩ = 88 _____     i. ♪ = 120 _____

e. ♩ = 160 _____     j. ♩ = 116 _____

RESPONSES

| | | | | | |
|---|---|---|---|---|---|
| a. | ♩ = 64 | *Larghetto* | f. | 𝅝 = 98 | *Andante* |
| b. | ♪ = 132 | *Allegro* | g. | ♩ = 102 | *Andante* |
| c. | ♩ = 200 | *Presto* | h. | ♪ = 48 | *Largo* |
| d. | ♩ = 88 | *Adagio* | i. | ♪ = 120 | *Allegro* |
| e. | ♩ = 160 | *Presto* | j. | ♩ = 116 | *Andante* |

---

**98**   To indicate that the established tempo within a composition should gradually become faster, the term **accelerando** (sometimes abbreviated **accel.,** and meaning *accelerate*) is written either above or below the notes. Conversely, the term **ritardando** (sometimes abbreviated **rit.**) is used to indicate that the established tempo should gradually become *slower*. The term **a tempo** (meaning *at the original tempo*) is used to indicate a return to the composition's original tempo. The rate of accelerando or ritardando is determined by the performer and the style of the music itself.

---

**99**   Here is an opportunity to apply the musical skills you have acquired in Chapter Two. Write three compositions, each at least six measures long. Use a simple time signature for one composition, a compound time signature for another, and a complex time signature for the third composition. Include in each composition:

a. Several different note and rest values (including dotted notes and rests).
b. Metronome markings and their appropriate tempo terms. (Write them at the beginning of your compositions—above the notes.)
c. Groups of measures using *accelerando, ritardando*, and *a tempo*. (Indicate terms.)
d. Counts under the notes.
e. Syncopations, through the use of rests, ties, and agogic accents.
f. Differences in dynamics: soft, medium, and loud.
g. *D.C. al Fine* and *D.S. al Fine* in two of the compositions.

Write your compositions in the spaces following this paragraph. Then, strike and count them. Play your slow compositions in a fast tempo. Did the beats change?

a.



b.



c.

---

**100**  Strike and count the following compositions of alternating time signatures, observing their tempo section terms. Write the counts below the notes.

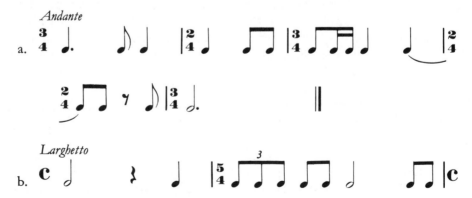

**Lively**

c.

Notice that the tempo remains constant throughout each composition, regardless of the change in time signatures.

RESPONSES

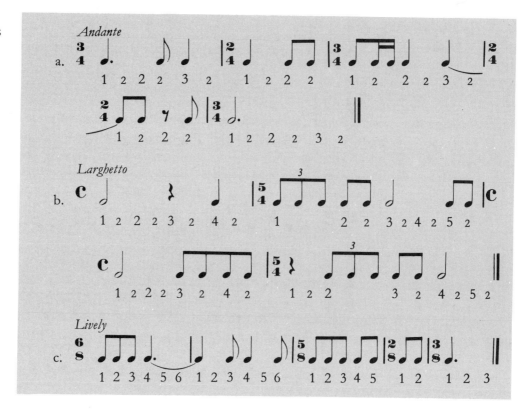

**101** Write three compositions, each at least five measures long. Alternate the time signatures within each composition, as in frame 100. Write the counts under the notes. Strike and count your compositions. Include tempo marks or metronome markings.

a.

b.

c.

Play all three compositions as one (that is, one after the other with no breaks). Use *accelerando, ritardando,* and *a tempo,* at your own discretion.

**102**  Strike (*without* counting) the following compositions. Vary the sound sources and the dynamics. Observe the tempo changes. Return to *a tempo* after the repeat signs.

Notice that all three compositions have the same time signature ( **C** ) and tempo ($\downarrow$ = 120). Since the time signatures and tempos of the compositions are identical, they can easily be played at the same time, thereby creating **part music** (three-part music, in this particular case).

**103**  Ask two other students to help you play the three-part composition in frame 100 (but eliminate the D.C. al Fine in composition c). Take turns playing the different parts. Use a variety of sound-producing combinations.

Now, write your own three-part composition with at least four measures for each part. Ask two students to help you play it. Use a variety of sound-producing combinations, and vary the dynamics. Remember that rests, accents, and syncopations are important devices in creating musical interest and variety. Write your composition in the space provided:

**104**   Fill in the blanks:

a. In $\frac{4}{4}$ time, a _____ note receives one count.

b. In $\frac{3}{4}$ time, this note 𝅗𝅥. receives _____ count(s).

c. Four of these notes ♪ equal this note _____ .

d. In $\frac{3}{2}$ time, this note 𝅗𝅥 receives _____ count(s).

e. In this time signature ₵, the _____ note receives one count.

f. Provide bar lines for the following composition:

g. A _____ bar line should be written at the end of a composition.

h. Musically speaking, altering the speed of the measures in f above is called altering the _____ of the music.

i. In $\frac{3}{8}$ time, these notes ♪ ♩ receive a total of _____ count(s).

j. This mark >, when placed under a note, is called an _____ .

k. *Accel.*, when it appears in the music, means that the established tempo should _____ .

l. To indicate a return to the established tempo, composers use the term
_____.

m. *Rit.,* when it appears in the music, means that the established tempo should
_____.

n. A _____ double bar line is drawn below the term, *D.C. al Fine.*

o. Groups of eighth, sixteenth, and thirty-second notes are connected by
_____.

RESPONSES

a. In $\frac{4}{4}$ time, a *quarter* note receives one count.

b. In $\frac{3}{?}$ time, this note ♩. receives *three* count(s).

c. Four of these notes ♪ equal this note ♩.

d. In $\frac{3}{2}$ time, this note ♩ receives *one* count(s).

e. In this time signature ¢ , the *half* note receives one count.

f. Provide bar lines for the following composition:

g. A *double* bar line should be written at the end of a composition.

h. Musically speaking, altering the speed of the measures in f above is called altering the *tempo* of the music.

i. In $\frac{3}{8}$ time, these notes ♪♩ receive a total of *three* count(s).

j. This mark >, when placed under a note, is called an *accent.*

k. *Accel.,* when it appears in the music, means that the established tempo should *speed up (or accelerate).*

l. To indicate a return to the established tempo, composers use the term

m. *Rit.,* when it appears in the music, means that an established tempo should *slow down.*

n. A *section* double bar line is drawn below the term, *D.C. al Fine.*

o. Groups of eighth, sixteenth, and thirty-second notes are connected by *beams.*

**105**

a. Divide this note ♪ into triplets _____, and then divide this note ♩ into triplets _____.

b. Divide this note $\mathbf{o}$ into five equal parts _____, and divide this note $\downarrow$ into four equal parts _____.

c. In a composition with the compound time signature of $\frac{9}{\flat}$, you could expect to see _____ groups of connected eighth notes in a measure.

d. With a compound time signature of $\frac{6}{8}$, music played at a *fast* tempo would have _____ beats or pulses per measure.

e. With a compound time signature of $\frac{12}{4}$, this note _____ receives one beat when the music is played in a *fast* tempo.

f. With a compound time signature of $\frac{6}{8}$, this note _____ receives one beat when the music is played in a *fast* tempo; but with the same time signature, this note _____ receives one beat when the music is played in a *slow* tempo.

g. Write the counts under the notes of the following measure. Show both halves of each count (e.g., 12 22, etc.).

h. Circle the syncopated notes:

i. Add a top number to the following time signatures so that each time signature will be complex:

   4    2    1   $\flat$   $\flat$

j. In these two measures, create syncopation by placing accents under the appropriate notes (anywhere except under a first count):

k. Now create syncopation in those same measures by using ties to connect appropriate notes (anywhere except first and second notes of a measure):

b. Divide this note 𝅝 into five equal parts 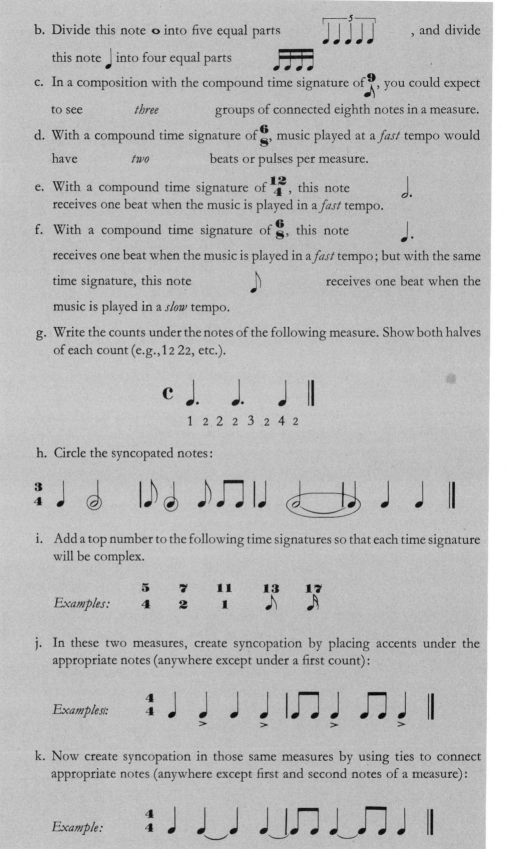 , and divide this note ♩ into four equal parts

c. In a composition with the compound time signature of $\frac{9}{8}$, you could expect to see _three_ groups of connected eighth notes in a measure.

d. With a compound time signature of $\frac{6}{8}$, music played at a *fast* tempo would have _two_ beats or pulses per measure.

e. With a compound time signature of $\frac{12}{4}$, this note ♩. receives one beat when the music is played in a *fast* tempo.

f. With a compound time signature of $\frac{6}{8}$, this note ♩. receives one beat when the music is played in a *fast* tempo; but with the same time signature, this note ♪ receives one beat when the music is played in a *slow* tempo.

g. Write the counts under the notes of the following measure. Show both halves of each count (e.g., 1 2 2 2, etc.).

**c** ♩. ♩. ♩ ‖

1 2 2 2 3 2 4 2

h. Circle the syncopated notes:

i. Add a top number to the following time signatures so that each time signature will be complex.

*Examples:* $\frac{5}{4}$ $\frac{7}{2}$ $\frac{11}{1}$ $\frac{13}{♪}$ $\frac{17}{♪}$

j. In these two measures, create syncopation by placing accents under the appropriate notes (anywhere except under a first count):

*Examples:* 

k. Now create syncopation in those same measures by using ties to connect appropriate notes (anywhere except first and second notes of a measure):

*Example:*

**106**

a. When a composition begins with an incomplete measure, the note(s) in that measure is called an _____ or _____ note(s), and the unused part of that measure will be found at the _____ of the composition.

b. Rewrite this measure, replacing the second, fourth, and sixth notes with their equivalent rests:

c. Rewrite this composition, replacing the first, third, fourth, fifth, sixth, and ninth notes with their equivalent rests:

d. Create syncopation in this composition by displacing *some* notes with their equivalent rests:

e. In this measure, replace the dots with tied notes:

f. When the tempo of a composition is changed, sometimes the _____ or _____ of that composition will also change.

RESPONSES

a. When a composition begins with an incomplete measure, the note(s) in that measure is called an *anacrusis* or *pickup* note(s), and the unused part of that measure will be found at the *end* of the composition.

71

b. Rewrite this measure, replacing the second, fourth, and sixth notes with their equivalent rests:

c. Rewrite this composition, replacing the first, third, fourth, fifth, sixth, and ninth notes with their equivalent rests:

d. Create syncopation in this composition by displacing *some* notes with their equivalent rests:

e. In this measure, replace the dots with tied notes:

f. When the tempo of a composition is changed, sometimes the *beats* or *pulses* of that composition will also change.

---

**107**

a. If a composer wishes to indicate how fast his music should be performed, he will write a _____ marking and/or a _____ _____ term above the music.

b. In your own language, write the equivalents of these tempo section terms:
*Largo* _____, *Allegro* _____,
*Presto* _____.

c. Rewrite these time signatures, using numbers: **C** ――――― **₵** ―――――.

d. Write a time signature to the left of the following measures:

1.

2.

3.

4.

5.

e. *Da Capo* means to return to the _____ of a composition, and *Dal Segno* means to return to the _____, which may be located anywhere in the composition.

a. If a composer wishes to indicate how fast his music should be performed, he will write a *metronome* marking and/or a *tempo section* term above the music.

b. In your own language, write the equivalents of these tempo section terms:
*Largo   slow,*                    *Allegro   fast,*
*Presto   very fast.*

c. Rewrite these time signatures, using numbers: **C**  **4/4**   **₵**  **2/2** .

d. Write a time signature to the left of the following measures:

1.  **3/4**

2.  **9/8**

3.  **4/2 or 8/4**

4.  **2/4**

5. $\frac{5}{4}$ ♫♫ ♩ ♫ ♩ ♪ 𝄽 ♪ 𝄾 ‖

e. *Da Capo* means to return to the *beginning* of a composition, and *Dal Segno* means to return to the *sign*, which may be located anywhere in the composition.

---

**108** Before beginning your *Involvement with Music* program, you identified popular songs simply by listening to them. But now that you understand rhythmic notation, you will be able to identify many of those songs from that notation alone. The ability to recognize a song by its rhythmic notation is an important step forward in thinking musically.

The following rhythmic examples are taken from the first few measures of well-known popular songs. Examine them, play them, and then match each one with the correct song title from this list. It should be quite an experience for you to see these familiar song passages in rhythmic notation. All of the titles will be used, and each will be used only once. The correct title is printed upside down below each example.

BRIDGE OVER TROUBLED WATERS
MRS. ROBINSON
MARIA (WEST SIDE STORY)
OVER THE RAINBOW
BY THE TIME I GET TO PHOENIX
I DON'T KNOW HOW TO LOVE HIM
FOR ALL WE KNOW
AQUARIUS

a. Title _____

A rock opera by Andrew Lloyd Webber and Tim Rice. Copyright © 1970 by Leeds Music Limited.
"I Don't Know How to Love Him" (Jesus Christ, Superstar).

b. Title _____

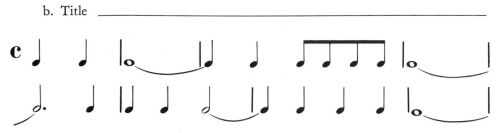

Copyright © 1966, 1967, 1968. James Rado, Gerome Ragni, Galt MacDermot, Nat Shapiro, United Artists Music Co., Inc. All rights administered and controlled by United Artists Music Co., Inc., 729 Seventh Ave., New York, N.Y. Used by permission.
"Aquarius."

c. Title _____

Lyric: E. Y. Harburg; music: Harold Arlen. Copyright © 1938; renewed 1966 Metro-Goldwyn-Mayer, Inc. Copyright © 1939; renewed 1967 Leo Feist Inc. Rights throughout the world controlled by Leo Feist Inc. Used by permission.
"Over the Rainbow."

d. Title _____

Copyright © 1969 Paul Simon. Used with permission of the publisher, Charing Cross Music, Inc.
"Bridge Over Troubled Waters," by Paul Simon.

e. Title _____

Copyright © 1967 by Dramatis Music Corp. All rights reserved. Used by permission only. Words and music by Jimmy Webb.
"By the Time I Get to Phoenix."

f. Title _____

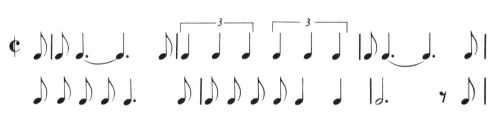

Copyright © 1957 by Leonard Bernstein and Stephen Sondheim. Used by permission of G. Schirmer, Inc.
"Maria," (West Side Story).

g. Title _____

Copyright © 1968 Paul Simon. Used with permission of the publisher, Charing Cross Music, Inc.
"Mrs. Robinson," by Paul Simon.

h. Title _____

"For All We Know."

---

**109**

Follow the same procedure as you did in frame 108 and match these rhythmic excerpts with the appropriate titles from this list:

      SCARBOROUGH FAIR
      I LEFT MY HEART IN SAN FRANCISCO
      UP, UP AND AWAY
      GAMES PEOPLE PLAY
      BOOKENDS
      LET THE SUNSHINE IN (HAIR)
      FIVE HUNDRED MILES
      I FEEL PRETTY (WEST SIDE STORY)
      JEAN

a. Title _____

"Five Hundred Miles," by Hedy West.

b. Title _____

"I Left My Heart in San Francisco," by Douglas Cross and George Cory.

c. Title _____

"I Feel Pretty," (West Side Story).

d. Title _____

"Up, Up and Away."

e. Title _____

"Scarborough Fair," Adapted by Albert Gamse.

f. Title _____

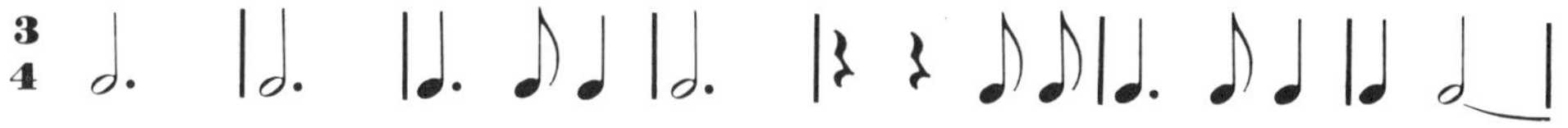

"Jean," by Rod McKuen.

g. Title _____

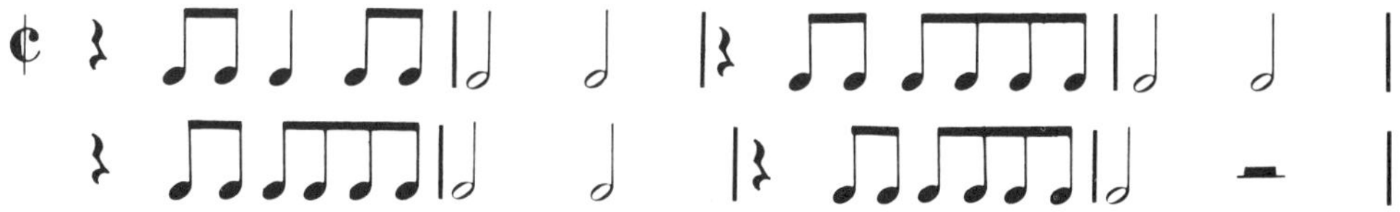

"Games People Play," by Joe South.

h. Title _____

"Bookends," by Paul Simon.

i. Title _____

"Let the Sunshine In."

**110**  Although the thrust of *Involvement with Music* is neither to make you a pop recording star (although the authors wish you success if you try) or a classical concert musician (which takes many years of dedicated training), you have now acquired sufficient rhythmic facility to deal with a variety of concert materials.

The following rhythmic examples are extracted from some of the most well-known and best-loved concert literature. For the most part, they are found at the beginning of a specific **movement** of a composition. (A movement is one section of a fairly long composition.)* Perform these concert excerpts and count as you see fit.

Since the names of the musical works and composers are given, and all these compositions are recorded, you might enjoy following up your rhythmic experiences by listening to some of the available recordings.

* Definitions of any other terms used in these examples may be found in the *Harvard Dictionary of Music* by Willi Apel (Cambridge, Mass.: Harvard University Press).

## SYMPHONY No. 5

First movement                                   Ludwig van Beethoven (1770–1827)

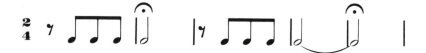

## SYMPHONY No. 9

Fourth movement, "Ode to Joy"                                              Beethoven

## SYMPHONY No. 8 ("Unfinished")

First movement, second theme                          Franz Schubert (1797–1828)

## SYMPHONY No. 7 ("Great")

First movement                                                            Schubert

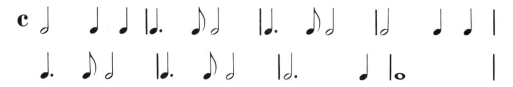

## SYMPHONY No. 1

Fourth movement, main theme                    Johannes Brahms (1833–1897)

## ACADEMIC FESTIVAL OVERTURE

Fifth theme                                                      Brahms

## SYMPHONY No. 6 ("Surprise")

Second movement                          Franz Joseph Haydn (1732–1809)

## FIREBIRD SUITE (Ballet)

Finale                                        Igor Stravinsky (1882–1971)

## SYMPHONY No. 40

First movement                    Wolfgang Amadeus Mozart (1756–1791)

## THE MESSIAH (Oratorio)

"And the Glory of the Lord"          George Frederick Handel (1685–1759)

And    the    glo - ry,    the    glo - ry   of    the    Lord

## THE MESSIAH

"Hallelujah Chorus"                                              Handel

Hal - le - lu - jah!   Hal - le - lu - jah!   Hal - le - lu - jah!   Hal - le - lu - jah!


## DIE WALKÜRE (Opera)

"Ride of the Valkyries"                          Richard Wagner (1813–1883)


## SYMPHONY  No.  1 ("Classical")

Sergei Prokofiev (1891–1953)

## SYMPHONY  No.  5 ("From the New World")

Second movement ("Going Home" theme)      Antonin Dvořák (1841–1904)


## SYMPHONY  No.  4 ("Italian")

First movement                                  Felix Mendelssohn (1809–1847)

## PRELUDE No. 15 ("Raindrop") FOR PIANO

Frédéric François Chopin (1810–1849)

## BALLADE No. 1 FOR PIANO

Two themes                                                                Chopin

## SYMPHONY No. 3 ("Eroica")

First movement                                                         Beethoven

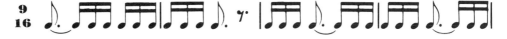

## BRANDENBURG CONCERTO No. 4

Johann Sebastian Bach (1685–1750)

## PARTITA No. 4 FOR PIANOFORTE

Gigue                                                                 J. S. Bach

## SYMPHONY No. 6 ("Pathetique")

Second movement                        Peter Ilyich Tchaikovsky (1840–1893)

SYMPHONY No. 5

Second movement                                                          Tchaikovsky

BILLY THE KID (Ballet)

Street in a Frontier Town, third theme          Aaron Copland (1900–     )

MATHIS DER MAHLER SYMPHONY

First movement                                    Paul Hindemith (1895–1963)

EL AMOR BRUJO (Ballet)

(Love, the Magician)

Pantomime                                          Manuel de Falla (1876–1946)

SYMPHONY No. 2

Second movement, third theme*                    Robert Schumann (1810–1856)

* These are triplets but have not been so indicated in original notation.

---

**111** In frames 108–110, you have been performing rhythmic excerpts from popular and classical compositions. In Appendices B and C, you will find a sampling of many different types of songs (folk, traditional children's songs, spirituals, hymns, popular). There are over seventy complete songs, most of which may be familiar to you and also which have direct application to the elementary school classroom.

Select at least six of these songs that interest you and perform them rhythmically. You may decide to arrange them for different combinations of rhythm instruments.

By playing only the rhythms of these songs, the task of learning the complete song will be reduced substantially. Also, you will be pleased to discover that there is not a song in either appendix that should give you much difficulty.

For further practice, play and identify each of the rhythmic examples in frames 112 and 113.

---

**112**  Play each of the following rhythmic examples. Choose the correct title from the three titles that are provided for each example. The correct title is printed below each example.

     (1) ELEANOR RIGBY
   a. (2) AMAZING GRACE
     (3) AMERICA (WEST SIDE STORY)

"America" (West Side Story).

     (1) WINDY
   b. (2) THE IMPOSSIBLE DREAM (MAN OF LA MANCHA)
     (3) MATCHMAKER (FIDDLER ON THE ROOF)

"Windy."

     (1) JOY (JESU, JOY OF MAN'S DESIRING)
   c. (2) BLOWIN' IN THE WIND
     (3) AND WHEN I DIE

"Joy" (Jesu, Joy of Man's Desiring) by J. S. Bach.

d.
   (1) BORN FREE
   (2) SAY IT LOUD—I'M BLACK AND I'M PROUD
   (3) DAY BY DAY (GODSPELL)

e.
   (1) RAINDROPS KEEP FALLING ON MY HEAD
   (2) JUDAS (JESUS CHRIST, SUPERSTAR)
   (3) LOVE STORY

f.
   (1) SUNNY
   (2) DO YOU KNOW THE WAY TO SAN JOSÉ?
   (3) WALK A MILE IN MY SHOES

g.
   (1) MONDAY, MONDAY
   (2) LET THERE BE PEACE ON EARTH
   (3) MIDNIGHT COWBOY

(1) EVERYTHING IS BEAUTIFUL

h. (2) GEE OFFICER KRUPKE (WEST SIDE STORY)

(3) THE LOOK OF LOVE

"Gee Officer Krupke" (West Side Story).

(1) THE IMPOSSIBLE DREAM (MAN OF LA MANCHA)

i. (2) WHAT THE WORLD NEEDS NOW IS LOVE

(3) SUNRISE, SUNSET (FIDDLER ON THE ROOF)

"The Impossible Dream" (Man of La Mancha).

(1) MISTY

j. (2) MOON RIVER

(3) MIDNIGHT COWBOY

"Midnight Cowboy."

(1) EVERYTHING'S ALRIGHT (JESUS CHRIST, SUPERSTAR)

k. (2) PROUD MARY

(3) I FEEL THE EARTH MOVE

"Everything's Alright" (Jesus Christ, Superstar).

(1) SOMETHING

l.    (2) BOTH SIDES NOW

(3) (I NEVER PROMISED YOU A) ROSE GARDEN

"(I Never Promised You a) Rose Garden," by Joe South.

---

**113**  Play each of the following rhythmic examples. Choose the correct title from the three titles that are provided for each example.

(1) WHERE DO I GO (HAIR)

a.    (2) YESTERDAY

(3) HEY, JUDE!

"Where Do I Go."

(1) NEVER ON SUNDAY

b.    (2) SHADOW OF YOUR SMILE

(3) CLASSICAL GAS

"Classical Gas," by Mason Williams.

(1) CHOIR (JESUS CHRIST, SUPERSTAR)

c.    (2) WICHITA LINEMAN

(3) SPINNING WHEEL

"Choir" (Jesus Christ, Superstar).

(1) IF I WERE A RICH MAN (FIDDLER ON THE ROOF)

d. (2) SOMEWHERE MY LOVE

(3) DIDN'T WE

(1) MONDAY, MONDAY

e. (2) SUMMER RAIN

(3) SOONER OR LATER

(1) PUT YOUR HAND IN THE HAND

f. (2) IF I WERE A CARPENTER

(3) OVERTURE (TOMMY)

(1) CHERISH

g. (2) MIDNIGHT COWBOY

(3) A NATURAL WOMAN

h.
(1) THE WINDMILLS OF YOUR MIND
(2) YOU'VE GOT A FRIEND
(3) SOMETHING'S COMING (WEST SIDE STORY)

i.
(1) CLOSE TO YOU
(2) AMAZING GRACE
(3) CANDYMAN

Traditional Hymn
"Amazing Grace."

j.
(1) A TASTE OF HONEY
(2) WALK ON BY
(3) SOMEWHERE (WEST SIDE STORY)

k.
(1) M*A*S*H
(2) SHAFT
(3) LEAVING ON A JET PLANE

l.
(1) SUMMERTIME (PORGY AND BESS)
(2) PEOPLE (FUNNY GIRL)
(3) TONIGHT (WEST SIDE STORY)

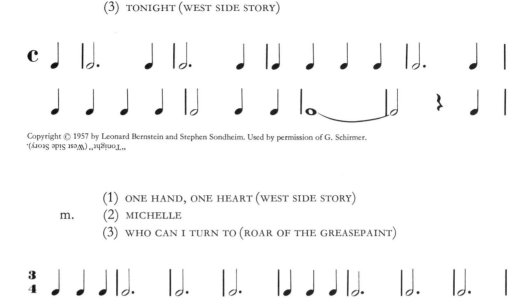

m.
(1) ONE HAND, ONE HEART (WEST SIDE STORY)
(2) MICHELLE
(3) WHO CAN I TURN TO (ROAR OF THE GREASEPAINT)

**114** Congratulations! By completing this chapter you have overcome the number one obstacle in learning music: the understanding and notation of sounds in time. At this point, your concepts of musical notations and rhythms probably are equal to those of many music students. Talk to them, and they might well agree with you. They certainly will agree (unless they're drummers) that rhythm gives them the hardest time of all! For you this should not be so.

Pick up any popular song (folk, rock, show, country). Look at it carefully and you should be able to strike and count that song with rhythmic accuracy. This same facility will enable you to perform rhythmic excerpts from the standard concert literature. Furthermore, you will find that you can work quite easily with the song materials encountered in the many children's music series.

CHAPTER THREE

Songs in Time:

Melody at the Keyboard

# Songs in Time: Melody at the Keyboard

*In Chapter Three, through the use of a keyboard instrument, you will begin to discover and understand such concepts as pitch, interval, melody, two-line harmony, key signature, transposition, and the pentatonic scale.*

*You will learn to identify and play all pitches from notation on the grand staff. You will compose melodies and accompaniments, write lyrics, and also devise finger patterns for playing these creations.*

*The central focus of Chapter Three is the in-depth performance of three folk songs (built on pentatonic scales and played on the black keys) which you can approach in a variety of ways to learn a variety of musical concepts.*

*Fourteen additional pentatonic songs (all on black keys) in Appendix B are available for expansion of your repertoire. At the end of Chapter Three, you will be capable of playing any of the fifty-five song melodies found in Appendix C.*

---

**115**    In Chapter One, you learned to create many different sounds and in Chapter Two, you learned to notate musical rhythms so that your compositions could be played by others, as well as by yourself. In this chapter, rhythms are combined with pitches at the keyboard.

---

**116**    Many of the sounds which were mentioned in Chapter One (for example, those sounds produced by the piano, organ, trumpet, bells, voice, etc.) are sounds of definite **pitch.** *Pitch refers to the highness and lowness of sounds, and is one of the most obvious characteristics of music.* Most people can readily distinguish differences in pitch. Sing a low pitch. Sing a higher pitch. Notice the difference. This difference is a result of the distance between the low pitch and the high pitch. The distance between any two pitches is referred to as an **interval.**

The piano is a pitch-producing instrument. When the piano keys are struck a variety of pitches (and also intervals) can be produced. The keys are arranged from left to right, from the lowest pitch to the highest pitch. The higher the pitch, the farther to the right is the key that produces it. Conversely, the lower the pitch, the farther to the left is the key that produces it.

---

**117**    Explore the keyboard. At random, produce high, low, and middle pitches. Notice the variety of intervals you can produce. A **horizontal interval** is produced when two pitches are played consecutively and a **vertical interval** is produced when two pitches are sounded together. The same two pitches, whether played horizontally or vertically, produce the same interval.

Experiment with both black and white keys, from the lowest pitches to the highest pitches. Notice that the black keys are easier to locate by touch. Why? Use both hands, first separately, then together, to produce keyboard pitches. Play single keys and then groups of keys with each hand. You may start with your hands next to each other on the keyboard, then gradually widen the interval between them. Or you may want to start with your hands wide apart and gradually move them closer together. Try a combination of these approaches.

---

**118** In your random exploration of the piano keyboard, you were concentrating on the pitches, not the fingers which were producing them. However, in order to perform successfully at the piano (and with ease), it is necessary to have your fingers under control.

Hold up your right hand. Move your thumb. In piano fingering, the thumb is considered the "first finger" (1). Move your little finger. This is your "fifth finger" (5). Move fingers 2, 3, and 4. Repeat this process until you automatically associate the fingers with their appropriate numbers.

Hold up your left hand. Move your thumb (1). Move your little finger (5). Move fingers 2, 3, and 4. Repeat this process until you automatically associate the fingers with their appropriate numbers.

Place your palms together so that the corresponding fingers on each hand are touching completely. In this exercise, strike the tips of each set of fingers indicated three times without letting any of the other fingers lose contact until it is their turn to strike.

Strike: Both 1's, 5's, 2's, 4's, 3's, 5's, 2's, 1's, 4's, 2's, 1's, 3's, 5's, 4's, 2's, 3's, 1's.

Practice this exercise both forward and backward several times, each time increasing the tempo, so that you can perform it as quickly and effortlessly as possible.

---

**119** Notice that the keyboard is organized into groups of black and white keys. The interval between any two **adjoining keys** is a **half step.** Study these diagrams:

half step
a. (black to white)

half step
b. (white to black)

half step
c. (white to white)

Place fingers 1 and 2 of your right hand on any black and white keys that are arranged the same way as the keys in diagram a. Explore the keyboard and play as many other examples of diagram a (black to white) as you can find. Repeat this process with fingers 2–3, 3–4, and 4–5 of your right hand (R.H.). Do the same with fingers 5–4, 4–3, 3–2, and 2–1 of your left hand (L.H.).

Following all of the above procedures, discover and perform examples of diagram b.

Repeat all of the procedures used for exploring diagrams a and b to discover and perform examples of diagram c.

---

**120**  When two keys are separated by either a black or a white key, they are **adjacent.** The interval between those keys is a **whole step.** Study the diagrams:

a.  whole step  
(white to white, with  
black between)

b.  whole step  
(black to black, with  
white between)

c.  whole step  
(black to white, with  
white between)

d.  whole step  
(white to black, with  
white between)

Place fingers 1 and 2 of your right hand on any white keys that are arranged the same way as the keys in diagram a. Explore the keyboard and play as many other examples of diagram a (white to white) as you can find. Repeat this process with fingers 2–3, 3–4, and 4–5 of your right hand. Do the same with fingers 5–4, 4–3, 3–2, and 2–1 of your left hand.

Following all of the procedures used for exploring diagram a, discover and perform examples of diagrams b, c, and d.

Now you should be familiar with intervals of half steps and whole steps as they relate to the keyboard. If these concepts are not completely clear to you, read frames 119 and 120 again.

---

**121**  Use the words from this list to answer questions a–e:

| | | |
|---|---|---|
| vertical | horizontal | little fingers |
| piano | interval | half |
| pitch | thumbs | whole |

a. _____ refers to the specific highness and lowness of sounds, and the distance between two pitches is called a(n) _____.

b. The _____ is a pitch-producing instrument.

c. Playing two piano keys, one after the other, creates a(n) _____ interval; playing both keys simultaneously results in a(n) _____ interval.

d. The _____ of both hands are considered the first fingers (1), and the _____ are the fifth fingers (5).

e. The interval between any two adjoining keys is a(n) _____ step. When a black or white key separates two adjacent keys, the interval is a(n) _____ step.

RESPONSES

a. *Pitch* refers to the specific highness and lowness of sounds, and the distance between two pitches is called a(n) *interval*.

b. The *piano* is a pitch-producing instrument.

c. Playing two piano keys, one after the other, creates a(n) *horizontal* interval; playing both keys simultaneously results in a(n) *vertical* interval.

d. The *thumbs* of both hands are considered the first fingers (1), and the *little fingers* are the fifth fingers (5).

e. The interval between any two adjoining keys is a(n) *half* step. When a black or white key separates two adjacent keys, the interval is a(n) *whole* step.

---

**122**  Carefully observe this diagram and notice that the black keys of the keyboard are aligned in groups of two's and three's.

Place fingers 1 and 2 of your right hand (R.H.) on the group of two adjacent black keys located in the middle (approximately) of the keyboard.

Place fingers 3, 4, and 5 of your right hand (R.H.) on the group of three adjacent black keys. Place the fingers of your left hand on the keyboard as marked in the diagram.

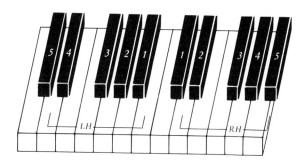

The fingers of both hands should be in a curved position on the keyboard, as if each hand were holding an apple or a ball. The *tips* of each finger should strike the keys. The bottom of each wrist should line up with the tops of the white keys.

In your own tempo, count and play the rhythm of the following composition with the second finger of your right hand. Keep all the other fingers of both hands stationary on the black keys, observing the hand and finger positions which have been described:

Play the same rhythm with the fifth finger of the left hand. Play the same rhythm with both hands together (L.H.-5 and R.H.-2). Play the same rhythm in the right hand, first with finger 1, then 3, then 4, then 5. Since your right hand is in the diagrammed position, each finger will play the rhythm on a different key. All fingers, except the one(s) with which you are playing, should remain stationary on top of the other keys.

Follow the right-hand procedures (described in the preceding paragraph) with the left hand. Play the same rhythm with both hands together, using any combination of fingers you desire (for example, L.H.-4 and R.H.-3; L.H.-2 and R.H.-5, etc.). Experiment performing this rhythm with different pitch and finger combinations.

---

**123**  Observe that the entire composition in frame 122 is based on only three rhythmic patterns (measures 1, 2, and 4) and their repetitions. Learn these three measures and you have, for all practical purposes, learned the entire composition.

You will find that many compositions, particularly popular and folk pieces, are rhythmically built on just a few patterns. These patterns may recur consistently throughout a particular composition. Your awareness of these patterns can reduce the mechanics of learning the entire composition. Noticing when these repeated *rhythmic* patterns coincide with repeated *pitch* patterns, as they often do, will further reduce any difficulties encountered in learning the music. Before trying to learn any composition, let your eyes first become familiar with the repeated patterns.

**124** Now you will use all of the pitches of the composition in frame 122. Position your right hand on the keyboard as diagrammed in frame 122. In the diagram below, the fingering for each piano key is indicated. Curve your fingers as if you were holding an apple. Remember, the bottom of the wrist should line up with the tops of the white keys. The numbers indicate the proper fingering and, since your right hand is in the stationary position diagrammed in frame 122, they also indicate the appropriate piano keys. Count out loud as you play the composition; play without counting the second time. *Whenever possible, keep your eyes on the music and not on the keys.*

**125** Position your left hand on the keyboard as diagrammed in frame 122 and play the same composition with the left hand:

**126** By this time you have noticed that repeated rhythmic/pitch patterns also frequently use repeated finger patterns. (Notice the second and sixth measures of frames 124 and 125.) Recognizing repeated finger patterns also facilitates learning.

**127** The music which you played in frames 124 and 125 is called a **melody** or a **tune.** *A melody is a succession of intervals which are arranged with a perceptible degree of coherence and logic.* A melody or a tune often is referred to as a **theme** when it is used repeatedly in a longer composition.

**128** Play and count the following melody with your left hand (L.H.) on the black keys, as indicated in the diagram.

L.H. fingers: 5  4  3  2  5  4  3  2  5  4  3  2  5  4  3 2 1

**129** Now, with your right hand (R.H.) play the melody you learned in frames 122–125. With your left hand (L.H.), accompany this melody with the music you have just played in frame 128. If your keyboard instrument does not have enough keys to accommodate both hands together, practice each hand separately on your instrument while moving the fingers of the other hand as if it were on the instrument. This exercise will prepare you to transfer your performance to a larger keyboard instrument.

Curve your fingers. Vary the dynamics. Play the composition slowly the first time; then play it faster the second time.

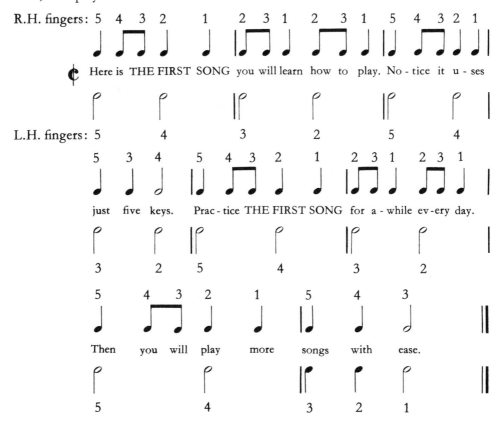

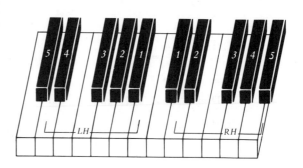

Listen to the recording of THE FIRST SONG. If you have any difficulty performing it, practice with the recording a few times. Then try practicing on your own. *Do not proceed to frame 130 until you have mastered* THE FIRST SONG.

---

**130**

In two-part piano music, such as the composition you just performed, the higher sounding part is usually referred to as the **treble** and the lower sounding part is called the **bass.** This combination of two parts produces **harmony.** Harmony is created by the sounding of two or more pitches simultaneously. Thus, any vertical interval (see frame 117) produces harmony. In the two-part composition in frame 129, as in most compositions, you used the right hand to play the treble part and the left hand to play the bass part. You played the melody in the treble and an accompaniment in the bass. This particular bass accompaniment acts as a **counterpoint** to the melody. A counterpoint is a succession of pitches which may be used to accompany a melody but which has *both* melodic and rhythmic independence from that melody. (The adjective for counterpoint is **contrapuntal.**) When a contrapuntal accompaniment consists of short rhythm/pitch patterns which are consistently repeated, it is known as an **ostinato.** Ostinato accompaniments can appear in the treble as well as in the bass, but are more often seen in the bass. They are common in jazz, rock, country, and Latin American music, as well as in the music of the seventeenth and eighteenth centuries.

Notice that the ostinato accompaniment in the composition in frame 129 (THE FIRST SONG) is generally moving in an upward direction while the melody in the treble is essentially moving downward. This type of movement in opposite directions is known as **contrary motion.** Contrary motion is another device that adds variety and interest to music.

The composition in this recording uses three *different* ostinato bass accompaniment patterns. Listen for each of them, and notice how all of them are consistently repetitive.

---

**131**

With your right hand (R.H.), play the ostinato accompaniment to THE FIRST SONG in the treble; with your left hand (L.H.), play the melody in the bass. Use the keyboard diagram below to locate the positions of your right hand and left hand fingers.

Notice that, although you have reversed hands, the melody and the ostinato are still in contrary motion.

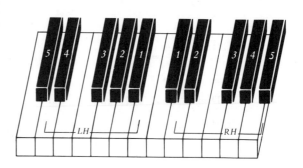

**134**  Using the keyboard diagram in frame 131 as a guide create your own simple, contrapuntal accompaniment (black keys) to THE FIRST SONG melody:

a. Write your *new* counterpoint (along with the melody, as in frame 133) for either right or left hand and sing and play your arrangement of THE FIRST SONG.

b. Now create your own melody: write a *new* melody to go along with your *new* counterpoint and the words you created in frame 133, and sing and play your new composition.

Write your arrangement (a) and composition (b) in the space provided, marking the fingerings for both treble and bass.

a.

b.

**135**  Use the words in this list to answer questions a–i.

| | |
|---|---|
| song | coherence |
| logic | intervals |
| treble | counterpoint |
| curved | bass |
| ostinato | harmony |
| theme | tips |
| lyrics | contrary motion |

a. A melody or tune often is referred to as a(n) _____ when it is used repeatedly in a longer composition.

b. A melody is a succession of _____ which are arranged with a perceptible degree of _____ or _____.

c. In two-part piano music, the higher sounding part is usually referred to as the _____, and the lower sounding part is called the _____.

d. A(n) _____ consists of short, rhythm/pitch patterns which are consistently repeated.

e. Any vertical interval produces _____.

f. A melody with words is called a(n) _____, and the words are sometimes referred to as _____.

g. When playing a keyboard instrument the fingers should be _____ in such a way that only the _____ strike the keys.

h. _____ is characterized by a certain degree of melodic and rhythmic independence from a simultaneous melody.

i. The device by which treble and bass melodies move in opposite directions is known as _____.

RESPONSES

a. A melody or tune is often referred to as a(n) *theme* when it is used repeatedly in a longer composition.

b. A melody is a succession of *intervals* which are arranged with a perceptible degree of *coherence* or *logic*.

c. In two-part piano music, the higher sounding part is usually referred to as the *treble*, and the lower sounding part is called the *bass*.

d. A(n) *ostinato* consists of short, rhythm/pitch patterns which are consistently repeated.

e. Any vertical interval produces *harmony*.

f. A melody with words is called a(n) *song*, and the words are sometimes referred to as *lyrics*.

d. When playing a keyboard instrument the fingers should be *curved* in such a way that only the *tips* strike the keys.

h. *Counterpoint* is characterized by a certain degree of melodic and rhythmic independence from a simultaneous melody.

i. The device by which treble and bass melodies move in opposite directions is known as *contrary motion*.

ship applies to all octaves (e.g., C → C) of all tones. This is a physical description which explains the highness and lowness of the pitches forming an octave, but it is not offered as an explanation of the octave's unique sound quality.

---

**141**  In this diagram, the finger numbers on the white keys show the new position (L.H.) in which you played THE FIRST SONG in frame 137:

The finger numbers on the black keys show the original position (L.H.) in which you played the same melody. Pay close attention to this original position. How many *different* black keys are there? Undoubtedly you have answered, "five." The sequence of the group of two black keys followed by the group of three black keys is called a **scale.** *A scale is any fixed sequence of keys in a specific intervalic relationship.*

This particular type of scale is known as a **pentatonic scale** ("penta" means "five"). Pentatonic scales may be played on both the white and black keys, but it is easier to build a pentatonic scale on the black keys, since there are only five different black keys. To build a complete pentatonic scale, start on any black key and then add the other four black keys. Starting on a different black key each time, you can build five different pentatonic scales—the *number* of keys will remain the same (five) but the sequence of intervals will be different in each of these five pentatonic scales. Play all five of these pentatonic scales in both hands and discover the different interval relationships in each one.

Although most people tend to associate the sound of the pentatonic scale with music of the Far East, this scale is also quite common in the folk music of other cultures. You will hear it in cowboy songs, American Indian songs, Hungarian, Irish, English, etc., songs.

When you played THE FIRST SONG on the white keys, you used the same pentatonic scale as in the original version on the black keys, but you transposed it down by a half step. Notice that you used only five white keys and that they were in the same interval relationship as the original five black keys. Examine this relationship carefully by referring to the keyboard diagram at the beginning of this frame.

Each of the five pentatonic scales can be transposed by starting on any white key and playing the specific sequence of intervals for that scale. Many of these transposed pentatonic scales must use combinations of black and white keys in order to maintain the fixed interval relationships of the original scales.

**142**  Your playing experience began on the black keys, and they have been a consistent reference point for you in relating to such concepts as transposition and the pentatonic scale. To learn the names of the black keys, observe the keyboard below:

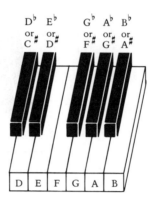

You will notice that every black key can have two names: a letter name followed by a sharp (♯), or a letter name followed by a flat (♭). Also notice that the letter name for each black key is the same as its left or right adjoining white key. A sharp *raises* a note by a half step; therefore when a black key is referred to as a sharp (e.g., F♯), it derives its letter name from the adjoining white key a half step below, which has been raised. When that same black key is referred to as a **flat** (e.g., G♭), its letter name is derived from the adjoining white key a half step above. Whatever the key is called, if it is the same key, it *sounds* the same. Different names for the same sounds are called **enharmonic equivalents.**

Enharmonic equivalents apply to white keys also. For instance, C can be called B♯; B can be called C♭, etc. They appear infrequently that way, but when they do, there is always a logical reason for altering the name. Remember—only the name changes; the sound remains the same (equivalent).

All sharps, flats, and other symbols which alter the sound produced by any given key through raising or lowering it are called **accidentals.**

Play the following keys, observe their accidentals, and give the enharmonic equivalent of each: C♯, A♯, F♯, B♭, D♯, D♭, E♯, C♭.

RESPONSES   C♯ = D♭; A♯ = B♭; F♯ = G♭; B♭ = A♯; D♯ = E♭; D♭ = C♯; E♯ = F; C♭ = B.

**143**  Write true or false to the left of the following statements. If the statement is false, change the italicized word(s) to make the statement true.

_____ a. If a musical composition sounds the same when played on two different groups of keys, this composition has been *transposed*.

_____ b. When transposing a musical composition, the *keys* remain constant.

_____ c. When transposing a musical composition, the *intervals* remain constant.

_____ d. The range used in the melody of THE FIRST SONG is *less* than an octave.

_____ e. The distance from the lowest to the highest pitch in a song is referred to as the *octave* of that song.

_____ f. The musical alphabet has *eight* different letters.

_____ g. If the key F were 1, the next F above would be *seven*.

_____ h. The interval from the key G to the next G below is an *octave*.

_____ i. Most people tend to hear both tones of an octave as sounding essentially *the same*.

_____ j. The number *5* is associated with an octave.

_____ k. When the treble and bass melodies move in opposite directions, they are said to be moving in *parallel* motion.

_____ l. If the note A vibrates at 440 cps, the A an octave above it will vibrate at *600* cps.

_____ m. If the note C vibrates at 512 cps, the C an octave below it will vibrate at *1024* cps.

_____ n. Within an octave, there are *five* different black keys arranged in groups of *twos* and *threes*.

_____ o. Scales are *random* sequences of keys in *random* intervalic relationships.

_____ p. A pentatonic scale is a five-tone scale with a *random* arrangement of intervals.

_____ q. A pentatonic scale has *two* possible starting points on the black keys.

_____ r. The pentatonic scale *cannot* be transposed to the white keys.

_____ s. Every black key can be called by *one* name(s) and *one* accidental(s).

_____ t. The black key a half step above G is called G♯ or G♭.

_____ u. The black key a half step below D is called D♭ or C♯.

_____ v. D followed by A creates a(n) *vertical* interval.

_____ w. G♭ and B♭ sounding together create a(n) *horizontal* interval.

_____ x. C and F, when sounded together, create *harmony*.

_____ y. E♭ and D♯ sound *differently* on the keyboard.

_____ z. Every white key has *one name*.

_____ aa. G♯ and A♭ are enharmonic equivalents.

_____ bb. E♯ and F sound *alike* on the keyboard.

_____ cc. B♭ and B♯ *are* enharmonic equivalents.

RESPONSES     *true*    a. If a musical composition sounds the same when played on two different groups of keys, this composition has been *transposed*.

                  *false*    b. When transposing a musical composition, the *keys* remain constant. (*intervals*) *true*    c. When transposing a musical composition, the *intervals* remain constant.

*false*    d. The range used in the melody of THE FIRST SONG is *less* than an octave. (*more*)

*false*    e. The distance from the lowest to the highest pitch in a song is referred to as the *octave* of that song. (*range*)

*false*    f. The musical alphabet has *eight* different letters. (*seven*)

*false*    g. If the key F were 1, the next F above would be *seven*. (*eight*)

*true*    h. The interval from the key G to the next G below is an *octave*.

*true*    i. Most people tend to hear both tones of an octave as sounding essentially *the same*.

*false*    j. The number *5* is associated with an octave. (*8*)

*false*    k. When the treble and bass melodies move in opposite directions, they are said to be moving in *parallel* motion. (*contrary*)

*false*    l. If the note A vibrates at 440 cps, the A an octave above it will vibrate at *600 cps*. (*880*)

*false*    m. If the note C vibrates at 512 cps, the C an octave below it will vibrate at 1024 cps. (*256*)

*true*    n. Within an octave, there are *five* different black keys arranged in groups of *twos* and *threes*.

*false*    o. Scales are *random* sequences of keys in *random* intervalic relationships. (*fixed*)(*specific*)

*false*    p. A pentatonic scale is a five-tone scale with a *random* arrangement of intervals. (*specific*)

*false*    q. A pentatonic scale has *two* possible starting points on the black keys. (*five*)

*false*    r. The pentatonic scale *cannot* be transposed to the white keys. (*can*)

*false*    s. Every black key can be called by *one* name(s) and *one* accidental(s). (*two*)

*false*    t. The black key a half step above G is called G♯ or G♭. (*A♭*)

*true*    u. The black key a half step below D is called D♭ or C♯.

*false*    v. D followed by A creates a(n) *vertical* interval. (*horizontal*)

*false*    w. G♭ and B♭ sounding together create a(n) *horizontal* interval. (*vertical*)

*true*    x. C and F, when sounded together, create *harmony*.

*false*    y. E♭ and D♯ sound *differently* on the keyboard. (*the same*)

*false*    z. Every white key has *one name*. (*two names*)

*true*    aa. G♯ and A♭ are enharmonic equivalents.

*true*    bb. E♯ and F sound *alike* on the keyboard.

*false*    cc. B♭ and B♯ *are* enharmonic equivalents. (*are not*)

---

**144**    For more experience with pentatonic songs, play the folk songs from Appendix B (pages 287–300).

**145** Place the fingers of your right hand and your left hand in the position shown below (black keys), making certain that the second finger of your left hand is on the D♭ in the middle of the keyboard.

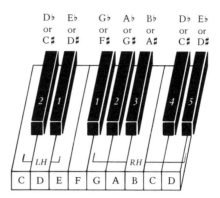

In your own tempo, count and play the rhythm of the following composition first with the second finger of your left hand, then with the fourth finger of your right hand, and finally, with both hands together. Notice the pickup notes at the beginning. For additional practice in coordinating the fingers of both hands, perform this composition again, following the procedures described in frame 122.

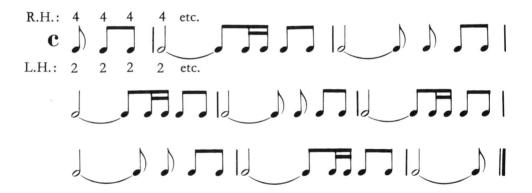

How many counts are there in the last measure? In the first measure? Notice that the composition is based on measures of repeated rhythm patterns.

RESPONSE     There are two and one-half counts in the last measure because of the pickup notes (one and one-half counts) at the beginning of this composition.

**146** Count and play this pentatonic melody. Play without counting the second time. Refer to the keyboard diagram in frame 145 for finger positions. Notice that some of the notes are played with the **left-hand fingers.**

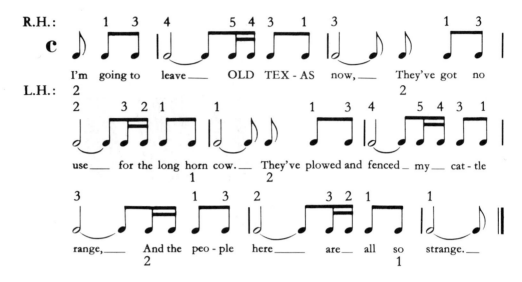

**147** Place the fingers of your right and left hands in the position diagrammed below (white keys), making certain that the second finger of your left hand is on the C in the middle of the keyboard. This C is referred to as **middle C.**

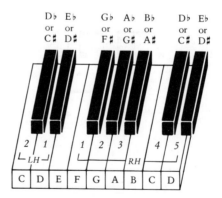

Play this transposed version of the pentatonic melody following the same rhythmic and finger patterns shown in frame 146.

**148** The composition you have been playing is the cowboy song, OLD TEXAS. Here are the lyrics:

> 1. I'm going to leave OLD TEXAS now,
> They've got no use for the long horn cow.
> They've plowed and fenced my cattle range,
> And the people here are all so strange.
>
> 2. I'll take my horse, I'll take my rope,
> And hit the trail with a lazy lope;
> Say "Adios" to the Alamo,
> And turn my face toward Mexico.

Sing the two **verses** of OLD TEXAS as you play the melody on the keyboard. Establish your own tempo.

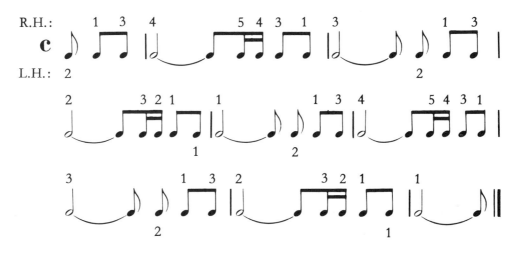

**149** Place the fingers of both hands in the position diagrammed below (white keys), making certain that the fifth finger of the left hand is resting on middle C. Notice that the F above middle C will sometimes be played with the left hand (second finger) and other times with the right hand (first finger).

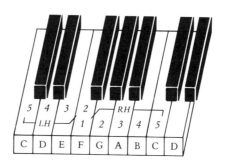

Learn this two-handed accompaniment (an ostinato) for OLD TEXAS. Practice each hand separately, then combine them. When you can play the treble and bass together smoothly, sing OLD TEXAS along with the harmonic accompaniment. Be aware of the two-measure instrumental introduction preceding the entrance of the sung melody.

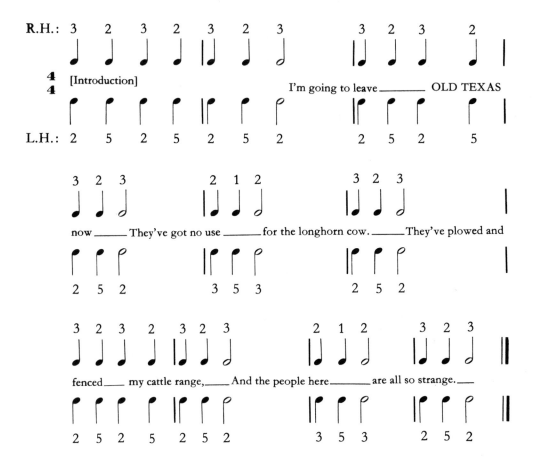

Listen to the recording of OLD TEXAS and pay particular attention to the relationship of the melody to the accompaniment.

---

**150**  In order to understand time notation in relation to pitches at the keyboard, it is important that you learn *pitch notation* also. In all of the exercises you have completed so far in this chapter, numbers were used to indicate which keys were to be played. Now pitch notation will be used to indicate the appropriate piano keys to be played; numbers will only be used to suggest the best fingering for that particular notation. Always remember that notation or notes refer to *visual* symbols of pitches. Notes are *not* pitches or tones. *Notes are read, but pitches are heard.*

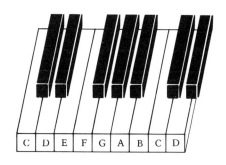

This is a diagram of the octave C-C in the middle of the keyboard (with a D added). This diagram concentrates on the white keys. Below the diagram is a series of five lines and four spaces called a musical **staff.** The symbol 𝄞 located at the far left of the staff is known as a **treble clef** or a **G clef.** A clef sign is used to indicate the specific pitch which is the focal point for locating all of the pitches on that staff. For example, the G clef is so called because its big, open loop circles the second line of the staff and indicates that the note on that line is the G above middle C. The short line through middle C is a substitute for a longer line across the staff and is called a **ledger line.** Ledger lines are used to indicate those pitches which occur above or below the staff.

At random, play all of the keys indicated by letter names on the keyboard diagram and familiarize yourself thoroughly with the locations of their respective notes on the staff below the keyboard diagram. Notice that the notes, like the keys, are consecutively named from line to space and from space to line. As you play each pitch sing its letter name.

**151**  Play and sing the letter names in the following pitch notation of OLD TEXAS. The fingerings are indicated; all are R.H. unless indicated L.H. Do not be confused by a stem going downward ( ♩ ). This is only a visual convenience and *does not* change the note in any way. Hold your hand and fingers in the positions which you have learned.

Notice the numbers ⌐1. and ⌐2. above the measures at the end of this song. ⌐1 represents the first ending and ⌐2. represents the second ending. Near the end of the song, :‖ instructs the performer to go back to ‖: and repeat the song starting at that point, but this time the singer should skip the measure marked ⌐1. (first ending) and end the song with the measure marked ⌐2. (second ending).

Notice the *f* above the first note. This is a **dynamic marking** and it is the abbreviation for **forte** (pronounced for′ tă), which means "loud" in Italian. You are to play this song loudly until the **p** (located above the C in the second complete measure). **p** is the abbreviation for **piano,** which means "soft" in Italian. The song remains soft until the *f* in the fourth measure.

Realize, of course, that *f* and **p** and all other dynamic markings are relative terms. There are no absolute louds and softs in music. However, as you might guess, *ff* (*fortissimo*) is louder than *f*, and **pp** (*pianissimo*) is softer than **p**. These relationships are established by the performer(s). What sounds loud to one musician or listener may seem comparatively soft to another. The use of dynamics, like so many other characteristics of music, are highly subject to individual tastes.

Observe the use of the tie in OLD TEXAS. Remember that the tie connects two notes to extend the duration of the original note. It is important to realize that the tie extends the duration of the *same* pitch. What is the range of OLD TEXAS?

RESPONSE    The range of OLD TEXAS is

**152**    Now play OLD TEXAS one octave lower. Place the fingers of both hands on the white keys with the same letter names as those diagrammed in frame 150, but located an octave lower. What you have just played can be notated this way:

This version of OLD TEXAS is notated in the **F clef** or **bass clef.** The F clef 𝄢 is so called because its two dots surround the fourth line and indicate that the note on that line is the F below middle C. Notice the differences in the two notations of OLD TEXAS, despite the fact that the song sounds the same (but an octave lower). The F clef is designed to facilitate reading notes which occur *below* middle C.

Observe the **mf** dynamic marking in the second complete measure: **m** is the abbreviation for **mezzo** (pronounced met′ so), which means "medium" in Italian. Therefore, **mf** is "medium loud."

Study this staff and its relationship to the keyboard diagram below. Notice middle C on the ledger line above the staff and D on the space above middle C.

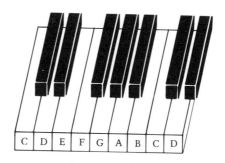

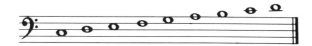

The notes in this diagram are the same as the notes in the diagram of frame 150, except that they sound an octave lower. Compare the two diagrams.

Play these notes at random on the keyboard and match the pitches with your own voice, singing their letter names. Familiarize yourself thoroughly with their locations on the staff.

---

**153**   The combination of the G clef staff and the F clef staff is known as the **grand staff.** Notice that middle C is literally in the middle of the grand staff.

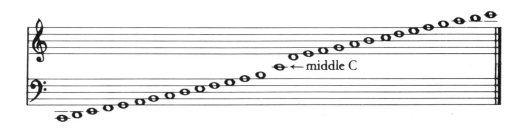

At the keyboard, experiment in locating and playing every note on the grand staff. Remember that a ledger line is musical shorthand for a longer line across the staff.

Each ledger line is necessary in order to notate that pitch properly. For instance: if a note is to be located on the second ledger line above or below the staff (observe the highest and lowest notes on the grand staff), the first ledger line *must* be shown, so that the reader will be certain to know that the note is on the second ledger line. If either of these lines is omitted, the note will be unrecognizable and incorrect.

**154** By now, you have seen that pitches can move in only two directions: up, or down (or remain the same). Pitch notation symbolizes this movement. Play, sing, and analyze these examples:

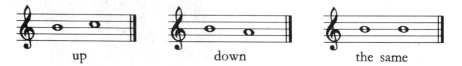

Pitches, and therefore notation, can move up and down by **steps** (half steps and whole steps) or **skips** (anything larger than a whole step). For example:

If you have any difficulty identifying these notes in the bass clef, study frame 153 more closely. Notice that sharps (♯) and flats (♭) are placed to the left of notes. Sharps and flats *do not* change the letter names of notes; when performed, they *do* change pitches by a half step (up or down).

**155** Notice (diagram in frame 153) that all steps (half and whole) notated on the staff move from a line to the nearest space (above or below), or from a space to the nearest line (above or below). Remember: *When moving from line to space or space to line, notes move only one letter name away.* However, in order to determine whether one letter name away is a half step or a whole step, relate the notes to the keyboard. Study the half and whole steps in example a:

A half step does not *always* move one letter away. In this case, one of the notes must be preceded by a sharp or a flat. Intervals in which both notes remain on the same line or space are called **primes**. For example:

b.

     half step        half step        half step        half step

**156** Intervals (vertical and horizontal) which move from line to space or from space to line are named **seconds.** For example, all of the intervals illustrated below are seconds.

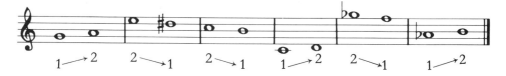

For seconds, always consider the lower note of the interval as 1 and the higher note as 2. The name of any interval is the same as the number of its higher note, and since the number of the higher note in the above examples is 2, the intervals are named seconds.

**157** Notice that all skips notated on the staff move at least from line to line or from space to space above or below the first note. *When moving from line to line or from space to space, one letter name is skipped*. For instance:

Play the above examples with your left hand. The second time, sing them as you play.

**158** Intervals (vertical and horizontal) which move from line to line (skipping a space), or from space to space (skipping a line), are named **thirds.** For example, all of the intervals illustrated below are thirds.

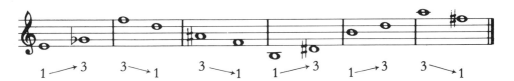

For thirds, always consider the lowest note of the interval as 1 and the highest as 3. In all cases, 2 with its equivalent letter name is the note skipped between 1 and 3. Remember, the name of any interval is the same as the number of its highest note (the lowest note always is 1). For example, $_1\nearrow^3$ is a third, $^2\searrow_1$ is a second, $_1\nearrow^5$ is a fifth, and so forth.

*If you are having trouble understanding these intervals, review frames 154-158.*

---

**159** Play this two-handed accompaniment for OLD TEXAS (fingerings are indicated next to the notes). Practice each hand separately, then combine them. Do not play the melody which is written in the middle; it is rhythmically notated here to show you where it fits with the accompaniment. In some large orchestral works, there are as many lines of music as there are different instruments.

When you can play the two-handed accompaniment smoothly, sing OLD TEXAS along with the harmonic accompaniment (the melody begins on middle C).

OLD TEXAS
(Accompaniment)

Introduction                                          Cowboy song

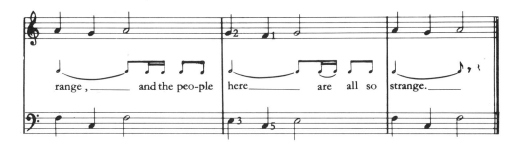

\* If the Pianica/Melodica is used, play bass clef notes an octave higher.

In the treble clef only one kind of interval is used. What is it? If you said "second," you are correct. If you did not say "second," reexamine frames 156 and 157.

In the bass clef of this accompaniment, find examples of thirds. If you located them in the fifth and ninth measures, you understand the concept of thirds very well. If you had difficulty in finding them, reexamine frames 157 and 158.

What interval appears most often in the bass clef staff? You have not been introduced to this interval yet, but if you decided "fourth," you are correct. Notice that the **fourth** in the bass clef staff moves from $F_{\searrow C}(^4_{\searrow 1})$ and $_C\nearrow^F(_1\nearrow^4)$. This pattern is consistent throughout the bass clef staff.

Observe that a fourth is comprised of two whole steps plus one half step. Starting on each white key (C, D, E, etc.) play these steps moving upward to find intervals of a fourth. Do this exercise with your right hand, left hand, and then both hands, singing the intervals as you play them. Only one black key will be used in this entire exercise. Which one and why? Repeat this exercise, building fourths starting on each black key. Only one white key will be used. Which one and why?

Most songs and compositions are based on certain patterns of intervals, just as the bass clef of the OLD TEXAS accompaniment is based on patterns of fourths and thirds. A good musician looks for these patterns and studies the best possible fingering for them before performing a piece of music, because this preparation can facilitate the reading and performing of the entire composition.

RESPONSES     In order to maintain the correct number of steps (two and one-half), the fourth starting on F must move upward to the black key of B♭.

When building fourths on the black keys, the only ascending fourth that requires the use of a white key is F♯–B. The correct number of steps must be maintained.

Listen to the recording of OLD TEXAS. If you are having any difficulty performing it, practice with the recording a few times. Then try practicing it on your own.

**160**     Play and sing the letter names of OLD TEXAS from the following notation. The fingerings are indicated; all are R.H. unless indicated L.H. The **mp** in the second complete measure is **mezzo-piano,** which means "medium soft" in Italian.

All pitches in this arrangement of OLD TEXAS are located a half step higher than the original (frame 151). You probably noticed that nearly all of the notes have flats (♭) to the left of them. If a particular note did not have a flat sign, you may have guessed from the sound that the note was meant to be flatted. When the flat sign was omitted (e.g., the second and fourth notes in the first complete measure above), it was because that specific note had already been flatted in that particular measure. *Once shown in a measure, a flat sign, or any other accidental, need not be repeated in that same measure.* However, if the accidental is to be played again in a *following* measure, it must be notated again. For example:

Although they are to be flatted, flat signs are not needed.

If they are to be flatted, the flat signs must be repeated.

---

**161**  Observe below the new arrangement of OLD TEXAS. Notice the group of six flats to the right of the G clef. This grouping is called a **key signature.** A key signature shows the number of sharps (♯) or flats (♭) to be used in a musical composition. It means that any note which is shown as flatted or sharped in the key signature, must be played as flatted or sharped throughout the composition. The key signature tells you in advance what will happen to a note when it appears in the music. It eliminates the necessity for placing accidentals to the left of each note as in frame 160. In the notation below, there are six flats in the key signature. From left to right, they are B, E, A, D, G, and C. Whenever any one of these notes appears in the composition, it should be flatted—unless a **natural** sign (♮) is placed to the left of that note. A natural is also an accidental; it cancels a flat or a sharp. For instance, a natural sign placed to the left of the B in the second complete measure of OLD TEXAS would cancel the flat shown in the key signature (but only for that *one* measure).

When looking at a key signature with as many as six flats (OLD TEXAS), it might be easier—since there are only seven different letters in the musical alphabet—to simply remember the one note which is *not* flatted. What note is it? If you said "F," you are correct.

Play this new arrangement of OLD TEXAS, using the fingering from frame 160. Sing the letter names as you play.

**162**  In the following diagram, write the letter names on the white keys and write the letter names on the black keys (include the appropriate flat *or* sharp symbol). On the staff below the diagram, notate the pitches (quarter notes) that correspond to the white keys in this diagram:

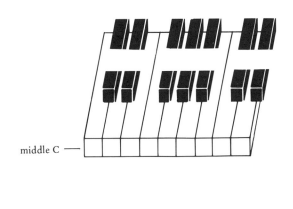

On the staff below, notate the pitches which sound an octave lower than the pitches you notated on the previous staff.

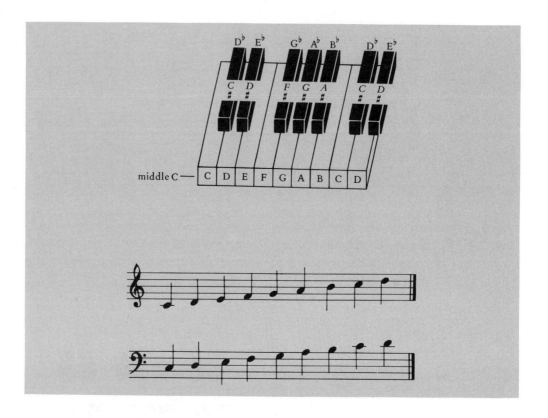

**163**  Using OLD TEXAS as a model (frame 160), develop a set of fingerings for WAYFARING STRANGER which requires the use of both hands alternating as in frame 160. Each hand remains in a fixed position.

*In order to play smoothly, you should always devise finger patterns in which the fingers can play as many keys as possible without having to change the particular hand position. Consecutive keys usually are played by consecutive fingers.*

Place R.H. finger numbers above the notes and L.H. finger numbers below the notes. Because this song is pentatonic, and because you have been using pentatonic finger patterns (one finger per key), you should have little trouble devising appropriate fingerings. Notice that all the tones of this song will be played on the black keys—since all tones (except F) are flatted (see key signature). Since the same finger will play the same key each time in the two-hand arrangement, you only need to indicate that finger when it is helpful to do so. A sample arrangement appears in the response frame.

## WAYFARING STRANGER

Spiritual

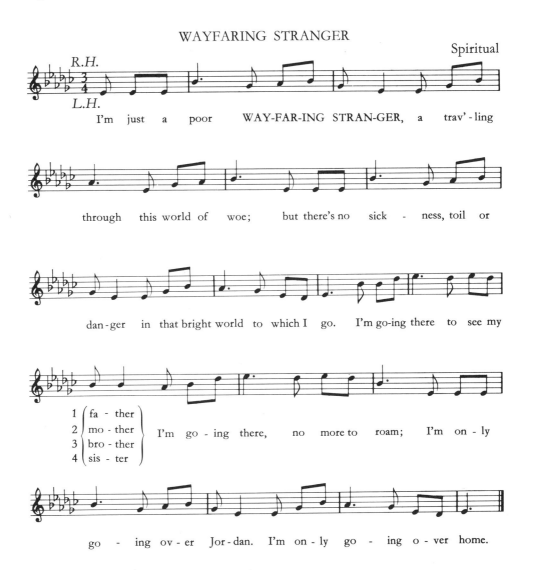

Here is another version of WAYFARING STRANGER which introduces you to using each hand in more than one position. Play WAYFARING STRANGER from beginning to end with the right-hand fingering only. Then play it with the left-hand fingering only. Now try it with both hands together. Observe the dynamic markings. Notice the *accelerando, a tempo* and *ritardando*. Your interpretation of these markings should be based on the melody and lyrics.

## WAYFARING STRANGER

After you have played this song, sing it also (the verses are the same except for "father," "mother," "brother," and "sister").

How many times does the main melodic pattern occur (ends at "woe" in measure 4) and in what measures? Are there any differences in this pattern when it does occur? How many times does the contrasting melodic pattern occur? In what measures? What is the range of this song?

# WAYFARING STRANGER

Spiritual

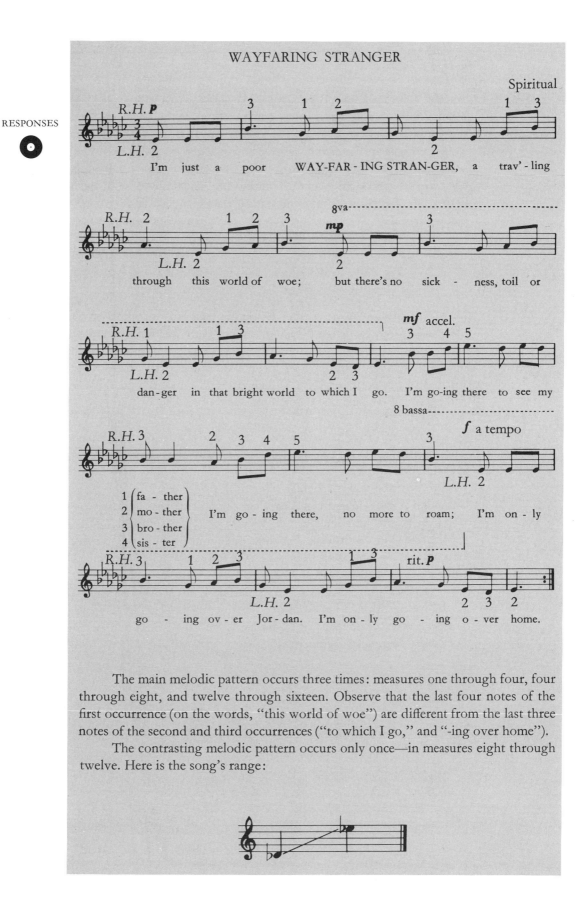

The main melodic pattern occurs three times: measures one through four, four through eight, and twelve through sixteen. Observe that the last four notes of the first occurrence (on the words, "this world of woe") are different from the last three notes of the second and third occurrences ("to which I go," and "-ing over home").

The contrasting melodic pattern occurs only once—in measures eight through twelve. Here is the song's range:

**164**
After you have played and sung WAYFARING STRANGER as written, notice the symbols **8va** and **8 bassa** above and below some sections of the music. 8va means to perform the music an octave higher; 8 bassa means to perform the music an octave lower. These symbols are frequently written to avoid the excessive use of ledger lines. Play WAYFARING STRANGER again, observing the symbols *8va* and *8 bassa*. Often the *va* and *bassa* are eliminated from the notation and only 8 is written. If the octave higher is desired, the 8 is placed above the staff; if the octave lower is desired, the 8 is placed below the staff.

**165**
What interval appears at the beginning of each main melodic statement? If you answered "fifth," you are correct. Observe that a **fifth** is comprised of *three whole steps plus one half step*. Starting on each white key (C, D, E, etc.) play these steps moving upward to find intervals of a fifth. Do this exercise with your right hand, left hand, and then both hands, singing the intervals as you play them. Only one black key will be used in this entire exercise. Which one and why? Repeat this exercise, building fifths starting on each black key. Only one white key will be used. Which one and why?

Fifths and fourths have a very close sound relationship. Reverse the order of D–A (a fifth) to A–D (a fourth). The interval of the fourth (two and one-half steps) and the fifth (three and one-half steps) are referred to as **perfect intervals**—a term used to describe their particular acoustical properties. Sing and play both intervals. Although at first you may only hear their similar characteristics, paying close attention will help you to hear their subtle differences. Which interval sounds wider? Why? Familiarize yourself with the comparative sounds of fifths and fourths. The character of both of these intervals will be especially noticeable when contrasted with narrower intervals such as thirds and seconds.

Octaves are also referred to as perfect intervals. Historically (from the ninth to the fourteenth century), the most frequently used intervals (fourths, fifths, and octaves) were considered perfect intervals, and the other intervals were considered somewhat dissonant (or imperfect).

RESPONSES

In order to maintain the correct number of steps (three and one-half), the fifth starting on B must move upward to the black key of F♯.

When building fifths on the black keys, the only ascending fifth that requires the use of a white key is B♭–F. The correct number of steps must be maintained.

The interval of the fifth is wider than the fourth, since the fifth has a larger number of steps between its two pitches.

**166**   Notate, play, and sing a transposition of WAYFARING STRANGER, starting a half step above the original note. Remember to carefully check the key signature in frame 163 to see if the original note is flatted or sharped. Do not use that key signature in this frame or it will make your transposition incorrect. You will need to use a different key signature. Remember, your transposition is only a half step above the original.

What is your new starting note? Use the fingerings from frame 163. Write the lyrics under the notes.

WAYFARING STRANGER

WAYFARING STRANGER

Spiritual

In the above transposition, notice that the key signature of six flats has been replaced by a key signature with a single sharp. This replacement has the effect of raising all the pitches of WAYFARING STRANGER by one half step. (All the notes which were flatted are now natural and the F which was natural is now sharped.) *Be certain you understand this concept before continuing to the next frame.*

**167** Notate, play, and sing a transposition of WAYFARING STRANGER starting a half step below the original note. Write the lyrics under the notes. What is your new starting note?

## WAYFARING STRANGER

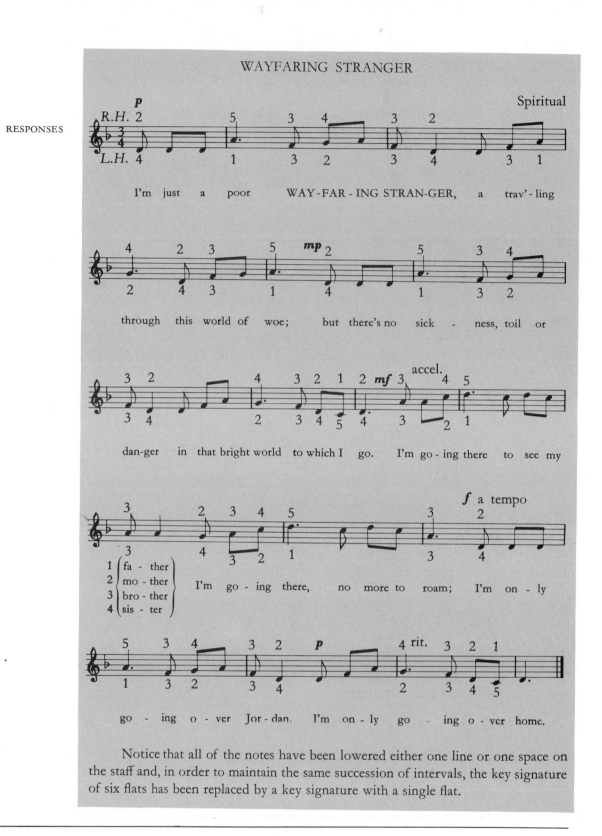

WAYFARING STRANGER

Notice that all of the notes have been lowered either one line or one space on the staff and, in order to maintain the same succession of intervals, the key signature of six flats has been replaced by a key signature with a single flat.

**168**   In this arrangement, the melody of WAYFARING STRANGER is notated as transposed in the response for frame 166. On the two bottom staffs, create your own accompaniment (ostinato type counterpoint) to WAYFARING STRANGER similar to the accompaniment for OLD TEXAS in frame 159. Both clefs are accompaniment.

Use only the five tones found in the melody as the basis for your accompaniment.

Be certain that your accompaniment is rhythmically more simple than the melody of WAYFARING STRANGER so that it will offer contrast. (It will also be easier to sing the melody with such an accompaniment.) Notate your accompaniment in both the treble and bass clefs, and indicate appropriate fingerings.

Sing WAYFARING STRANGER accompanied by your own original arrangement.

## WAYFARING STRANGER

1 fa - ther
2 mo -ther
3 bro -ther
4 sis - ter

I'm go - ing there, no more to roam; I'm on - ly

go - ing o - ver Jor-dan. I'm on - ly go - ing o - ver home.

Your accompaniment to WAYFARING STRANGER will probably be slightly different from the accompaniment notated here. Listen to the recording of this version, as you watch the music. Be certain that in your accompaniment you have only used the five tones found in the melody. Compare this arrangement and the one you have written. Which one do you think is better suited to the melody?

WAYFARING STRANGER

Spiritual

I'm just a poor WAY-FAR-ING STRAN-GER, a trav'-ling

R.H. 3  1          4  3

L.H. 4  3  2

through this world of woe; but there's no sick - - ness, toil or dan-ger in that bright world to which I go. I'm go-ing there to see my

1 ⎰fa - ther⎱
2 ⎱mo - ther⎰
3 ⎰bro - ther⎱
4 ⎱sis - ter⎰

I'm go-ing there, no more to roam; I'm on-ly go - ing o - ver Jor-dan. I'm on-ly go - ing o - ver home.

**169**  Match the most appropriate term or symbol from the following list to each description below (a–gg). Each term will be used at least once, and some will be used more than once.

sharp
***p***
ledger lines
***ff***
second
***mp***
third
grand staff
perfect intervals
fourth
***f***
accidentals

***pp***
middle C
natural
staff
skips
steps
key signature
prime
***mf***
tie
8va
8 bassa
flat

_____ a.   Extends duration of the note
_____ b.   Interval: F moving up to F♯
_____ c.   The G and F clefs combined
_____ d.   Whole and half
_____ e.   Interval: G moving up to C
_____ f.   Middle C is literally in the middle of it
_____ g.   ♯, ♭
_____ h.   Play an octave higher
_____ i.   Used in notating pitches above and below the staff
_____ j.   Interval: C moving down to A
_____ k.   Intervals that remain on the same line or space
_____ l.   Raises note a half step
_____ m.   Lowers note a half step
_____ n.   Cancels flats and sharps
_____ o.   The five lines and four spaces
_____ p.   Shows the number of sharps or flats
_____ q.   Interval: B♭ moving down to A
_____ r.   Interval: C moving up to E
_____ s.   Intervals larger than a whole step
_____ t.   Notated on one ledger line below the treble clef staff
_____ u.   ♭
_____ v.   Interval: D moving up to E
_____ w.   Six flats located on the staff to the right of the clef
_____ x.   ♯
_____ y.   _Forte_ (loud)
_____ z.   _Piano_ (soft)
_____ aa.  _Mezzo piano_ (medium soft)
_____ bb.  _Mezzo forte_ (medium loud)
_____ cc.  _Fortissimo_ (very loud)

_____ dd. *Pianissimo* (very soft)

_____ ee. Play an octave lower

_____ ff. Always appear to the left of the note

_____ gg. Fourths, fifths, octaves and primes

RESPONSES

| | | |
|---|---|---|
| *tie* | a. | Extends duration of the note |
| *prime* | b. | Interval: F moving up to F♯ |
| *grand staff* | c. | The G and F clefs combined |
| *steps* | d. | Whole and half |
| *fourth* | e. | Interval: G moving up to C |
| *grand staff* | f. | Middle C is literally in the middle of it |
| *accidentals* | g. | ♯, ♭ |
| | | |
| *8va* | h. | Play an octave higher |
| *ledger lines* | i. | Used in notating pitches above and below the staff |
| *third* | j. | Interval: C moving down to A |
| *prime* | k. | Intervals that remain on the same line or space |
| *sharp* | l. | Raises note a half step |
| *flat* | m. | Lowers note a half step |
| *natural* | n. | Cancels flats and sharps |
| *staff* | o. | The five lines and four spaces |
| *key signature* | p. | Shows the number of sharps or flats |
| *second* | q. | Interval: B♭ moving down to A |
| *third* | r. | Interval: C moving up to E |
| *skips* | s. | Intervals larger than a whole step |
| *middle C* | t. | Notated on one ledger line below the treble clef staff |
| *flat* | u. | ♭ |
| *second* | v. | Interval: D moving up to E |
| *key signature* | w. | Six flats located on the staff to the right of the clef |
| *sharp* | x. | ♯ |
| *f* | y. | *Forte* (loud) |
| *p* | z. | *Piano* (soft) |
| *mp* | aa. | *Mezzo piano* (medium soft) |
| *mf* | bb. | *Mezzo forte* (medium loud) |
| *ff* | cc. | *Fortissimo* (very loud) |
| *pp* | dd. | *Pianissimo* (very soft) |
| *8 bassa* | ee. | Play an octave lower |
| *accidentals* | ff. | Always appear to the left of the note |
| *perfect intervals* | gg. | Fourths, fifths, octaves, and primes. |

**170** Select any rhythmic composition which you created in Chapter Two; use it as the basis for creating and notating (both clefs) a composition. Include melody and lyrics in the G clef and an accompaniment in the bass clef. Limit your song to eight measures, if possible. Include dynamic marks and fingerings. If appropriate, use rit., accel., accents, metronome markings, etc.

# Songs in Time:

# Melody and Harmony at the Keyboard,

# Ukulele, and Autoharp/Chromaharp

# Songs in Time: Melody and Harmony at the Keyboard, Ukulele, and Autoharp/Chromaharp

*In Chapter Four, you will learn to recognize and play all major and minor chords both from chord symbols and staff notation. The chords are first introduced in root position and then in inversions. Special emphasis is placed on the major seventh chord because of its frequent use in popular music. Diminished and augmented chords also are presented.*

*You will learn to play all of the major and minor scales, and you will develop an understanding of their relationship to chords. Specific criteria are established for the selection of certain harmonies to accompany particular melodies. The ear, however, is stressed as the final decision-maker in choosing chord patterns. Diversity of harmonic possibilities is demonstrated and encouraged.*

*You will be presented with a number of new concepts such as form, phrase, sequence, nonchord tones, arpeggio, key tone, legato, and staccato.*

*At the end of Chapter Four, you will find yourself able to play both the melody and harmony of almost any song in Appendix C.*

---

**171**

### KUMBAYAH!
### (Come By Here)

*Slowly, with feeling*

Folk song

KUM-BA-YAH, my Lord, KUM-BA-YAH! KUM-BA-YAH, my Lord, KUM-BA-

YAH! KUM-BA-YAH my Lord, KUM-BA-YAH! Oh, Lord___ KUM-BA-

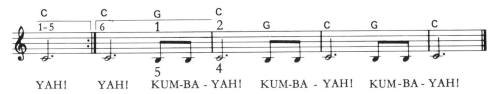

YAH! YAH! KUM-BA-YAH! KUM-BA-YAH! KUM-BA-YAH!

1. Someone's sleeping, Lord, KUMBAYAH!
Someone's sleeping, Lord, KUMBAYAH!
Someone's sleeping, Lord, KUMBAYAH!
Oh, Lord, KUMBAYAH! (chorus)

2. Someone's praying, etc.  (as above) (chorus)
3. Someone's crying, etc.   (chorus)
4. Someone's smiling, etc.  (chorus)
5. Someone's laughing, etc. (chorus)
6. Someone's shouting, etc. (chorus)

KUMBAYAH!, like most folk songs, has an unusual heritage. It is often referred to as an African folk song. More accurate reports say that this song actually started in the Southern United States, then went to Africa, and finally came back via the West Indies. KUMBAYAH! has been recorded by many popular singers—it is well known and well liked in many different countries.

---

**172**  Strike and count KUMBAYAH!. Notice how many times the rhythmic figure ♩♪ appears in this song. Be certain that you understand how to count this figure. Here is an easy way:

Play KUMBAYAH! on the keyboard—first with your right hand (fingerings above the notes), then with your left hand (fingerings below the notes), and finally with both hands, an octave apart. Now sing the letter names of the music in the proper rhythm. Then sing the song with words, varying the dynamics to reflect the lyrics.

Notice that the same ending is used for verses 1–5, but verse 6 uses an extended ending which is not part of the regular eight-measure melody. This extended ending is called a **coda.** (In Italian, coda means "tail".) In today's popular music, the coda is consistently used. The fadeout endings heard on many recordings are codas.

Not all codas, however, are fadeout endings. Joseph Haydn (1732–1809), Wolfgang Amadeus Mozart (1756–1791), and Ludwig van Beethoven (1770–1827) are composers who sometimes added very elaborate and lengthy codas at the ends of their compositions. It was not unusual for these composers to write codas of over thirty-two measures—longer than any of the songs which appear in *Involvement with Music.*

Follow the notes as you listen to the recording of the ♩♪ figure. Strike and count this figure until you can play it perfectly in several tempos.

---

**173**  As you recall from Chapter Three, harmony is created by the sounding of two or more pitches together. Notice the letters above the measures of KUMBAYAH! in frame 171. They refer to an **harmonic accompaniment** suggested by the melody. One way to provide an harmonic accompaniment for a melody is by using **chords.** A chord is a group of *at least* three different pitches which sound at the same time. The letters C and G above the measures of KUMBAYAH! are **chord symbols,** specifying the particular chords to be played at those points in the melody. Play the C major chord with your left hand (L.H.) and listen carefully to its sound:

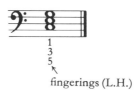

fingerings (L.H.)

This chord with only three pitches is called a **triad.** Notice that in this C major triad, the lowest note is C. The note C is the **root** of this triad and the symbol C takes its name from the root. Sing the C major triad (using the letter names of the notes) from the root to the highest tone and back to the root.

---

**174**  Play this G major triad with your left hand. Listen carefully to its sound:

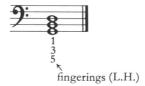

fingerings (L.H.)

Notice that in this G major triad the lowest note is G. Therefore, G is the root of this triad. Sing the G major triad (using the letter names of the notes) from the root to the highest tone and back to the root.

---

**175**  Examine the formation of the C major triad on the keyboard. *The root of any triad is called 1.*

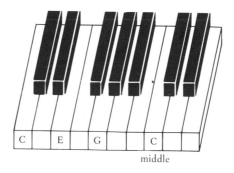

middle

143

In the C major triad above, the tone C is the root and is located on a space. E is called 3, because it is the interval of the third from the root. (See frames 157 and 158.) G is called 5, because it is the interval of a fifth from the root. Notice that the interval from 3 to 5 (E to G) is also a third. *All triads*—considering the root *as the lowest note— are built with one third upon another.* Because triads are built on thirds, the pitches will either all be found on spaces or they will all be found on lines. The C major triad illustrated above is built on spaces and the G major triad (frame 174) is built on lines. Now sing the C major triad, this time replacing the letter names with the numbers of the notes. Sing the triad up (1, 3, 5) and down (5, 3, 1). Sing the G major triad the same way.

**176**   Here are two groups of rhythm patterns:

Play the C major triad in the above rhythm patterns. Use the left hand alone, then the right hand alone, then both hands together (right hand on a higher C major triad, left hand on a lower C major triad).

Play the G major triad in the above rhythm patterns (R.H., L.H., B.H.).

**177**   You may have noticed that there are two kinds of thirds which make up major triads: (1) two whole steps and (2) one and one-half steps. Thirds which consist of two whole steps are referred to as **major thirds**; thirds which consist of one and one-half steps are referred to as **minor thirds**. Every major triad in root position (with root as 1) is built with a major third on the bottom and a minor third on the top. Count the steps in the C major triad:

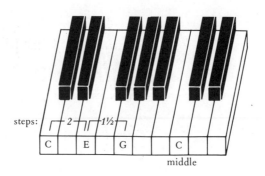

Count the steps in the G major triad:

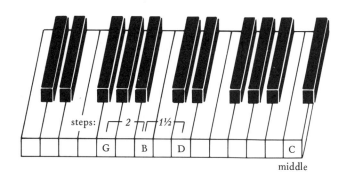

**178** Build major triads on the roots indicated below the staff. Remember when a major triad is in root position, the major third (two whole steps) is on the bottom and the minor third (one and one-half steps) is on the top:

Play these triads with your left hand, then with your right hand.
Play them with both hands together in the rhythm patterns of frame 176.

RESPONSES

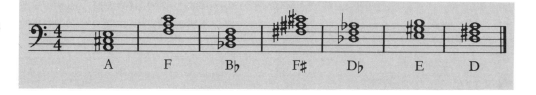

**179** Now you are ready to play KUMBAYAH! with a triadic accompaniment, using the C major and the G major triads.* For the present ignore the symbol (F). Practice the song until you can play it without making any mistakes.

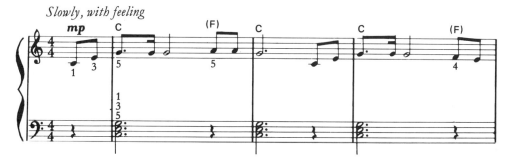

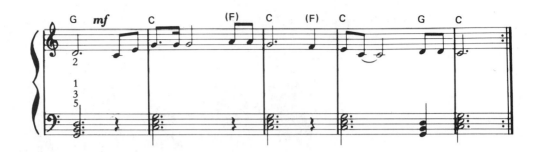

\* If the range of your keyboard instrument is not sufficient to play all the notes of the compositions in *Involvement with Music* (the student Pianica™, for instance, has only two octaves, F–F), play as many notes as you can. The basic chords of your accompaniment will remain the same, but they will not sound as full because fewer pitches are available on your instrument. Sometimes changing the octave of the melody (when convenient) will allow for a fuller triadic accompaniment.

Listen to the recording of KUMBAYAH! as you follow the music. Did you play this song correctly?

**180** Write true or false to the left of the following statements. If the statement is false, change the italicized word(s) to make the statement true.

_____ a. The letters above the measures of a composition refer to an *harmonic accompaniment* suggested by the melody.

_____ b. A chord with only three pitches is called a *root*.

_____ c. A *chord* with only three pitches is called a triad.

_____ d. *Chord symbols* specify the particular chords to be played at that point in the melody.

_____ e. The *third* of a chord is called 1.

_____ f. All *harmonic accompaniments* are built with one third upon another.

_____ g. The *root* of a chord is called 3.

_____ h. The *fifth* of a chord is called 5.

_____ i. A major triad in root position is built with a *minor third* on the bottom and a *major third* on top.

_____ j. There are *one and one-half steps* in a minor third.

_____ k. There are *two whole steps* in a major third.

RESPONSES

*true*  a. The letters above the measures of a composition refer to an *harmonic accompaniment* suggested by the melody.

*false*  b. A chord with only three pitches is called a *root*. (*triad*)

*true*  c. A *chord* with only three pitches is called a triad.

**181**    Play the arrangement of KUMBAYAH! in frame 179 again. This time play all the F major chords as shown by the chord symbols (in parentheses). Substitute them for the rests in the bass clef.

Have you given any thought as to why the F major chords were added to the harmonization of KUMBAYAH!? Remember that this variety is essential to musical interest. Harmonic variety contributes to this interest.

Play the song again, but replace the F major chords with E major chords. Do the E major chords sound like they *belong* with the melody? Repeat the song, but this time substitute A♭ major chords for the F major chords. Do they go with the melody?

Your ears probably regarded the E and A♭ major chords as unacceptable alternatives for the F major chords. The reason your ears ruled out these substitute chords in favor of the F major chords is that the melody pitches do not appear in either of the substitute chords. However, these melody pitches (A and F) do represent 3 and 1 of the F major triad. In other words, the decision to use a certain chord is usually based on the existence of one or more melody tones present in the chord. The more melody tones which appear in a particular chord, the stronger the reason for selecting that chord. For example, the beginning notes of KUMBAYAH! (C, E, and G) are all contained in the C major chord.

**182**    Now that you have learned to play KUMBAYAH! and its harmony on the keyboard, you might enjoy playing that same harmony on other instruments.

One of the principal instruments used to play chords is the **ukulele.** There are two types of ukuleles: the soprano (small, high-pitched instrument) and the baritone (larger, lower-pitched instrument). Because of the great influence of the guitar on modern music and because the four strings of the baritone ukulele are tuned to the same pitches as the four highest-pitched strings of the guitar (D, G, B, E), the baritone is the ukulele described in this text.

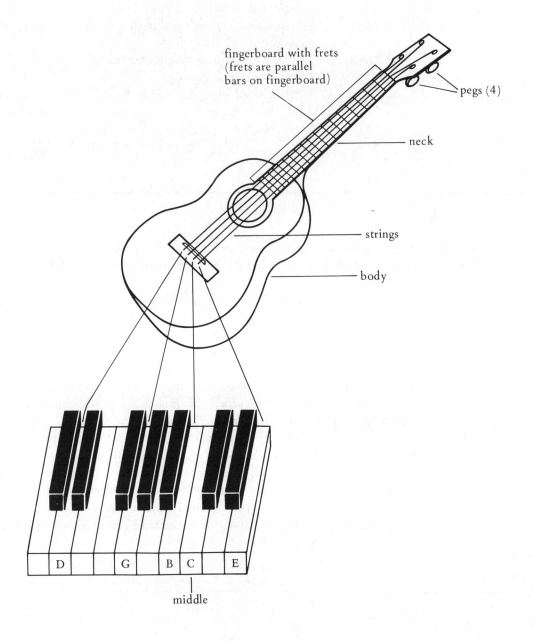

fingerboard with frets
(frets are parallel
bars on fingerboard)

pegs (4)

neck

strings

body

D   G   B C   E

middle

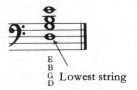

E
B
G
D  Lowest string

When playing the ukulele, the frets are pressed with the left-hand fingers and the strings are strummed with the right-hand fingers. To tune your ukulele, match each **open string** (a string which is sounded without any frets being pressed) to its respective pitch on the keyboard. The pitch of each string can be altered by turning its corresponding peg on the top of the neck of the ukulele. For example, match the pitch of the lowest-sounding string to the pitch of the D below middle C on the keyboard. When these two D's have the same pitch, they are said to be in **unison.** Tune the other strings so that when they are played open, they will also be in unison with their respective tones on the keyboard, G, B, and E (see diagram above).

As an aid to remembering the sound of the tuning, sing this much of OLD TEXAS:

D   G   B  (D)  E

"I'm going to (leave) old . . ."

Sing "leave" silently and sustain the higher tone on "old." These tones are D, G, B, and E as written above the words. What are the intervals between each of these tones? Sing these intervals again and try to remember them. Knowing the sounds of these intervals will help you to remember the tuning.

Once you have tuned the open D string to a piano or some other instrument, you can tune the other strings in relation to the D string without using another instrument. Press the D string on the fifth fret (counting from the pegboard) and pluck the string. The tone produced is G. Using the appropriate peg, adjust the second string until it sounds in unison with G (see diagram A). Press the fourth fret of the G string and pluck the string. The tone produced is B. Adjust the third string until it sounds in unison with B (see diagram B). Press the fifth fret of the B string and pluck the string. The tone produced is E. Adjust the fourth string until it sounds in unison with E (see diagram C).

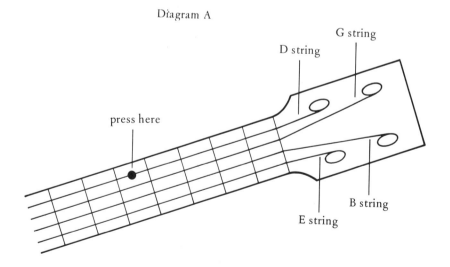

Diagram A

G string

D string

press here

E string

B string

Diagram B

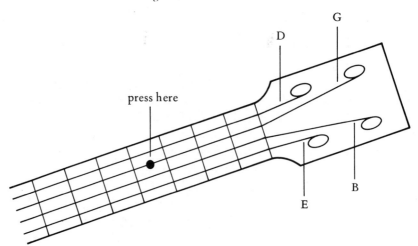

Diagram C

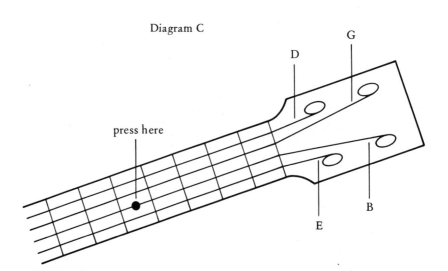

Sometimes you will not have access to an instrument so that you can tune the open D string properly. The lack of the D tone should not deter you from playing the ukulele properly. If you *estimate* the D pitch and follow the tuning procedures described in the previous paragraph, your ukulele will be in tune with itself. However, it may not be in tune with other instruments, simply because your estimate of D was either too high or too low. What is most important is that the strings are tuned in the proper relationship to each other.

**183**  Here are the C, G, and F major chords for the ukulele:

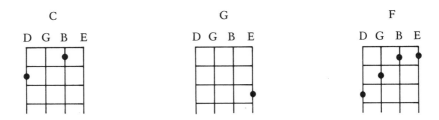

The dots illustrate where to press the strings with the fingers of your left hand. Press the strings firmly against the keyboard. From one fret to the next is a half step. The closer the frets are to the body of the ukulele, the higher the pitch.

Knowing this rule, it is now possible for you to play any melody or scale. You may do this on one or more strings—whichever way you find more convenient. If you plan to play a melody on one string, the only limitation is that the lowest tone of the melody cannot go lower than the pitch of that string when played open. The entire playable range of each of the four strings is the interval of an octave plus the interval of a fourth.

Examine the diagrams below. What tones are being played by each string?

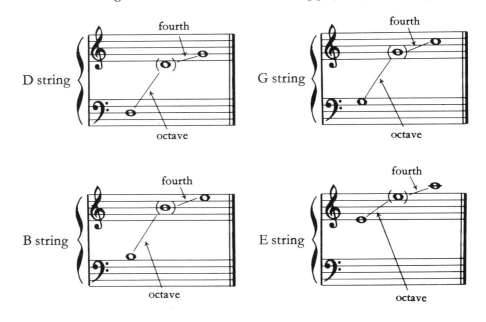

RESPONSES

Tones played by each string (in the diagrams):

D string: D—(D)—G
B string: B—(B)—E
G string: G—(G)—C
E string: E—(E)—A

**184**

Notice that in the above example the F major chord has four tones. There are two Fs: the root and an F one octave higher than the root. Up to this point, you have been playing triads on the keyboard. Now you are dealing with four-tone chords, because the ukulele has four strings. When in root position, the root of a four-tone chord is the one that is usually doubled one octave higher.

    Examine the C major chord. It is not in root position, since the C is not the lowest tone. When a tone other than the root is the lowest tone, the chord is said to be **inverted.** In this particular C major chord, the E (the third of the C major chord) is the lowest tone. This position of a chord (with the third as the lowest tone) is referred to as **first inversion.** What tone has been doubled?

    Examine the G major chord. It is not in root position, since the G is not the lowest tone. This chord is also inverted, but the D (the fifth of the G major chord) is the lowest tone. This position of a chord (with the fifth as the lowest tone) is referred to as **second inversion.** What tone has been doubled?

RESPONSES

In the C chord, E has been doubled. In the G chord, G has been doubled. In the F chord, F has been doubled. Listen to these chords played on the ukulele.

---

**185**    Use rhythms a and b below to practice each chord separately (C major, F major, and G major) on the ukulele. Gently strum the strings (over the opening on the body) downward with the fingernail side of the index finger (R.H.). Then repeat the rhythms using all three chords. Change chords every measure. The order of chords is your choice. You may want to try several combinations.

    Repeat the rhythms again, but change chords at random *within* the measures.

---

**186**    Sing KUMBAYAH! and accompany yourself on the baritone ukulele. Read only the treble staff and the chord symbols above it. The bass staff is a piano accompaniment. There are no limitations regarding how many or how few times you should play a particular chord in a particular measure. Let your ears and your musical taste help you to make these decisions.

# KUMBAYAH!

*Slowly, with feeling*                                                    Folk song

Listen to the accompaniment played by the ukulele in this recording of KUMBAYAH!.

---

**187**   Play the piano arrangement of KUMBAYAH! in frame 186. Look at the G chords and compare their structure to the G chords in frame 179. Your analysis will show that the G chords in frame 186 do not have G as their lowest note, but G is the lowest note in the G chords of frame 179. B is the lowest note in the G chords of frame 186; therefore, each G chord of frame 186 is in the _____ inversion. Look at the F chords in frame 186. Each F chord is in the _____ inversion.

As you practice this arrangement of KUMBAYAH! on the keyboard you will find that it is much easier to play than the arrangement of frame 171 (which uses the C, F, and G chords in root position).

RESPONSES   Each G chord of frame 186 is in the *first* inversion. Each F chord is in the *second* inversion.

**188** Chord inversions are important in music. Their chief contribution is to add variety to the music, particularly when the same chord must be repeated a number of times.

There is also a very practical reason for the use of inversions. As you discovered from playing the two different arrangements of KUMBAYAH!—when playing the piano —the use of inversions along with root position chords makes it easier for the fingers to move smoothly from one chord to the next. Inversions eliminate many of the wide skips encountered in a series of root position chords. The use of inversions can create an **anchor tone:** a tone which is common to successive chords. In the example below, the anchor tone C is circled. It is common to both the C and the F chords and therefore it does not require a change in finger position. The fifth finger remains anchored while the other fingers move in stepwise motion:

In the next example the C and F chords are both in root position. The C no longer acts as an anchor tone, and therefore the entire hand must move awkwardly.

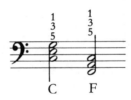

*In general, the use of some inversions along with root position chords will facilitate the playing of most songs.*

---

**189** Using the same harmony, you can learn an accompaniment for KUMBAYAH! on the **autoharp™** (or **chromaharp™**).

The autoharp/chromaharp is the easiest instrument on which to play chords. All that it requires is that you press the appropriate chord button and strum the strings with either the fingernail side of your index finger (R.H.) or with a pick.

Place the autoharp/chromaharp on a table with the lowest (longest) string nearest your body. Adjust the angle of the autoharp/chromaharp to the most comfortable position. The chord buttons should be within easy reach of your left-hand fingers. On these instruments, the right hand usually strums the strings by crossing over the left hand. However, you may devise your own method of playing.

There are several ways to play the autoharp/chromaharp, but the techniques illustrated below are the ones most often employed:

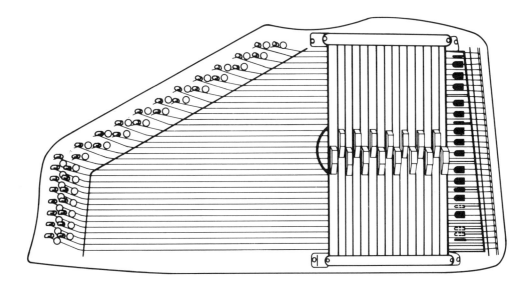

**190**  Use rhythms a and b below to practice the C, F, and G major chords separately on the autoharp/chromaharp. Then repeat the rhythms using all three chords in sequence (change chords every measure). The order of chords is your choice. You may want to try several combinations.

Repeat the rhythms, but select chords other than the C, F, and G major chords. Play them in any order that appeals to you. Try changing chords *within* measures.

Sing KUMBAYAH! and accompany yourself on the autoharp/chromaharp, using the chords indicated in frame 186.

**191**  Fill in the missing word(s):

a. The pitches of the four baritone ukulele strings are (starting with the lowest) _____, _____, _____, and _____.

b. Fill in the fingerings for the following ukulele chords:

C   G   F

c. The playable range of each ukulele string is the interval of a(n)
_____ plus the interval of a(n) _____.

d. When in root position, the _____ of a four-tone chord is usually doubled.

e. When a tone other than the root is the lowest tone, the chord is said to be
_____.

f. When the third of a chord is the lowest tone, the chord is in _____ inversion.

g. When the fifth of the chord is the lowest tone, the chord is in _____ inversion.

h. Another instrument like the autoharp is the _____.

i. On the autoharp, the right hand usually strums the strings by _____ the left hand.

j. When you have established the lowest tone D on the ukulele, how do you tune the remaining three strings to each other? (Describe.) _____
_____
_____
_____

k. A tone which is common to successive chords is a(n) _____ tone.

a. The pitches of the four baritone ukulele strings are (starting with the lowest) D, G, B, and E.

b. Fill in the fingerings for the following ukulele chords:

c. The playable range of each ukulele string is the interval of a(n) *octave* plus the interval of a (n) *fourth*.

d. When in root position, the *root* of a four-tone chord is usually doubled.

e. When a tone other than the root is the lowest tone, the chord is said to be *inverted*.

f. When the third of a chord is the lowest tone, the chord is in *first* inversion.

g. When the fifth of the chord is the lowest tone, the chord is in *second* inversion.

h. Another instrument like the autoharp is the *chromaharp*.

i. On the autoharp, the right hand usually strums the strings by *crossing over* the left hand.

j. When you have established the lowest tone D on the ukulele, how do you tune the remaining three strings to each other? (Describe.) *Tune the G string to the sound of the fifth fret of the D string; tune the B string to the sound of the fourth fret of the G string; tune the E string to the fifth fret of the B string (or equivalent answer).*

    k. A tone which is common to successive chords is a(n) *anchor* tone.

**192**   Throughout this Chapter you have been working with the C, F, and G major chords, using them to accompany the song, KUMBAYAH!.

    A measure-by-measure analysis of the melody (KUMBAYAH!) will explain why these three chords have been used exclusively in this chapter.

    The first three tones (C, E, G) of the song form the C major triad; consequently, the C major chord is used. The next different tone is A and it is the third of the F major triad. Traditionally, at least one note of a triad (preferably the root or the third) should be in the melody to justify the use of that chord. Consequently, the A (being the third of the F major triad) justifies the use of the F major triad.

    In measure two, the C chord is used again because all of the tones of the C major triad are in the melody. Measure three (including the pickup notes from measure two) again justifies the use of the C major triad. The F major chord is used because the F in the melody is the root of the F chord.

    Do not worry about the E (last half count of measure three). It is a **nonchord tone** (not present in either the F major triad or the upcoming G major triad). Nonchord tones will be examined later.

    The G major triad is used in measure four because the D is the fifth of the G major triad. The pickup notes C and E in the measure belong to the C major triad of measure five, which is identical to measure one. The C major triad is used on the note G in measure six because G is the fifth of the C major triad. The F in measure six is the root of the F major triad.

    In measure seven, the E and C represent the third and root of the C major triad. The D (last count of measure seven) is the fifth of the G chord.

If you understand this **harmonic analysis,** you are well prepared for further exploration of harmony. Start by analyzing the *coda* of KUMBAYAH!.

---

**193**     The C, F, and G major chords have a specific and important relationship to the **major scale.**

You will recall that a scale is any fixed arrangement of keys in a specific interval relationship. Frame 194 illustrates the structure of a major scale.

---

**194**

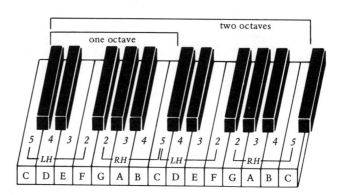

Observe the keyboard diagram above. Place your left- and right-hand fingers on the keys as illustrated, from middle C to the octave above. Play the C major scale up and down (one octave). Maintain a smooth and even beat, as you gradually increase the tempo of your scale.

Now play the C major scale up and down for two octaves. After the L.H. has played the first four keys in the first octave, cross the L.H. over the R.H. and prepare it immediately for its new position in the next octave by holding it directly above the keys it is to play. After the R.H. has played the second four keys in the first octave, cross the R.H. over the L.H. and prepare it immediately for the second octave. Change hand positions smoothly so that the flow of the music is uninterrupted. Maintain a smooth and even beat as you gradually increase the tempo of your two-octave scale. Practice this scale daily to improve your finger dexterity and coordination.

**195**   Carefully examine the formation of the C major scale in relation to this C major chord:

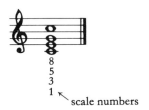

scale numbers

Notice that the C major chord is 1, 3, 5, and 8 of the C major scale:

scale numbers:   1      2      3      4      5      6      7      8

All major chords are 1, 3, 5, and 8 of their respective major scale. When 1, 3, 5, or 1, 3, 5, and 8 are played successively rather than simultaneously (either in root position or in an inversion), the chord is called an **arpeggio** (pronounced är pĕ j′ ō) or a **broken chord.** Arpeggiated chords are commonly used in accompaniments.

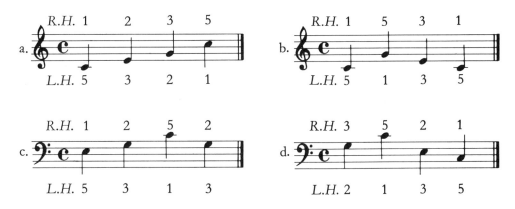

Examine and play each of the above **arpeggiated** C major chords up and down in L.H., R.H., and B.H. (one octave apart). Now move all of your fingers to the right one half step and play these **arpeggiated** patterns in their new positions, using L.H., R.H., and B.H. After you have played these transposed versions of examples a–d, move all your fingers a half step to the right again and play the **arpeggiated** patterns in these new positions. Continue transposing these broken chords a half step higher than the previous ones until you arrive at the C major chord one octave above the original C major chord. This experience will help you to develop finger agility. Remember that each of these broken chord patterns uses the 1, 3, 5, and 8 of a major scale in either root position order or in an inversion.

---

**196** Number 1 of any major scale is the **key tone** or **home tone.** Play the C major scale once more using the fingering in frame 194. Notice that the melody of KUMBAYAH! is based upon the tones of the C major scale. In this song, C is the home tone or key tone. Observe that KUMBAYAH! ends on the home tone. An analysis of familiar folk songs will reveal that over 90% of them end on their home tone and many of them also begin on their home tone. In most songs, the home tone appears frequently throughout the song.

Examine the C major scale. Notice that there are adjoining white keys between 3–4 (E–F) and 7–8 (B–C); all of the other keys are adjacent keys (separated by one key). In other words, there are half steps between 3–4 and 7–8 and all other steps in the major scale are whole steps. Observe the half steps in the keyboard diagram:

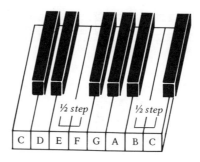

*Every major scale is built the same way: half steps only between 3–4 and 7–8, whole steps between the other keys.* When building major scales other than C, it will become necessary to use flats or sharps to maintain the half steps between 3–4 and 7–8. Sharps and flats are never mixed in a major scale. Observe the following examples and name the home tones:

*Bb major scale*                                             *Home tone =*

scale numbers:   1    2    3    4    5    6    7    8

Play the D and Bb major scales on the keyboard, up and down for one and then two octaves each. Use the same L.H./R.H. fingering positions as you did for the C major scale. Gradually increase the tempo, but do not sacrifice smooth playing to gain speed.

Now play the D and Bb major scales on the ukulele, using the most convenient strings.

On the keyboard, play the D and Bb major chords (L.H., R.H., B.H.) in root position and in all their inversions. Play several different broken chord patterns (L.H., R.H., B.H.) built on these chords (refer to frame 195, if necessary). Use the most comfortable fingerings.

RESPONSES

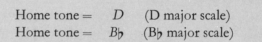

Home tone =   *D*   (D major scale)
Home tone =   *Bb*   (Bb major scale)

---

**197**  Write major scales in half notes for the home tones indicated below in both the treble and bass clef staffs. Where necessary, include flats or sharps to the left of the respective notes; do not mix flats and sharps in any given scale. Be certain that you provide half steps between 3–4 and 7–8. Play each of these scales up and down (one and two octaves), using the fingerings you have learned. Play each of these scales on the ukulele.

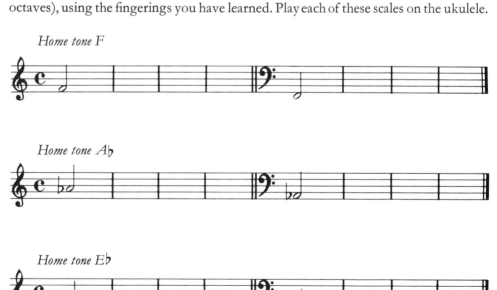

*Home tone F*

*Home tone Ab*

*Home tone Eb*

Home tone B

Home tone A

Home tone G

RESPONSES

Home tone F

Home tone A♭

Home tone E♭

Home tone B

Home tone A

*Home tone G*

**198** Instead of writing flats and sharps to the left of each note which needs to be altered, the appropriate key signature can be written next to the clef sign:

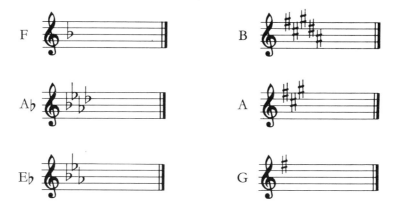

The sharps or flats of key signatures are not necessarily arranged in the same order as they appear in their respective scales. For instance, in the E♭ scale, the flats appear in this order:

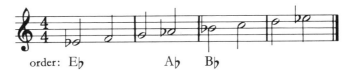

order: E♭      A♭   B♭

But in the E♭ key signature, the flats appear in this order (reading from left to right):

order: B♭ E♭ A♭

Logically, it would seem that the flats should appear in the key signature in the same order as they appear in the scale. But only in the major keys of F, B♭, G, and D do the key signatures coincide with the order of flats or sharps in their respective scales.

Understanding the relationship of the key signature to the composition will facilitate the performance of that music. Besides indicating which notes are to be sharped or flatted, the key signature also suggests the home tone, the particular scale, and which chords are most likely to occur.

No matter where a sharp or a flat is located in the key signature, it means that any note bearing that letter name will be sharped or flatted. For example:

The flat applies to all Bs, regardless of the octave.

---

**199**    **Key Signature Order: Rules for Constructing Flat Key Signatures**

    a.  Every flat key signature starts with B♭.

    b.  The flats that follow B♭ are in the relationship of the interval of a fourth up, then the interval of a fifth down:

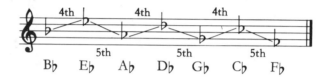

---

**200**    **Key Signature Order: Rules for Identifying the Home Tone of a Major Scale with a Flat Key Signature**

    a.  The last flat on the right is on 4 of its major scale. The home tone is (1) of that major scale.

    b.  A simpler rule is that the next to last flat on the right is on the home tone (1) of the major scale.

Obviously, rule b does not apply to the key signature having only one flat; therefore, use rule a:

---

**201**    Write the flat key signatures for the home tones indicated, then write the corresponding major scale (from 1 to 8) and indicate the locations of the half steps with a bracket. Example:

*Home tone F*

scale numbers: 1    2    3    4    5    6    7    8

Write the appropriate scale numbers below the notes. Play each major scale on the keyboard in one and two octaves, using the R.H./L.H. fingerings illustrated in frame 194. Gradually increase your speed as you practice these scales. Curve your fingers.

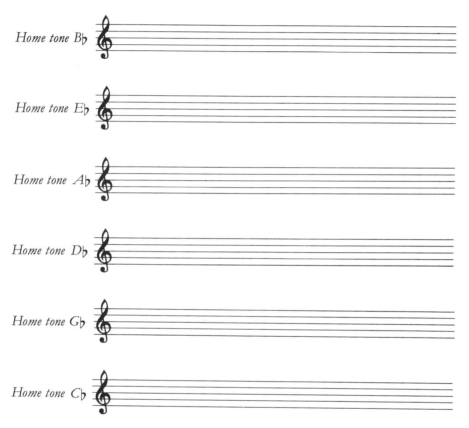

*Home tone B♭*

*Home tone E♭*

*Home tone A♭*

*Home tone D♭*

*Home tone G♭*

*Home tone C♭*

After you feel comfortable playing each of these major scales separately, play them consecutively (with no breaks between the scales—only one octave). As you are playing with one hand, prepare the other hand for its next position in order to make a smooth and uninterrupted transition from scale to scale. This exercise will help you to develop coordination and agility at the keyboard.

Play each of the scales on the ukulele.

*Home tone B♭*

1    2    3    4    5    6    7    8

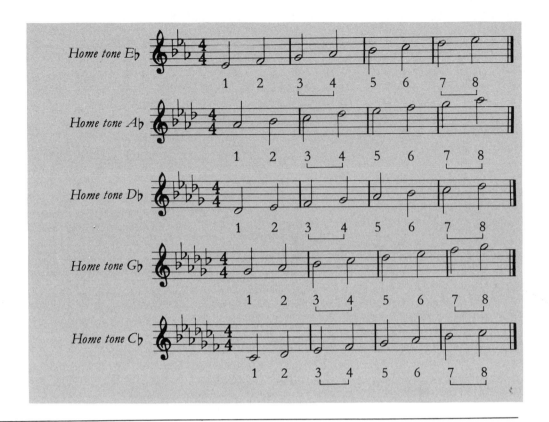

---

## 202    Key Signature Order: Rules for Constructing Sharp Key Signatures

     a. Every sharp key signature starts with F♯.

     b. After F♯, the sharps that follow are in the relationship of the interval of a fourth down, then the interval of a fifth up.* For example:

   * This rule is the exact opposite of the rule for construction of flat key signatures (frame 199).
      Notice that the A♯ is located on the second space, rather than on the line above the staff. This avoids the use of a ledger line above the staff.

---

## 203    Key Signature Order: Rules for Identifying the Home Tone of the Major Scale with a Sharp Key Signature

     a. The last sharp on the right is on 7 of its major scale. The home tone is 1 of that major scale.

     b. Since the home tone is 8 (or 1), it is located one half step above 7. For example:

Home tone G

**204** Write the sharp key signatures for the home tones indicated, then write the major scale (from 1 to 8) and indicate the locations of the half steps with a bracket. Example:

Home tone G

1    2    3    4    5    6    7    8

Write the appropriate scale numbers below the notes. Play each major scale on the keyboard in one and two octaves, using the R.H./L.H. fingerings illustrated in previous frames. Gradually increase the tempo.

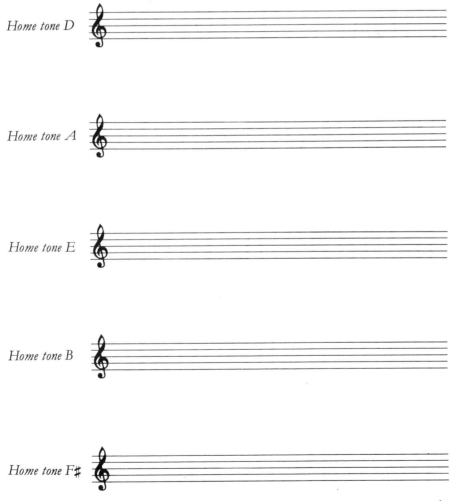

Home tone D

Home tone A

Home tone E

Home tone B

Home tone F♯

*Home tone C♯*

After playing each of these major scales separately, follow the procedure in frame 201 and play them consecutively. Try to play these exercises as smoothly and evenly as possible. Notice that the last four notes of each scale (5, 6, 7, and 8) are the first four notes (1, 2, 3, and 4) of the next scale. Recognizing this pattern will enable you to prepare your hands more readily.

Play these scales on the ukulele.

RESPONSES

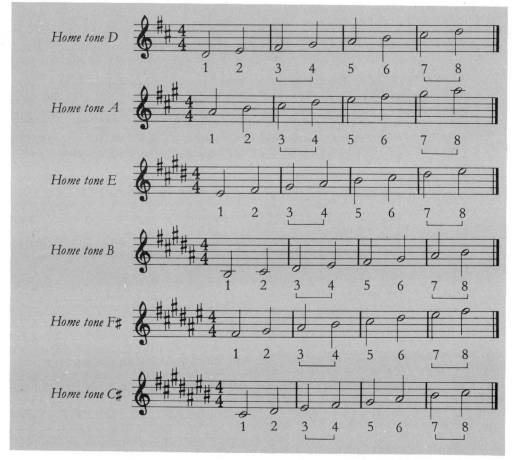

**205**   Now that you are familiar with all of the major scales and their key signatures, you will be able to understand the specific and important numerical relationships between the C, F, and G major chords which were used for the harmony of KUMBAYAH!.

Since KUMBAYAH! is in the key of C major (home tone C) the C chord is built on C, which is 1 of the C major scale. The F major chord is built on 4 of the C major scale; and the G major chord is built on 5 of the C major scale. Hereafter, chords built upon scale numbers will be illustrated: ℭ, ℭ, ℭ, and they will be referred to as the **primary chords.** The chord relationships are also shown by these symbols. The **C** which partially encloses the scale number is the first letter of the word,

168

"chord." Therefore, C1 = *any* chord built on 1 of the scale; C4 = *any* chord built on 4 of the scale; C5 = *any* chord built on 5 of the scale. In other texts, chords built on scale numbers are designated with Roman numerals. For example, C1 as used in this program is traditionally written I; C5 is V, etc.

---

**206** Notate C1, C4, and C5 in the following major keys, include the key signatures, and write the chord symbols above the chords. Example:

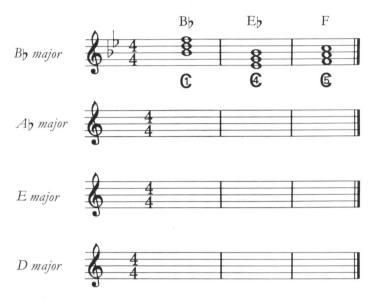

Play the above chords on the keyboard (R.H.). Play them an octave below (L.H.). Now play the chords with B.H.

RESPONSES

**207** Transpose the melody and harmony of KUMBAYAH! into the keys of G major and B♭ major, using the original arrangement in C major as your guide. Write your transpositions on the staffs provided in this frame. Write the appropriate chord symbols above the measures and also include 𝄴, 𝄵, and 𝄶 below the chords.

The most important step in transposing a melody is to be certain that the starting note in the new key is the *same* scale number as the starting note in the original key. In other words, a transposition *always* starts on the same scale number as the original arrangement—but the note itself is different. For example: if an original arrangement is in the key of C and starts on 3 (E), then a transposition in the key of F would also start on 3—but the note would be A. All notes in a transposition have scale numbers which are identical to those in the original arrangement.

KUMBAYAH!
Original Arrangement, Key of C

## KUMBAYAH!
### G Major Transposition

## KUMBAYAH!
### B♭ Major Transposition

Play both transpositions of KUMBAYAH! on the keyboard and also on the auto-harp/chromaharp. Play the chords for the G major transposition on the ukulele.

RESPONSES Compare your transpositions of KUMBAYAH! to the ones in this frame. Then, listen to the recorded B♭ major transposition of KUMBAYAH! accompanied by the autoharp/chromaharp.

KUMBAYAH!
G Major Transposition

KUMBAYAH!
B♭ Major Transposition

Slowly, with feeling

Folk song

**208** Write true or false to the left of the following statements. If the statement is false, change the italicized word(s) to make the statement true.

_____a. A major scale is built with half steps between *2–3 and 6–7*.

_____b. An *arpeggio* or *broken chord* may be composed of 1, 3, 5, and 8 of the major scale.

_____c. The key tone or home tone of any major scale is *5*.

_____d. Ⓒ₁ , Ⓒ₂ , and Ⓒ₃ are primary chords.

**209** Sing and play (keyboard) the melody of this beautiful spiritual, ALL NIGHT, ALL DAY. Then sing the melody and play the chords written in the bass clef staff (L.H.). Now play both the melody and the chords together, as you sing.

If you were to transpose this song into the key of F major, what would be the starting note? Why? Play it.

What would be the starting note in the key of D major? Why? Play it.

What would be the first chord in the key of A major? Why? Play it.

What would be the first chord in the key of E♭ major? Why? Play it.

In the key of C major, what would be the second chord in the second measure? Why? Play it.

RESPONSES    If ALL NIGHT, ALL DAY were transposed into F major, the starting note would be C. The starting note of the original arrangement in frame 209 is D, which is 5 of the G major scale. Therefore, in the key of F major, 5 of that scale is C. If this procedure is not clear, review frame 207.

Therefore, in D major, the starting note would be A.

The first chord in A major would be an A major chord in second inversion, since that chord is Ⓒ in the key of A major—just as the G major chord is Ⓒ in the key of G major. Remember that chord numbers in a transposition are identical to those in the original arrangement.

The third chord in the key of C major would be a G major chord.

Listen to the recording of ALL NIGHT, ALL DAY as you follow the music. Observe the changes in dynamics. Did you play the rhythm correctly?

Practice ALL NIGHT, ALL DAY until you can play it with no mistakes.

**210**    Notice the use of the G major chord in second inversion (D, the fifth, is in the bass) throughout the arrangement of ALL NIGHT, ALL DAY in frame 209. The D in the bass consistently serves as an anchor tone for the D and G major chords.

Are there any inversions of the other chords? If there are others, identify them as first or second inversion.

The use of inversions and anchor tones makes this arrangement easier to play than if root position chords were used exclusively.

The accompaniment uses repeated chords, and its rhythm contrasts with the melody, thereby creating musical interest.

This arrangement only uses the 𝕀, 𝕀𝕍, and 𝕍 chords. *These primary chords are the most frequently used chords in music.* Of the three chords 𝕀 occurs most often because it is the home tone, then 𝕍 and 𝕀𝕍, in that order.

Notice the D7 chord symbol in measures 4 and 7. This means that the tone C is added to the D major triad, making a **four-tone chord.** The number relationship of D to C is 1:7—thus the use of the number 7 for the added tone:

D7

This fourth tone is called the **common seventh**\* because it is the seventh which is most frequently added to chords. It is always found a whole step below the octave of the letter name of the chord. For example, the common seventh of a B♭7 chord is A♭ (a whole step below the octave B♭). What is the common seventh of an E♭7 chord? Of an A7 chord? Of an E7 chord? Play the E♭7, A7, and E7 chords (L.H., R.H., B.H.). When the seventh is the lowest tone of the chord, the chord is in the **third inversion.** Play each of the preceding chords in their third inversions. Play each of these seventh chords as *arpeggios* (L.H., R.H., B.H.) in root position *and* in third inversion.

\* In most texts, this seventh is referred to as the *dominant seventh* when it is used in conjunction with the 𝕍. A more flexible term used in many sources is the X7 chord.

---

RESPONSES    The C major chord in ALL NIGHT, ALL DAY is used in first inversion.

The common seventh of an E♭7 chord is D♭:

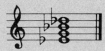

Common seventh of an A7 chord is G:

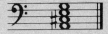

Common seventh of an E7 chord is D:

Remember that the common seventh is located a whole step below the octave of the letter name (or root) of the chord.

---

**211**    When the common seventh is used in conjunction with a Ⓖ chord (Ⓖ7), it is most often found at the end of a **phrase.** A phrase is a group of measures containing a single musical thought which seems to have a beginning and a temporary or a final point of repose. A phrase has a certain degree of tension which moves toward some degree of release. *Musical compositions, like other art forms, are usually constructed so that they convey feelings of tension and release.* Unrelieved tension offers little musical variety; but tension followed by release creates variety in a musical composition.

Most of the music in our culture is composed of connecting groups of phrases. ALL NIGHT, ALL DAY is composed of two phrases—the first phrase terminates at measure four and the second terminates at measure eight. The first phrase will be referred to as phrase A. The second phrase will be referred to as A′, because it is similar to phrase A. Thus the **form** of ALL NIGHT, ALL DAY is AA′. *Form is the musical organization of same and different phrases.* In folk songs, phrases usually consist of four or eight measures.

The end of a phrase is harmonically strengthened by certain chords which, together, form what is known as a **cadence.** When a phrase ends on the Ⓒ chord (home tone chord), it is called a **full cadence.** Full cadences provide complete release from tension. If the *last* chord of a cadence is Ⓖ or Ⓖ7 (or any chord other than Ⓒ), it is referred to as a **temporary cadence** (sometimes called a half cadence). Temporary cadences only give a feeling of *momentary* repose, while preparing the listener to move ahead to other phrases. Play ALL NIGHT, ALL DAY once again; listen for the difference between the temporary cadence at the end of the first phrase (measure 4) and the full cadence at the end of the second phrase (measure 8).

---

**212**    Notice the curved line ‿ below the notes B and A in measures two and six of ALL NIGHT, ALL DAY (frame 209) and below the notes E and D in measure four. This curved line is called a **slur.** At first you might have thought that the curved line was a tie. However, remember that a tie connects the *same* notes (refer to OLD TEXAS, frame 151, whereas a slur has a very different function. The slur tells the performer to make a smooth connection between two or more *different* notes. The slur is used both instrumentally and vocally. In vocal music, it is most often used when a word or a syllable is sung on more than one tone—such as the words "ALL," and "Lord" in ALL NIGHT, ALL DAY (two tones are required—B and A for "ALL" and E and D for "Lord"). The slur is a very common device throughout all music. It is applied only to small groups of tones.

When a composer wishes a large section of a composition—or the entire composition itself—to be played as smoothly as possible, he will use the term **legato** (pronounced le gä′ tō, meaning "bound" in Italian). The opposite of *legato* or smoothly is **staccato** (pronounced sta kä′ tō, meaning "detached" in Italian). Since they are performed as detached, nonsustained sounds, staccato notes sound shorter than their written values indicate. At the keyboard, the finger quickly bounces off the key to achieve *staccato*. A composer will indicate his desire for *staccato* playing or singing by using the word itself or by writing dots above or below the notes ( ). The use of *legato* and *staccato* add variety to a musical composition.

---

**213** Play and/or sing the melody of ALL NIGHT, ALL DAY (frame 209). Perform it first in legato style, then in staccato style. Which style seems more appropriate for ALL NIGHT, ALL DAY? Why? Notice the temporary cadence at the end of the first phrase (measure four) and the full cadence at the end of the second phrase (measure eight).

---

**214**

ALL NIGHT, ALL DAY

Spiritual

Play and sing this arrangement of ALL NIGHT, ALL DAY at the keyboard. Compare it to the arrangement in frame 209. Did you notice that some of the same chords are used differently? They are occasionally broken up to give a more flowing quality to the music.

In measures three and five, the C and G major chords are broken into *arpeggios* (see frame 195), providing a thinner **chordal texture.** Chordal texture refers to the density of the chordal structure in a musical composition. Specifically, the more tones in a chord and the closer together these tones are, the thicker or more dense the texture. In contrast to the thin texture of measures three and five, observe the thicker chordal texture in measures two, four, and six. Pay particular attention to the four-note chords—both of which are common sevenths.

Broken chord patterns could be used exclusively in ALL NIGHT, ALL DAY. However, for an effective contrast, other patterns have also been used. Select one or two of these patterns, or devise some of your own, and use them to play your own arrangement of ALL NIGHT, ALL DAY.

After you can play this arrangement of ALL NIGHT, ALL DAY with no mistakes, continue to the next frame.

---

**215** Play the chords of ALL NIGHT, ALL DAY on the baritone ukulele and on the autoharp/chromaharp. You already know how to play the C, F, and G chords on the ukulele (frame 183); but in order to play ALL NIGHT, ALL DAY on the ukulele, you must add the D and D7 chords to your chord vocabulary:

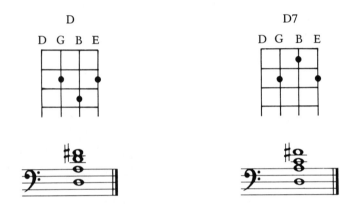

When playing the ukulele or the autoharp/chromaharp, change chords only when the symbols change. Use your own musical discretion to devise rhythm patterns and to determine how many times in a measure you should play each chord.

---

**216** Both the baritone ukulele and the autoharp/chromaharp readily lend themselves to the playing of broken chord patterns. Play ALL NIGHT, ALL DAY (frame 214) on both of these instruments using some broken chord patterns and some vertical chord patterns. You will find that variety in *chordal texture*—when used judiciously—creates more musical interest.

**217** Write true or false to the left of the following statements. If the statement is false, change the italicized word(s) to make the statement true.

_____ a. A phrase is a group of measures containing *several* musical thoughts.

_____ b. A phrase has a *temporary or a final* point of repose.

_____ c. The musical organization of same and different phrases is called *form*.

_____ d. If the last chord of a cadence is a 🅖 or 🅖7, it is referred to as a *temporary* cadence.

_____ e. The *full* cadence ends on 🅒.

_____ f. A curved line 🎵 which connects two different notes is called a *staccato*.

_____ g. *Staccato* indicates that the notes should be played smoothly; and *legato* indicates that the notes should be played in a detached style.

_____ h. The *major* seventh is always found a whole step below the octave of the letter name of the chord.

_____ i. A *thin* chordal texture is one in which as many tones as possible are used in a particular chord or group of chords.

RESPONSES

*false*  a. A phrase is a group of measures containing *several* musical thoughts. *(a single)*

*true*  b. A phrase has a *temporary or a final* point of repose.

*true*  c. The musical organization of same and different phrases is called *form*.

*true*  d. If the last chord of a cadence is a 🅖 or 🅖7, it is referred to as a *temporary* cadence.

*true*  e. The *full* cadence ends on 🅒.

*false*  f. A curved line 🎵 which connects two different notes is called a *staccato*. *(slur)*

*false*  g. *Staccato* indicates that the notes should be played smoothly; and *legato* indicates that the notes should be played in a detached style. *(legato) (staccato)*

*false*  h. The *major* seventh is always found a whole step below the octave of the letter name of the chord. *(common)*

*false*  i. A *thin* chordal texture is one in which as many tones as possible are used in a particular chord or group of chords. *(thick)*

## 218 — ALL THE PRETTY LITTLE HORSES

*Peaceful*

Folk song

Hush - a - by, don't you cry, go to sleep-y lit-tle ba - by.

When you wake, you shall have ALL THE PRET-TY LIT-TLE HORS-ES.

Black and bay, dap-ples and greys, coach and six-a lit-tle hors - es.

Hush - a - by, don't you cry, go to sleep-y lit -tle ba - by.

Play ALL THE PRETTY LITTLE HORSES on the keyboard (R.H.). Now sing the letter names of the music in the proper rhythm.

The chord symbols in ALL THE PRETTY LITTLE HORSES are unfamiliar to you, although you know that the chords are built upon the letter names of the symbols. The "m" to the right of a chord's letter name indicates that the chord is minor. Play these **minor triads** on the keyboard (L.H.) and listen carefully to the sound of the minor triad. Also sing the triads (once with letter names and again with the numbers of the notes) from the root to the highest tone, and back to the root:

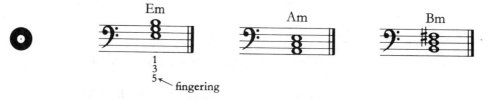

Now play and sing major triads built upon the same roots as the above minor triads.

Which kind of triad sounds brighter? Which kind of triad sounds darker? What single note did you change in each minor triad to make that triad major?

RESPONSES

Most musicians hear the major triad as sounding brighter than the minor triad.

In order to change the minor triads to major, you had to raise the third of each minor triad by one half step:

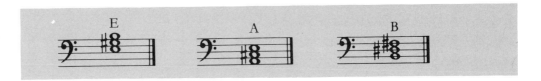

**219**  Notice that minor triads, like major triads, are also made up of combinations of minor thirds (one and one-half steps) and major thirds (two steps). Every minor chord in root position (with root as 1) is built with a minor third on the bottom and a major third on the top. Observe that this construction is precisely the reverse of the major triad.

**220**  Build minor triads on the roots indicated below the staff. Remember that a minor third consists of a minor third on the bottom, plus a major third on the top.

Cm    Dm    Gm    B♭m    C♯m    Fm    F♯m    Em

   Play each of these triads in root position, then in first and second inversion (L.H., R.H., B.H.). Now add a common seventh (refer to frame 210 if necessary) to each of the above minor triads (e.g., Cm7, Dm7, etc.). Play these minor chords (with sevenths) in root position and in third inversion. Break each of these minor chords into *arpeggiated* patterns (both with and without the sevenths) and play each pattern up and down three octaves, alternating hands for each octave. Play these patterns as *legato* as possible and vary the dynamics. This exercise will reinforce your understanding of minor chords and it will also help you to develop a technical facility at the keyboard.

*First inversion*

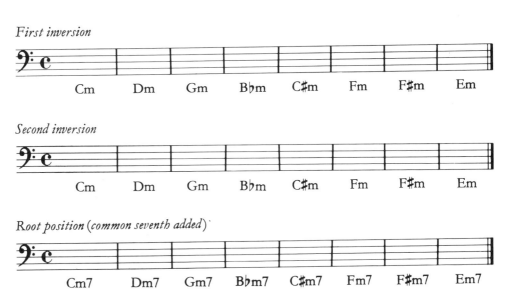

Cm    Dm    Gm    B♭m    C♯m    Fm    F♯m    Em

*Second inversion*

Cm    Dm    Gm    B♭m    C♯m    Fm    F♯m    Em

*Root position (common seventh added)*

Cm7    Dm7    Gm7    B♭m7    C♯m7    Fm7    F♯m7    Em7

*Third inversion* (*common seventh added*)

Cm7    Dm7    Gm7    B♭m7    C♯m7    Fm7    F♯m7    Em7

*Arpeggiated patterns* (*one octave*)

Cm    Dm    Gm    B♭m

C♯m    Fm    F♯m    Em

Cm7    Dm7    Gm7    B♭m7

C♯m7    Fm7    F♯m7    Em7

RESPONSES

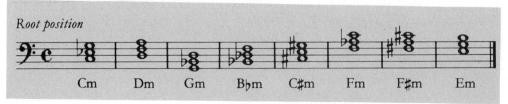

*Root position*

Cm    Dm    Gm    B♭m    C♯m    Fm    F♯m    Em

182

*First inversion*

Cm    Dm    Gm    B♭m    C♯m    Fm    F♯m    Em

*Second inversion*

Cm    Dm    Gm    B♭m    C♯m    Fm    F♯m    Em

*Root position (common seventh added)*

Cm7    Dm7    Gm7    B♭m7    C♯m7    Fm7    F♯m7    Em7

*Third inversion (common seventh added)*

Cm7    Dm7    Gm7    B♭m7    C♯m7    Fm7    F♯m7    Em7

Here are examples of arpeggiated patterns (three octaves)

Cm    1  3  5  etc.

5  3  1  etc.

R.H. 1    3    5

L.H. 5    3    1

Cm7    1  2  3  5  etc.

5  3  2  1  etc.

R.H. 1    2    3    5

L.H. 5    3    2    1

It may help you to play chords in arpeggiated patterns. Notate them on music paper, using the preceding examples as a general guide. You will have to devise your own fingerings for some of the patterns.

**221** In this chapter you have been working with harmonization of KUMBAYAH!, ALL NIGHT, ALL DAY, and ALL THE PRETTY LITTLE HORSES. The first two songs were built upon the major scales. ALL THE PRETTY LITTLE HORSES is built upon the **natural minor scale.** Now you will examine the formation of the natural minor scale. If you have suspected that there is a relationship between the natural minor scale and minor chords, your suspicion is absolutely correct.

---

**222**

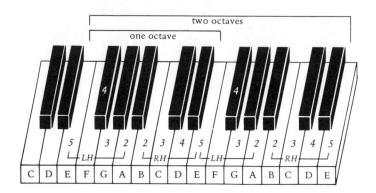

Place both hands on the keyboard using the fingerings illustrated above. Play the E natural minor scale up and down, using both hands. Play it twice: first time *legato*, second time *staccato*. Gradually increase the tempo until it is as fast and as accurate as possible.

Now play the same scale up and down for two octaves. Follow the same procedures as you did for the major scale in frame 194. Recall that finger 1 is not used in either hand.

Carefully examine the formation of the E minor (natural) scale in relation to the E minor chord:

Notice that the E minor chord is 1, 3, 5, and 8 of the E minor scale:

184

As in the major scale, 1 is the home tone in the minor scale. In the song, ALL THE PRETTY LITTLE HORSES, E is the home tone. If you know which letter name is the home tone of any natural minor scale—and you perform the sharps or flats as indicated in the key signature—you will be able to play any minor scale. The same procedure applies to the major scale.

**223**
○

*Every natural minor scale is built precisely the same way: half steps between 2–3 and 5–6, whole steps between the other keys.* As you build different natural minor scales, you will have to add flats or sharps to maintain the half steps between 2–3 and 5–6. Flats and sharps are *never* mixed in major or natural minor scales. Observe the following examples:

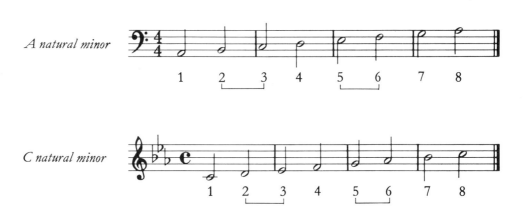

Play the A and C natural minor scales on the keyboard, using the fingerings and procedures described in frame 194 (two octaves).

Write and play the D and B natural minor scales. Add key signatures where necessary.

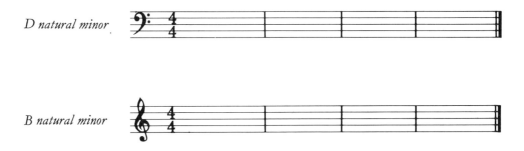

Play the A, C, D, and B natural minor scales on the ukulele, using the most convenient string(s). You will have to play the A natural minor scale an octave higher, since it is too low for the ukulele as it is notated above.

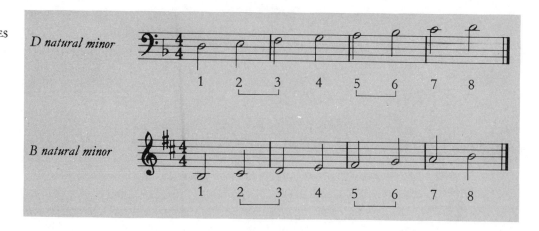

D natural minor

B natural minor

**224**

A harmonic minor

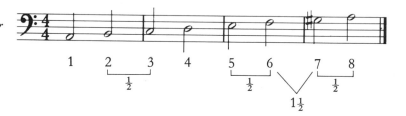

C harmonic minor

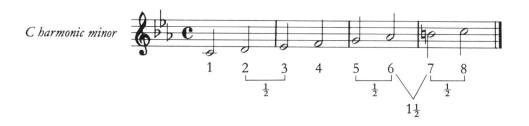

Play the above minor scales on the keyboard (use the keyboard diagram in frame 222 as a guide) and on the ukulele. Notice how they differ from the natural minor scales in frame 223. Your first response probably is that the scale tone 7 has been raised, through the use of an accidental, by one half step. Your second response is probably that another half step has been created between scale tones 7 and 8. Your third response probably is that there are now one and one-half steps between scale tones 6 and 7. These three characteristics distinguish an **harmonic minor scale** from a natural minor scale. *The key signature remains the same as that of the natural minor scale.* The only necessary addition is an accidental which raises the seventh note by one half step.

**225** Every key signature has two possible home or key tones—one key tone derived from the major scale and one key tone derived from the minor scale. The letter names of these home tones in major and minor keys are not the same. The key signature alone cannot show whether or not a composition is in a major or minor key. One must look more closely at the composition itself, especially:

a. the first tone which is frequently the key tone
b. the last tone, which most likely will be the key tone
c. the harmony, which probably will have a greater proportion of minor chords if the composition is in a minor key, and
d. the melody, which will tend to gravitate toward the key tone at the end of phrases.

---

## 226 Key Signature Order: Rules for Identifying the Home Tone of Minor Key Signatures

a. In the flat key signatures, the last flat to the right is on 6 of the natural *and* the harmonic minor scales. For example:

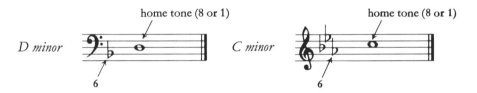

In the D minor example, B♭ is 6 of the D minor scale. What is the major scale which uses the same key signature? In the C minor example, A♭ is 6 of the C minor scale. What is the major scale which uses the same key signature?

b. In the sharp key signatures, the last sharp on the right is 2 of the natural *and* the harmonic minor scales. For example:

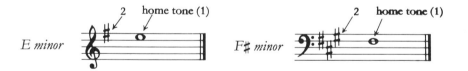

In the E minor example, F♯ is 2 of the E minor scale. What is the major scale which uses the same key signature? In the F♯ minor example, G♯ is 2 of the F♯ minor scale. What is the major scale which uses the same key signature?

RESPONSES    The F major scale uses the same key signature as the D minor scale and the E♭ major scale uses the same key signature as the C minor scale.
The major scale of G shares the key signature with the E minor scale and the major scale of A uses the same key signature as F♯ minor.

187

**227** There is a definite relationship between the major and minor scales which share the same key signatures. Can you determine this relationship? Use the following examples:

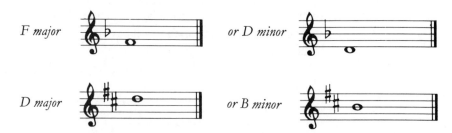

F major        or D minor

D major        or B minor

If you have determined that the minor scale is built upon scale tone 6 of the major scale that shares its key signature, you are correct.

What minor scale shares the key signature with G major? With B♭ major?

RESPONSES | The minor scale of E shares the key signature with the G major scale; the minor scale of G uses the same key signature as B♭ major.

---

**228** Write the following harmonic minor scales in half notes. Indicate the half steps and one and one-half steps with brackets. Don't forget to raise the seventh note with an accidental.

F harmonic minor

E harmonic minor

Play these scales on the keyboard (one and two octaves) and on the ukulele (an octave higher than written).

RESPONSES

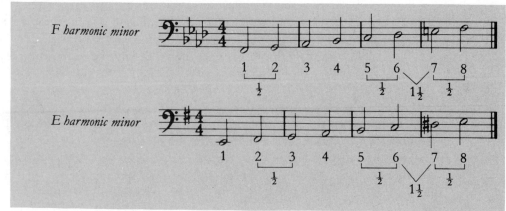

188

**229**  Play this arrangement of ALL THE PRETTY LITTLE HORSES on the keyboard.

### ALL THE PRETTY LITTLE HORSES

Folk song

How many phrases are in this composition and what is its form? Do the lyrics and the melody suggest a *legato* or a *staccato* approach?

RESPONSES    There are four phrases in ALL THE PRETTY LITTLE HORSES, each four measures long. The form is AABA. Notice that the melody in the last two measures of phrase B is identical to the last two measures of the A phrases.

Since this composition is a lullaby, it should be played *legato*.

## 230    Musical Analysis of ALL THE PRETTY LITTLE HORSES

*Measure 1:* The E minor chord is used because E and B (1 and 5 of the E minor chord) appear in the melody. The broken chord accompaniment in the bass clef includes the G (3 of the E minor chord) to complete the E minor chord.

*Measure 2:* The A minor chord is used because A (1 of the A minor chord) is the focal point of that measure. In the bass clef, the A minor triad is used in its first inversion. The G in the melody functions as a nonchord tone. A nonchord tone which moves stepwise up or down from the chord tone and returns to the same chord tone is called a **neighboring tone.**

*Measure 3:* The B minor chord is used since all tones of the B minor chord appear in the melody. Notice the open position of the B minor chord in the bass clef. The D (3 of the B minor chord) is not necessary in the bass clef because its harmonic presence is strongly felt by appearing as the first and longest melody note in the measure. The C in the melody functions as a nonchord tone. A nonchord tone which moves stepwise up or down from one chord tone and directly moves stepwise to *another* chord tone is called a **passing tone.** A passing tone connects two chord tones. The A and the G in the melody are **double passing tones,** because together they perform the same function as a single passing tone (they pass from one chord tone to the next).

*Measure 4:* The E minor and A minor chords are used in succession to harmonize the E which appears in the melody. Since the E is common to both chords (1 of the E minor chord; 5 of the A minor chord), it is possible to use these two different chords in the same measure to harmonize the same melody tone. This is a good example of one way to achieve **harmonic variety.** Strive for harmonic variety in your own accompaniments and notice the many more interesting sounds that develop. Observe the broken chord accompaniment of both the E minor and A minor (first inversion) chords.

*Measures 5 and 6:* These are the same as measures 1 and 2, thus lending textural unity to the accompaniment.

*Measure 7:* Other than a slight rhythmic change in the bass clef, this is the same as measure 3.

*Measure 8:* In contrast to measure 4, only the E minor chord is used this time to harmonize the melody. Further variety is gained by the use of the E minor *arpeggio.* Notice that this chord has been broken into eighth notes, which gives considerable rhythmic movement to the word "horses."

*Measure 9:* The B minor chord is used because B and D (1 and 3 of the B minor chord) are the melody tones.

*Measure 10:* The E minor chord is used because E and G (1 and 3 of the E minor chord) are the melody tones. Observe the change from a **closed position** (second inversion) E minor chord to an **open position** (still second inversion) E minor chord. Since G is the melody tone, it has been omitted from the open position chord. A closed position chord is one in which all members of the chord follow consecutively in the *same* octave from bottom to top. In this first E minor chord, B, E, and G do follow uninterruptedly in the same octave. There is no chord tone left out. The E is doubled by the melody in the treble. An open position chord is one in which all members of the chord usually appear, but not consecutively and *not* in the same octave. In the second E minor chord, E follows B, but G does not follow E in that same octave. G appears as the melody tone which does in effect complete the E minor chord, but not in the same octave. In this case, no tone is actually doubled.

*Measure 11:* Identical to measure 7.

*Measure 12:* Identical to measure 4.

*Measures 13 and 14:* Identical to measures 1 and 2, and measures 5 and 6.

*Measure 15:* With the exception of a slight rhythmic change in the bass clef, this measure is the same as measure 11.

*Measure 16:* The E minor chord is used throughout the entire measure to harmonize the E melody tone. Notice, however, that some harmonic variety is gained by the use of the second inversion E minor chord moving to an E minor chord in root position. The technique allows the lowest tone, the bass tone (B), of the inverted E minor chord to move up to a different tone (E) when it changes to a root position E minor chord. In a static (i.e., one-chord) harmonic situation, alternating inversions permits the bass tone to move, thereby increasing the harmonic interest. Although all harmonic lines are important, it is the juxtaposition of the **bass line** (formed by the bottom note of each chord) to the **melodic line** that determines the essential character of the harmonization. The use of inversions can help to create a smooth bass line or, for variety, add movement.

---

**231** Play ALL THE PRETTY LITTLE HORSES once again (frame 229), but this time only play the melody and the bass line. Compare this sound to your performance of ALL THE PRETTY LITTLE HORSES with the full accompaniment.

---

**232** Here are additional observations about ALL THE PRETTY LITTLE HORSES:
   a. Ritardando (rit.) in the last two measures, culminating in the **fermata** (or

hold, ⌢) on the last melody tone (E) and chord (E minor). A fermata or hold above or below a tone or chord means that these tones are sustained approximately twice as long as their assigned note values. The actual length of a *fermata* is interpreted by the performer.

b. In measures 9 and 10, ◁═══ means **crescendo,** or gradually becoming louder, starting at the dynamic level indicated ( *mp* at the beginning of measure 9) and proceding to the dynamic level indicated at the end of the crescendo ( *mf* in measure 11). Crescendo may also be indicated *cresc.* In measures 11 and 12, ═══▷ means **decrescendo** or **diminuendo,** the opposite of crescendo. These terms may also be indicated *decresc.* and *dim.*

c. *Accelerando* and *a tempo* in measures 9 and 11, respectively.

d. 𝓟𝓮𝓭. ╱╲___╱╲ under each measure in the bass clef means to use the **sustaining pedal** where indicated. The sustaining pedal is the pedal on the right in the set of pedals on the floor. The pedal should be depressed with the ball of the right foot (the heel remains stationary on the floor). Notice that the pedal is released at the end of one chord and immediately is depressed at the beginning of the next chord ( $\frac{\text{down} \quad \wedge \quad \text{down}}{\text{up}}$ ). *Legato* playing is facilitated by the use of the sustaining pedal.

---

**233**
Here is another arrangement of ALL THE PRETTY LITTLE HORSES. Many different chords have been substituted for the chords in frame 229. Although Ⓒ , Ⓒ₄ , and Ⓒ₅ are still included, Ⓒ₃ , Ⓒ₆ , and Ⓒ₇ have been added (with some alterations). You will discover that there is a logical basis for the selection of every chord.

You learned about the *coda* in KUMBAYAH! (frame 172). Observe the **coda signs** (⊕) used in this arrangement. The first coda sign advises you that there will be a *coda* at the end of this song. The second coda sign is placed at the beginning of the *coda* itself. D.C. al coda ("da capo"—pronounced dä kä′ pō—"al coda") means to repeat the composition, but only play to the first "coda" sign, then skip directly to the second "coda" sign and play to the end of the song.

Notice that both the chord changes and the pedal changes are more frequent here than in the previous arrangement (frame 229) so that one chord will not be held accidentally while the next chord is being played. If a composer wanted some chords to *spill* into each other, he would eliminate certain pedal changes. Some contemporary composers use this technique for a certain effect.

Play this arrangement of ALL THE PRETTY LITTLE HORSES. When fingerings are not indicated, they will be apparent from previous measures or because they fall naturally in the correct order.

# ALL THE PRETTY LITTLE HORSES

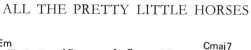

Listen to the recording of ALL THE PRETTY LITTLE HORSES. If you have any difficulty performing it, practice with the recording a few times. Then practice on your own until you can play the song without making any mistakes.

## 234 Musical Analysis of ALL THE PRETTY LITTLE HORSES

*Measure 1:* The basic chord is E minor; however, two types of sevenths have been added. The Em maj7 (or + 7) is spelled E, G, B, D♯. Any chord which adds the **major seventh** adds that tone which is located one half step below 8 of the chord. For example:

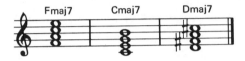

The major seventh is always one half step below 8 of the chord. Spell these major seventh chords:

The major seventh refers specifically to that interval from the root (letter name) to the seventh a *half* step below 8, just as the common seventh represents that interval from the root to the seventh a *whole* step below 8. The major seventh chord is used extensively in popular music. Many pianists, particularly jazz pianists, automatically add a major seventh to every major chord they play, even though they have not been directed to do so by the chord symbol. However, a pianist would not automatically add a major seventh to a minor chord—he would only do so if the chord symbol indicated it.

If a 7 follows a chord name, it indicates that a common seventh is to be added. To distinguish between the common seventh and the major seventh, a plus sign (+) or maj7 is usually placed before the 7 to indicate that a major seventh is to be added to that chord.

For example:

| | |
|---|---|
| A = A major | Am = A minor |
| A7 = A major with common seventh | Am7 = A minor with common seventh |
| A+7 = A major with major seventh (or Amaj7) | Am+7 = A minor with major seventh (or Am maj7) |

Notice in this measure the Em7 chord which follows an Em maj7 (or Em+7) chord.

*Measure 2:* The A7 chord (second inversion) is used because the melody tones A and G are 1 and 7, respectively, of the A7 chord. Then the Am7 chord (second inversion) is used because the melody tone A is the root of the Am chord as well as the A chord.

*Measure 3*  The D7 chord is used because the melody tones D and C are 1 and 7, respectively, of the D7 chord. The Cmaj7 chord is used because the melody tone B is the major seventh of the Cmaj7 chord. The melody tone A is a passing tone. The B7 chord is used because the F♯ melody tone is 5 of the B7 chord. The G melody tone that precedes the F♯ is a **suspension.**

A suspension is a nonchord tone which delays the arrival of a chord tone (in this case, the melody tone F♯). Suspensions are highly characteristic of today's *popular* music, particularly the type of suspension which when used in a chord replaces 3 of that chord with 4 (a nonchord tone) of the scale indicated by the chord's letter name. For example:

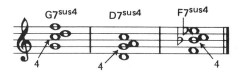

In each of the foregoing chords with suspensions, 3 was eliminated in favor of 4. Name the note in each chord that 4 replaced.

Those same chords often appear with abbreviated symbols in popular music. For example: G7^sus, D7^sus, F7^sus. The number 4 has been omitted, but the chords are still played the same way as if the number were there. Any chord using a suspension almost always replaces 3 with 4. Spell these chords:

*Measure 4:* The Fmaj7 chord, (third inversion, in which the seventh is in the bass) is used because the E melody tone is the seventh of the Fmaj7 chord. The C♯m chord (first inversion) is used on the second E because E is also the third of the C♯m chord. The E in the bass line appears in both the Fmaj7 and C♯m chords. The use of the anchor tone here helps make a smooth transition from one chord to the next.

*Measure 5:* The Em chord is used for the same reasons as in measure 1. A seventh has been added in the first E minor chord. In the second E minor chord, a **sixth** is added. The Em6 is spelled E, G, B, C♯. A sixth is a whole step above the fifth of a chord. For example:

Spell these sixth chords:

Added sixth chords are also used extensively in the playing of popular music. Many pianists add sixths to major and minor chords even when they are not indicated by the chord symbols. Instead of playing a C chord, a pianist might play a C6 chord; instead of playing a Fm chord, he might play an Fm6 chord, etc. The application of the sixth chord is somewhat less general than that of the major seventh chord. However, in today's music, its use with the minor chord is becoming very popular.

*Measures 6 and 7:* Identical to measures 2 and 3.

*Measure 8:* The A chord is used because the melody tone E is 5 of the A chord. The C chord is used because the melody tone E is also 3 of the C chord.

*Measure 9:* The G chord (open position) is used because the melody tones B and D are 3 and 5, respectively, of the G chord. The B minor chord (open position) is used because the melody tone D is also 3 of the B minor chord.

*Measure 10:* The C7 chord (open position) is used because the E and G melody tones are 3 and 5, respectively, of the C7 chord. The E♭maj7 chord is used because the melody tone G is 3 of the E♭maj7 chord.

*Measure 11:* The Bm7 chord is used because the melody tone D is 3 of the Bm7 chord. The B7 chord is used for the same reason as it was used in measure 3.

*Measure 12:* Compare this measure with measure 4. In measure 12, notice the second inversion of the Fmaj7 chord and the open position of the C♯ minor triad.

*Measures 13 and 14:* These are exactly the same as measures 1 and 2.

*Measure 15:* The first chord is the same as that chord in measure 11. However, there is no seventh on the B minor chord here (and the chord is in open position).

*Measure 16:* The C chord (open position) is used because the melody tone E is 3 of the C chord. The E minor chord is used because the melody tone E is 3 of the C chord. The E minor chord is used to end the composition because the home tone (or root) E is the melody tone.

*Measures 17–20:* For the most part, this *coda* alternates between the E minor and the D major chords. The E minor triad is used because the melody tones E and G are 1 and 3 of the E minor chord. The D major triad is used because the melody tones F♯ and D are 3 and 1 of the D major chord. In measure 19, the D major triad is used because the melody tones A, F♯, and D are 5, 3, and 1 of the D major chord. In measure 20, the C major chord is used because the melody tone, E, is 3 of the C major triad. The D is a neighboring tone, and the final chord is E minor because the coda ends on the home tone (E).

RESPONSES    In the Amaj6 chord, G♯ is the major 7th. Notice it is a half step below the root, A. In the Gm maj7 chord, F♯ is the major 7th. Notice it is a half step below the root, G.

As you can see, adding a major 7th does not alter the fact that the triad itself remains minor.

In the G7<sup>sus4</sup> chord, the B(3) was replaced by C(4).
In the D7<sup>sus4</sup> chord, the F♯(3) was replaced by G(4).
In the F7<sup>sus4</sup> chord, the A(3) was replaced by B♭(4).

In the D6 chord, B is the added 6th. Notice it is a whole step above the 5th, A.
In the E♭m6 chord, C is the added 6th. Notice it is a whole step above the 5th, B♭.

**235**  **Guidelines for Creating an Harmonic Accompaniment**

a. Examine the key signature, bearing in mind that it may specify either a major or a minor key.
b. Look at the last note of the melody and the ending notes of phrases.
c. Using guidelines 1 and 2, determine the home tone and character (major or minor) of the melody.
d. On a staff, write out the primary chords (𝗖, 𝗖, 𝗖) in root position, first inversion, second inversion, (and third inversion—if you are planning to use any type of sevenths).
e. Examine each measure of the melody for possible primary chord tones. Use this criterion as the basis for deciding which primary chord to use: The more notes of a particular chord that appear in the melody of a particular measure, the stronger the reason for using that chord. Study examples 1 through 4:

*Example 1*

C, E, G, Bb (in the key of C major) are 1, 3, 5, and 7 of the C7 chord. D is a nonchord tone (Passing tone = P).

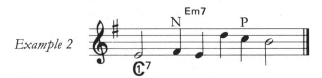

*Example 2*

E (which appears twice), B, and D (in the key of E minor) are 1, 5, and 7 of the Em chord. F♯ is a nonchord tone (Neighboring tone = N) and C is also a nonchord tone (Passing tone = P).

*Example 3*

Eb, Bb, G, and Eb (in the key of Bb major) are 8, 5, 3, and 1 of the Eb chord. Ab is a nonchord tone (Suspension = S) and F is also a nonchord tone (Passing tone = P).

*Example 4*

C♯ (key of D major) is 3 of the A chord. The B is a nonchord tone (Neighboring tone = N) and F♯ is also a nonchord tone (simply designated here as NC). It would have been possible to use the note B (now designated N) as the basis for another chord—the G (4) chord in key of D major, since the note B is 3 of the G chord. However, since the C♯ appears twice in this example—and on the strongest counts—it is the focal point of the measure. *As a general rule, when there is only one note of a primary chord in a measure, the best reason for selecting this chord is that the melody note is 1, 3, 5, or 7 (in that order of priority).* Of course, this is always considered within the context of the phrase and the entire composition.

f. Decide whether you will use one or more than one chord per measure. For example:

*Example 1. One chord:*

*Example 2. Two chords:*

     In example 1, F, A, and C are 1, 3, and 5 of the F chord, respectively. The G is a nonchord tone. In example 2, the same melodic pattern is harmonized with *two* chords: F and C, The melody notes F and A are 1 and 3 of the F chord and the G and C are 5 and 8 of the C chord. Play examples 1 and 2.

g. Determine the rhythm of your harmonic accompaniment. Decide how many times per measure you will play each chord. Provide rhythmic contrast between the melody and the accompaniment, especially when the same chord is used throughout the measure.

h. Decide when you will use inversions and when you will use root position chords.

i. Decide when to use *arpeggiated* patterns. Remember that broken chords can help to provide a more interesting accompaniment.

j. Determine when open position chords might sound effective.

k. If you are planning to use substitute chords to replace certain primary chords, disregard guideline e. If a melody note is either 1, 3, 5, or 7 of a particular chord, that one note is sufficient reason for your chord choice. The ultimate decision, however (*after* you have tried various chords based on the melody tone), will rest with your own musical taste.

l. If the same note appears at the beginning of two consecutive measures, variety can be achieved by using two different chords to harmonize that tone. Again, your own judgment is the chief determinant. Example:

m. The above guideline may also be applied to a particular tone which is consistently repeated within a measure. Example:

199

# 236 Guide to Chord Construction

a. A **major triad** = 1, 3, 5 of any major scale. The interval between 1 and 3 is a major third (two whole steps); the interval between 3 and 5 is a minor third (one and one-half steps). Example:

*C major triad*

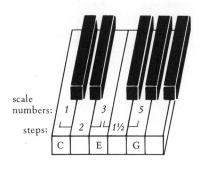

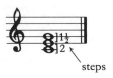

b. A **minor triad** = 1, 3, 5 of any minor scale. The interval between 1 and 3 is a minor third (one and one-half steps); the interval between 3 and 5 is a major third (two whole steps). Example:

*C minor triad*

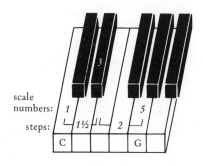

c. A **four-tone chord** in root position (major or minor) usually adds the octave (8) to the existing triad. These chords are shown in both a closed and an open position. Other chords may be similarly arranged. Examples:

*C major chord*

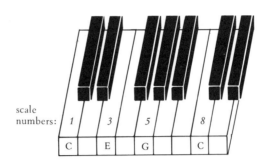

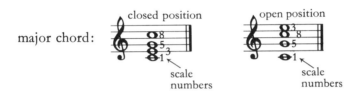

major chord:

*C minor chord*

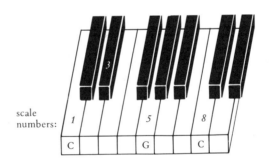

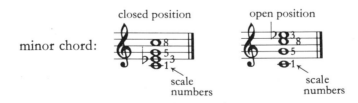

minor chord:

d. A **seventh** (common or major) can be added to any existing major or minor triad without any special justification (except for the desirability of that sound). The common seventh is located a whole step below the octave; the major seventh is found a half step below the octave.

*Example 1: Common seventh added (major triad)*

*Example 2: Major seventh added (major triad)*

*Example 3: Common seventh added (minor triad)*

*Example 4: Major seventh added (minor triad)*

e. A **sixth** can be added to any existing major or minor triad. The most useful sixth is found a whole step above the fifth.

*Example 1: Added sixth (major chord)*

*Example 2: Added sixth (minor chord)*

f. A **ninth** can be added to any existing major or minor triad. The most useful ninth is found a whole step above the octave. The common seventh is usually included in a ninth chord.

*Example 1: Added ninth (major chord)*

*Example 2: Added ninth (minor chord)*

A major seventh can also be a part of a ninth chord.

*Example 3: Added ninth (major chord)*

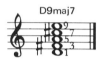

*Example 4: Added ninth (minor chord)*

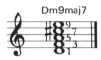

Notice that the ninth chord, like the seventh, is built upon thirds. Since there are so many notes in seventh and ninth chords, it sometimes becomes expedient to eliminate at least one tone. *The most dispensable tone of any chord is usually the fifth.* However, in today's popular music—particularly country-oriented styles—the seventh may be eliminated. Example:

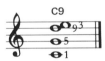

g. A **suspension** is a nonchord tone which replaces a chord tone in any existing major or minor chord. As applied particularly to popular music, the suspension usually replaces 3 of the chord with 4 of the scale indicated by the chord's letter name.

*Example 1: Suspension (major chord)*

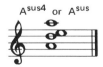

Observe: D (4) replaces C♯ (3).

*Example 2: Suspension (major chord with common 7th)*

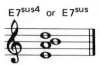

Observe: A (4) replaces G♯ (3).

*Example 3: Suspension (minor chord)*

Observe: F (4) replaces E♮ (3).

*Example 4: Suspension (minor chord with common 7th)*

Observe: G (4) replaces F (3).

h. Chords are not restricted to root position. Any member of the chord (1, 3, 5, 7, 9) may be the bass tone. *In today's popular music, the specific bass tone is often indicated along with the chord symbol. For instance G (D) means a G major chord with D (5) in the bass; Fm (A♭) means an F minor chord with A♭ (3) in the bass.* When any other member of a chord except 1 (the root) is found in the bass, the chord is inverted. The basic chord remains the same, but the tones are arranged in a different order:

*Example 1: Root position (1 in the bass)*

*Example 2: First inversion (3 in the bass)*

*Example 3: Second inversion (5 in the bass)*

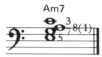

*Example 4: Third inversion (7 in the bass)*

Inversions serve the following functions:

(1) They add variety to the accompaniment.
(2) They create smoother bass lines.
(3) They minimize movement of fingers from one chord to another by the use of anchor tones. Example:

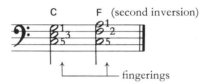

(4) They minimize the movement of fingers from one chord to another by emphasizing stepwise rather than skipwise movement. Although both of the examples below use the C and G chords, notice the difference in finger movement:

*Skipwise (root position)*

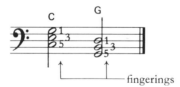

*Stepwise (first inversion)*

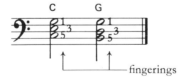

   i. To determine the root (and the name) of any notated chord, follow this simple procedure:

    (1) If the chord is a triad, designate the lowest note as 1, then see if 3 and 5

are found above it. If they are, then the lowest note is the root of that triad. If either 3 or 5 is missing, try designating each of the other triad tones as 1. Then find the 3 and 5 that complete the triad. Example:

If A is 1, C is 3—but F is not 5. Therefore, A cannot be the root in the above triad. If C is 1, there is no 3 or 5 in relation to C. If F is 1, A is 3, and C is 5. The triad, then, is an F major triad in first inversion (A = 3 and it is the lowest tone).

(2) If the chord is a seventh chord, the same procedure can be followed— except that four tones must be considered instead of three. Example:

For the above chord, follow procedure (1) and you will find that it is a Dm7 chord in the third inversion (C = 7 and it is the lowest tone).

j.   There are two types of chords which occur less frequently in music than the major and minor chords, but nonetheless they contribute considerably to harmonic variety. They are the **diminished** and the **augmented** chords.

   (1) A **diminished triad** contains *two minor thirds*: The interval between 1 and 3 is a minor third and the interval between 3 and 5 is also a minor third. The chord symbol for a diminished triad is either ° or dim. Example:

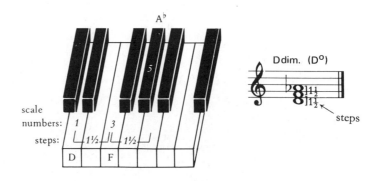

Root position chords are always *spelled* in thirds. When notating diminished triads, the spelling often requires the application of a new type of accidental: the **double flat** (♭♭). For example, the diminished triad based on the note E♭ is spelled E♭ (1), G♭ (3), B♭♭ (5). The B♭♭ actually sounds the same as A, but it must be notated as B♭♭ in order to preserve the 1, 3, 5 relationships of a triad. Example:

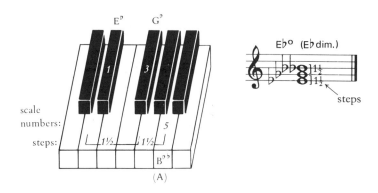

(2) A **diminished seventh chord** contains three minor thirds. It adds a minor third between 5 and 7. The chord symbol for a diminished seventh chord is the same as for a diminished triad (° or dim.) but with a 7 added. Example:

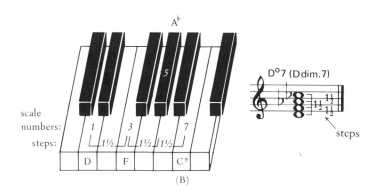

When a diminished chord symbol appears in the music, it is the performer's option to play either a diminished triad or a diminished seventh chord. Most musicians play a diminished seventh chord.

The double flat notation is used even more extensively in the spelling of the diminished seventh chord. For example, the diminished seventh chord based on the note F is spelled F (1), A♭ (3), C♭ (5), E♭♭ (7). The E♭♭ actually sounds the same as D, but it must be notated as E♭♭ in order to preserve the 1, 3, 5, 7 relationships of triadic harmony.

(3) An **augmented triad** contains two major thirds. The interval between 1 and 3 is a major third and the interval between 3 and 5 is also a major third. The chord symbol for an augmented triad is usually aug. or +.

207

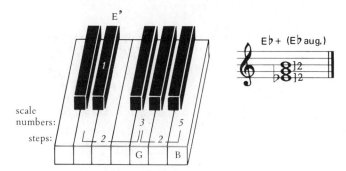

A four-tone augmented chord normally adds the octave just like in major or minor chords. Example:

An augmented triad may also have the common seventh or major seventh. Examples:

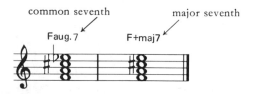

Whereas a plus sign (+) always means to "raise" something by a half step, a minus sign (−) always means to "lower" something by a half step. Examples:

This − sign is found consistently in today's popular music and usually follows the note which is meant to be lowered, such as the ninth and sixth respectively in the preceding examples. If there are two notes indicated, it will be the last one which is lowered. For instance, a frequent chord in popular music is a common seventh with a lowered ninth (e.g., D7 − 9). In this case, since the ninth appears last it would be lowered from E to E♭.

Examine a book of popular songs and find examples for yourself.

## 237  Baritone Ukulele Chords

Suggested fingerings for the left hand are written below the strings (O = open string, 1 = index finger, 2 = middle finger, 3 = ring finger, and 4 = little finger). However, you may want to devise your own fingerings for some of the chords.

### Major Triads

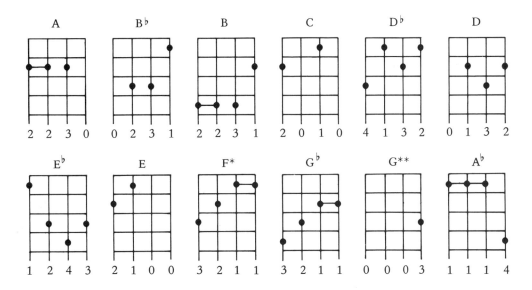

### Minor Triads

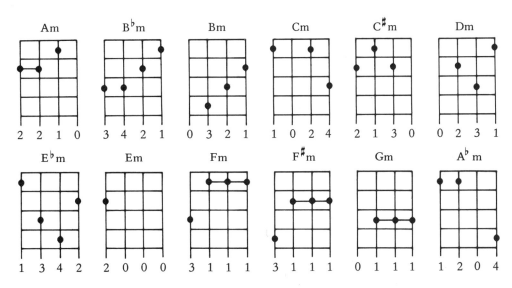

## Major Chords with Common Seventh

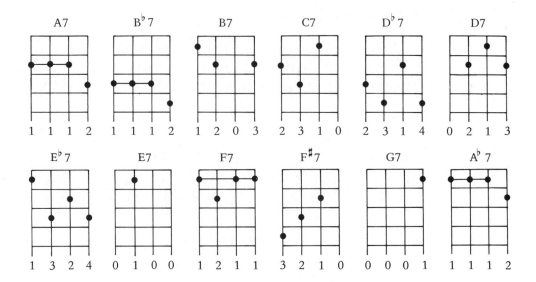

## Minor Chords with Common Seventh

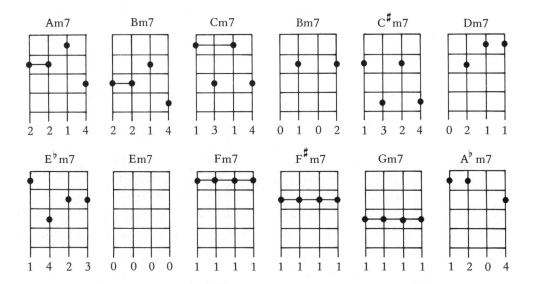

## Diminished Seventh Chords

Only three are possible, but each of the three chords may have four different names.

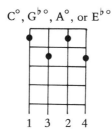

C°, G♭°, A°, or E♭°

1 3 2 4

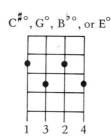

C♯°, G°, B♭°, or E°

1 3 2 4

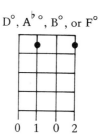

D°, A♭°, B°, or F°

0 1 0 2

## Augmented Triads

Only four are possible, but each of the four triads may have three different names.

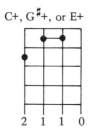

C+, G♯+, or E+

2 1 1 0

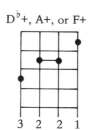

D♭+, A+, or F+

3 2 2 1

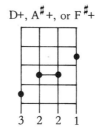

D+, A♯+, or F♯+

3 2 2 1

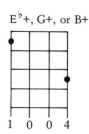

E♭+, G+, or B+

1 0 0 4

## Additional Hints

The F6 chord can be substituted for the F chord by leaving the first (D) string open. In both major "and" minor chords, the sixth may be added by substituting it for whatever triad tone is doubled. See **Guide to Chord Construction**, frame 236, guide e.

The Gmaj7 chord can be substituted for the G chord by playing the second fret (F♯) instead of the third fret (G). In both major "and" minor chords, the major seventh may be added by substituting it for whatever triad tone is doubled. See **Guide to Chord Construction**, frame 236, guide d.

a. If your melody is to be sung, make certain that all the tones fall within a comfortable vocal range. From middle C to the C an octave above is usually a good reference point, but this will always depend on the particular singer. However, on occasions, the melody may extend as high as E above the C octave and as low as A below middle C. Too many tones above or below the middle C to C range can strain the inexperienced singing voice.

b. Choose the type of scale (e.g., major, minor, pentatonic—you will learn other scales in Chapter 5) which you feel would sound most appropriate for the words you have created.

c. Decide upon the form of the melody (ABA, ABCA, etc.) and how long the phrases should be.

d. Select a time signature(s) which is appropriate for the melody. If the melody is to be sung, consider the words and how they will *fit* with the time signature.

e. When writing music to accompany words, make certain that the melody follows the natural rise and fall of speech patterns. In your melodies, try to approximate patterns of speech. For instance, the words, "I love you," are found in thousands of songs. Say these three words. In this speech pattern, the word, "love," normally ascends. It is most frequently the highest pitched word in the sentence, "I love you."

*Example 1*

I    love    you.

Observe the above example. This melodic fragment expresses "love" as the strongest word, because it has the highest and the longest pitch. Sing the words, "I love you," in the following ways:

(1) Emphasize "love" to an even greater degree than in the above example by singing it for a longer duration.

(2) Here is an example in which several pitches are used to sing one word, "love." Sing this melodic phrase.

*Example 2*

I    love _____ you.

Notice that "love" is emphasized differently than in Example 1. Do the two expressions of "I love you" (Examples 1 and 2) convey different *feelings?* Describe these differences.

(3) This melodic fragment places the strongest emphasis on the word, "I." Sing this example.

*Example 3*

I   love you.

Because it has the highest tone and the rest of the phrase moves downward, the word "I" conveys the strongest feeling. Experiment using several tones on the word "I." Does using more tones on "I" give a different feeling than Example 3?

(4) In the phrase below, notice that the strongest emphasis is now placed on the word "you." Sing this example.

*Example 4*

I____   love   you.

Because the word "you" is on the highest and longest tone and the phrase moves upward, "you" does convey the strongest feeling.

(5) Would a melodic phrase which used several tones to express the word "you" give a different feeling from that of Example 4? Sing this melodic fragment.

*Example 5*

I       love _   you. _____

(6) In Example 6, the original melodic phrase from Example 1 is used, but now it is repeated twice, each time starting on a different tone (D in measure 1; E in measure 2). In both repetitions, the intervals remain the same, since they are merely transposed.

*Example 6*

I   love   you,   I   love   you,   I   love   you.

This technique of transposing a melodic fragment and repeating it on different pitches is known as a **sequence**. There is no prescribed limit to the number of sequences that can appear in a melody.

Compose a short, sequential, melodic pattern on the words, "I love you."

f. *Two essential ingredients of an interesting melody are unity and variety—they should always be considered in the construction of a melody. Unity and variety are created in a melody by the repetition and contrast of tones and durations.*

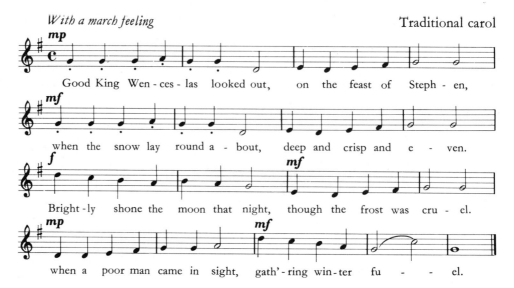

*With a march feeling*                      Traditional carol

Good King Wen-ces-las looked out, on the feast of Steph-en,

when the snow lay round a-bout, deep and crisp and e-ven.

Bright-ly shone the moon that night, though the frost was cru-el.

when a poor man came in sight, gath'-ring win-ter fu-el.

GOOD KING WENCESLAS is one of the most moving and human Christmas songs ever written—its lyrics express a beautiful thought with great sensitivity.

Notice the staccato dots under the quarter notes in measures 1–2 and 5–6. Where dots are not used, perform those notes in a more legato fashion.

Copy each line of the melody of GOOD KING WENCESLAS on the treble clef line of the staffs (or "staves," another word for the plural of staff) provided in this frame. Write verses 2 through 5 in the space provided under the treble staffs. Be careful to place each word or syllable under its corresponding note.

2. "Hither Page, and stand by me, if thou know'st it; telling,
   Yonder Peasant, who is he? Where and what his dwelling?"
   "Sire, he lives a good league hence, underneath the mountain;
   Right against the forest fence, by Saint Agnes' Fountain."

3. "Bring me flesh, and bring me wine, bring me pinelogs hither;
   Thou and I will see him dine, when we bear them thither."
   Page and Monarch forth they went, forth they went together;
   Through the rude wind's wild lament, and the bitter weather.

4. "Sire, the night is darker now, and the wind blows stronger;
   Fails my heart, I know not how, I can go no longer."
   "Mark my footsteps, my good Page, tred thou in them boldly;
   Thou shalt find the winter's rage freeze thy blood less coldly."

5. In his master's steps he trod, where the snow lay dinted;
   Heat was in the very sod, which the Saint had printed.
   Therefore, Faithful Men, be sure, wealth or rank possessing,
   Ye who now will bless the Poor, shall yourselves find blessing.

# GOOD KING WENCESLAS

Now compare your placement of the lyrics with the responses for frame 239.

When you have completed notating the melody and the words, add an harmonic accompaniment based on the Ⓒ, Ⓒ₄, and Ⓖ or Ⓖ 7 chords. Follow the **Guidelines for Creating an Harmonic Accompaniment,** frame 235. Also consult the **Guide to Chord Construction,** frame 236. Pay particular attention to smooth movement of the harmonic parts. Open and/or closed position chords may be used. Experiment.

Be certain to use some inversions in your accompaniment and identify the chords with symbols above the melody and with numbers below the bass. Also indicate nonchord tones with the appropriate symbols (P, N, S, or NC). Vary the dynamics to reflect the sentiments of the lyrics.

On a separate sheet of paper, write a measure-by-measure analysis of GOOD KING WENCESLAS which includes your rationale for the chord selections. As a model for your analysis, refer to ALL THE PRETTY LITTLE HORSES, frame 234.

Sing as you play your arrangement of GOOD KING WENCESLAS on the keyboard. Then accompany yourself on the ukulele (only play the melody). Sing GOOD KING WENCESLAS again, but this time use the autoharp/chromaharp (only play the chords) to accompany yourself. Do not proceed to frame 240 until you have mastered this frame.

RESPONSES

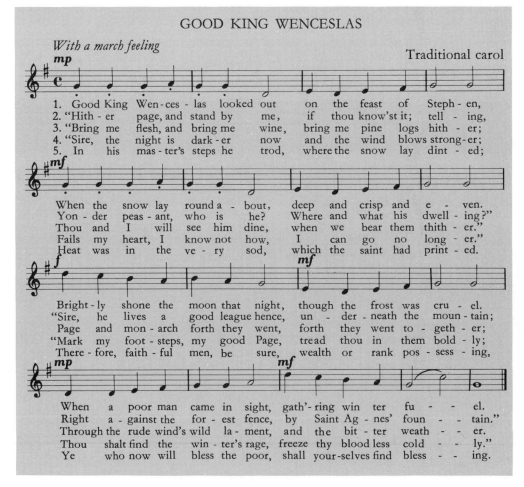

GOOD KING WENCESLAS

*With a march feeling*

Traditional carol

1. Good King Wen-ces-las looked out    on the feast of Steph-en,
2. "Hith-er    page, and stand by    me,    if thou know'st it;    tell - ing,
3. "Bring me    flesh, and bring me    wine,    bring me pine logs hith - er;
4. "Sire, the    night is dark-er    now    and the wind    blows strong-er;
5. In his    mas-ter's steps he    trod,    where the snow lay    dint - ed;

When the    snow lay round a - bout,    deep and crisp and    e - ven.
Yon-der    peas-ant, who is    he?    Where and what his    dwell - ing?"
Thou and    I will see him    dine,    when we bear them    thith - er."
Fails my    heart, I know not    how,    I can go no    long - er."
Heat was    in the ve-ry    sod,    which the saint had    print - ed.

Bright-ly    shone the moon that night,    though the frost was    cru - el.
"Sire, he    lives a good league hence,    un - der-neath the    moun - tain.
Page and    mon-arch forth they went,    forth they went to - geth - er;
"Mark my    foot-steps, my good Page,    tread thou in them    bold - ly;
There-fore,    faith-ful men, be    sure,    wealth or rank pos - sess - ing,

When    a poor man came in sight,    gath'-ring win ter    fu - - el.
Right    a - gainst the for - est fence,    by Saint Ag - nes' foun - - tain."
Through the rude wind's wild la - ment,    and the bit - ter    weath - - er.
Thou    shalt find the win - ter's rage,    freeze thy blood less    cold - - ly."
Ye    who now will bless the poor,    shall your-selves find    bless - - ing.

216

The following harmonic accompaniment to the GOOD KING WENCESLAS melody is based upon the C, C4, C5 and C57 chords. Listen to the recording of this arrangement as you follow the music. Play the music yourself. Notice the use of open position chords in measures 1–8 and 13–14. Closed position chords are used in measures 9–12 and 15–17. Compare the sound of open and closed position chords in this arrangement. Notice the inversions and anchor tones.

In measures 13, 14, and 16 (bass clef) two fingers have been assigned to the same chord tone. Whenever you see this, play the first finger and then switch to the other finger immediately. This facilitates movement to the next chord.

Is this arrangement very different from your own arrangement? In what ways (e.g., chords, nonchord tones)?

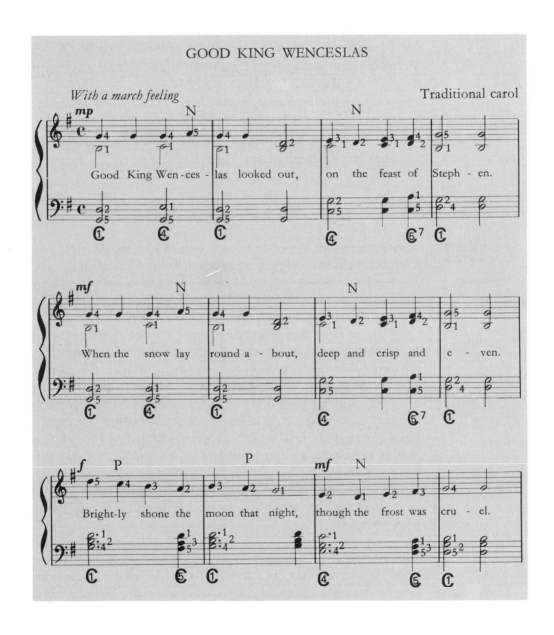

GOOD KING WENCESLAS

*With a march feeling*

Traditional carol

When a    poor man | came in   sight, | gath'-ring win - ter | fu -   el.

**240**    Examine the form of GOOD KING WENCESLAS. Compare phrases one (measures 1–4), two (measures 5–8), three (measures 9–12), and four (measures 13–17) for similarities and differences. Phrases may be identified by letter names (A, B, C, D, etc.). Similar phrases are identified with the same letter name. For example, four phrases might be identified ABAB, AABA, AABC, or ABCD, etc.

     One of the preceding forms is the exact phrase structure of GOOD KING WENCESLAS. Which one is it?

RESPONSE    The form of GOOD KING WENCESLAS is AABC.

**241**    Notate the melody for GOOD KING WENCESLAS in the staffs provided below. Create a substitute chord arrangement for this melody which not only uses the $\mathbb{C}$ , $\mathbb{C}$ , and $\mathbb{C}$ chords but also chords based on $\mathbb{C}$ , $\mathbb{C}$ , and $\mathbb{C}$ . Sixth and seventh chords may also be used at your discretion. Whatever your rationale might be, *change chords on every melody tone*. Again consult frames 235 and 236 for assistance.

     Use inversions in your accompaniment which facilitate the smooth movement of the harmonic parts. Identify chords with symbols above the melody and with numbers below the bass. Since you will be harmonizing each melody tone with a separate chord, there won't be any nonchord tones to identify.

     On a separate sheet of paper, write a measure-by-measure analysis of your new harmony to GOOD KING WENCESLAS. Include your rationale for each chord selection. Remember that the final criterion for the selection of any harmony is the *combined sound* of the melody and the harmony. Experiment further with open and/or closed position chords.

     Sing and play your substitute chord arrangement of GOOD KING WENCESLAS. Try to play this arrangement on the ukulele (chords only) and the autoharp/chromaharp (chords only).

# GOOD KING WENCESLAS

Good King Wen-ces - las looked out, on the feast of Steph - en,

When the snow lay round a - bout, deep and crisp and e - ven.

Bright-ly shone the moon that night, though the frost was cru - el.

When a poor man came in sight, gath'-ring win - ter fu - - el.

# GOOD KING WENCESLAS

*With a march feeling*　　　　　　　　　　　　　　　　Traditional carol

Listen to the recording of this arrangement of GOOD KING WENCESLAS as you follow the music. It uses a greater variety of chords and chord positioning than the previous arrangement does. Try to play it. Compare the harmonic treatment with that of your own arrangement (frame 239). Are there chords in your arrangement that you prefer?

**242**　On the staffs given, write an original composition: create your own melody, lyrics, and harmonic accompaniment incorporating as many aspects of melodic, harmonic, textural, and rhythmic variety as will make your composition interesting for the listener. You may want to review frames 235 (**Guidelines for Creating an Harmonic Accompaniment**), 236 (**Guide to Chord Construction**), and 238 (**Guidelines for Creating a Melody**) before composing the song.

Perform your composition for your colleagues and ask their opinion of its sound. Analyze and discuss your composition with the other students in your class.

---

**243** The following questions and problems will help focus your attention on the materials presented since frame 218. Most of your responses will be simple fill-ins.

    a. Though the "fermata" or "hold" has no absolute time value, when placed above ( 𝄐 ) or below ( 𝄑 ) a note, it usually means to sustain that note for approximately _____ its value.

b.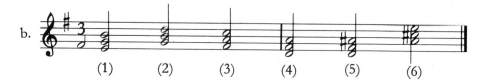

(1)     (2)     (3)     (4)     (5)     (6)

Classify the above triads as major, minor, diminished, or augmented. (Be sure to consider the key signature in your analysis.)

(1) _____

(2) _____

(3) _____

(4) _____

(5) _____

(6) _____

c.

(1)     (2)     (3)     (4)

Classify the sevenths in the above chords as common or major.

(1) _____

(2) _____

(3) _____

(4) _____

d. The chords in example c are _____ position chords.

e.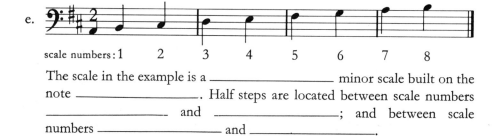

scale numbers: 1     2     3     4     5     6     7     8

The scale in the example is a _____ minor scale built on the note _____. Half steps are located between scale numbers _____ and _____; and between scale numbers _____ and _____.

f. If 7 is raised $\frac{1}{2}$ step in the preceding scale to make the note an _____ this scale now becomes a(n) _____ minor scale.

g.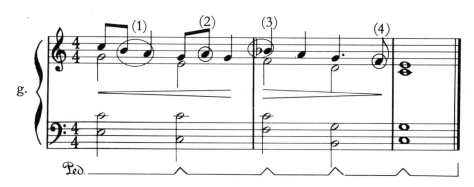

222

Identify the nonchord tones circled in example g as neighboring, double-passing, passing, or suspension.

(1) _____
(2) _____
(3) _____
(4) _____

h. The chords in example g are mostly _____ position chords.

i. In the same example,  ◁ means to become _____, and it is called a _____ sign.

j. ▷ means to become _____, and it is called a _____ or _____ sign.

k. 𝓟𝑒𝒹. in example g means to use the piano's _____ pedal (the pedal on the right).

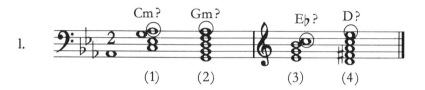

l.

Identify the circled notes in the above chords as added ninths or added sixths. Fill in the numbers *after* the chord symbols as well as in the spaces below.

(1) _____
(2) _____
(3) _____
(4) _____

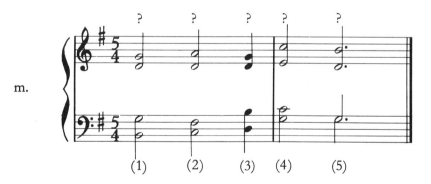

m.

Classify the above chords as first inversion, second inversion, third inversion, or root position. Place the chord symbol letter names above each chord.

(1) _____
(2) _____
(3) _____
(4) _____
(5) _____

n. The double-flat, when placed before a note (♭♭♩), means to play that note a(n) _____ step lower.

o.

Describe how to use the coda signs (⊕) and D.C. al Coda in the above example. _____

_____
_____
_____

(1)   (2)

p.

(3)

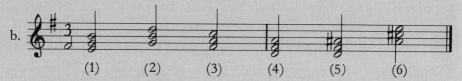

A melodic sequence is illustrated in example _____ above.

d. The chords in example c are *closed* position chords.

scale numbers: 1    2    3    4    5    6    7    8

The scale in the example is a *natural* minor scale built on the note *B*. Half steps are located between scale numbers *2* and *3*; and between scale numbers *5* and *6*.

f. If 7 is raised ½ step in the preceding scale to make the note an *A sharp,* this scale now becomes a(n) *harmonic* minor scale.

g.

Identify the nonchord tones circled in example g as neighboring, double-passing, passing, or suspension.

(1) *double-passing*
(2) *neighboring*
(3) *suspension*
(4) *passing*

h. The chords in example g are mostly *open* position chords.

i. In the same example, ◁ means to become *louder*, and it is called a *crescendo* sign.

j. ▷ means to become *softer*, and it is called a *decrescendo* or *diminuendo* sign.

k. 𝓟𝓮𝓭 in example g means to use the piano's *sustaining* pedal (the pedal on the right).

l.

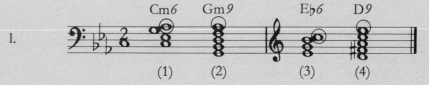

Cm6    Gm9        Eb6    D9

(1)    (2)        (3)    (4)

Identify the circled notes in the above chords as added ninths or added sixths. Fill in the numbers *after* the chord symbols as well as in the spaces below.

(1) *added sixth*
(2) *added ninth*
(3) *added sixth*
(4) *added ninth*

m.

Classify the above chords as first inversion, second inversion, third inversion, or root position. Place the chord symbol letter names above each chord.

(1) *first inversion*
(2) *third inversion*
(3) *second inversion*
(4) *second inversion*
(5) *root position*

n.  The double-flat, when placed before a note (♭♭●), means to play that note a(n) *whole* step lower.

o.

Describe how to use the coda signs (⊕) and D.C. al Coda in the above example. *Play to D.C. al Coda; return to beginning and play to first coda sign. Then skip to second coda sign and play to end of composition (or equivalent answer).*

p.

A melodic sequence is illustrated in example (*3*) above.

Congratulations! If you have successfully completed all of the assignments through Chapter 4, you are well on your way to becoming a musician. You are able to understand and conceptualize the structure of music as well as many music majors entering their first year in college. You should value this achievement. If you continue to build upon these musical skills and concepts, music will be a constant source of enrichment throughout your life.

CHAPTER FIVE

# Sounds in Time:

# Twentieth Century Contributions

# Sounds in Time: Twentieth Century Contributions

*In Chapter Five you will become acquainted with the blues progression through analysis, playing in a variety of keys, and composing a blues song.*

*Composition and analysis, with particular emphasis on contemporary sounds and techniques, is the main thrust of Chapter Five. You will create a number of short works using such concepts as twelve-tone row, modal scale, whole-tone scale, modulation, multimetric time signatures, nontriadic harmony (chords built on intervals other than thirds), and bitonality. Musique Concrète and electronic music are also discussed because of their place in twentieth-century music. The rondo form is introduced and explored.*

*By the end of Chapter Five you will find that your creative thinking processes have been expanded, and the continuum of skills and concepts which has developed from previous chapters is now in clearer perspective. At this point* Involvement with Music *will have come full circle . . . back to environmental sounds.*

---

**244**
Play P.M. BLUES on the keyboard, but first consider the following new notation: In measures 1, 3, 5, 7, and 9–11, you will see notes such as these ♪ connected by a slur marking ♪♩ to another note. These small notes ♪ are called **grace notes** or **appoggiaturas**. A grace note (or appoggiatura) is a nonchord tone which *delays* the sounding of the chord tone a half or a whole step above or below it. Its purpose is to complement and add interest to a melody. Grace notes must be played as quickly (and smoothly) as possible so that the regular notes receive practically their full time values. Only single grace notes are used in P.M. BLUES, but it is quite common (particularly in classical music) to see *groups* of grace notes preceding a regular note.

For easier fingering or a different sound, you may eliminate a tone of a chord when that tone is doubled either in the chord itself or in the melody. For example, in measure 5, the seventh is eliminated from the C7 in the left hand, since it is used in the melody (B♮ is the seventh).

Notice that the C7 is the only chord which is in root position in P.M. BLUES. All the other chords are inverted so that the fingers can *easily* move from chord to chord.

## P.M. BLUES

Original

● Listen to the recording of P.M. BLUES and follow the music.

**245**

A.M. ROCK

Original

A.M. ROCK is a blues piece (rock-type) which is especially reminiscent of the late 1950's and early 1960's (although it is still heard today). Play A.M. ROCK; compare it to P.M. BLUES. Notice that A.M. ROCK has more rhythmic variety in the bass and it uses fewer grace notes (because of its faster tempo). Observe the similarities between P.M. BLUES and A.M. ROCK. Pay particular attention to the chordal relationships in each composition. What are they?

In A.M. ROCK, there are no root position chords. *All* chords are inverted.

Listen to the recording of A.M. ROCK and follow the music.

---

**246**  You have probably discovered that P.M. BLUES and A.M. ROCK share the same chord progressions. Here is a measure-by-measure analysis of the chord progressions:

P.M. BLUES and A.M. ROCK

| Measures: | 1 | 2 | 3 | 4 |
|---|---|---|---|---|
| Chords: | Ⓒ or Ⓒ⁷ | Ⓒ or Ⓒ⁷ | Ⓒ or Ⓒ⁷ | Ⓒ or Ⓒ⁷ |

| Measures: | 5 | 6 | 7 | 8 |
|---|---|---|---|---|
| Chords: | Ⓕ or Ⓕ⁷ | Ⓕ or Ⓕ⁷ | Ⓒ or Ⓒ⁷ | Ⓒ or Ⓒ⁷ |

| Measures: | 9 | 10 | 11 | 12 |
|---|---|---|---|---|
| Chords: | Ⓖ or Ⓖ⁷ | Ⓕ or Ⓕ⁷ | Ⓒ or Ⓒ⁷ | Ⓒ or Ⓒ⁷ |

**247** This chord progression is known as a *blues progression*. It is the harmonic core of blues, jazz, rock, and gospel music, and it is one of the most permanent and striking contributions of the black musical heritage. Contemporary jazz artists employ a wide variety of blues forms, but the most characteristic form is the **twelve-bar blues progression** outlined in frame 246. The progression may be summarized:

Four measures of Ⓒ or Ⓒ⁷
Two measures of Ⓕ or Ⓕ⁷
Two measures of Ⓒ or Ⓒ⁷
One measure of Ⓖ or Ⓖ⁷
One measure of Ⓕ or Ⓕ⁷
Two measures of Ⓒ or Ⓒ⁷

The chords which make up the twelve-bar blues progression are traditional chords—what makes this progression sound contemporary is the progression itself (the specific order and relationship of these chords).

---

**248** Play the twelve-bar blues progression in the following keys, using the L.H.: F, D, and B♭. Use chords both with and without common sevenths. Use convenient inversions.

Play the twelve-bar blues progression on the chromaharp/autoharp in the following keys: C, D, F, and G. Use the common seventh chord whenever desirable and/or necessary. Within your twelve-bar blues, assign a slightly different rhythm pattern for each of the three chords.

Play the twelve-bar blues progression on the baritone ukulele in the following keys: C, D, and G. Vary the rhythm as above.

It is not necessary to notate these progressions. Simply follow the summary in frame 247.

RESPONSE  Here is a simple example of a twelve-bar blues progression in the key of F major. Play it with your left hand:

---

**249** If you examine the melodies of P.M. BLUES and A.M. ROCK, you will find that they are composed exclusively of chord tones—with the exception of the grace notes. Such blues compositions are relatively easy to compose. It is very characteristic of blues-oriented music to use grace notes to *slide* into the chord tones from a half or a whole step above or below. Your musical ear, once again, determines how often you should use these appoggiaturas. Use them discriminately.

On the staffs provided in this frame, compose your own twelve-bar blues progression. Include a melody in the treble clef staffs and write one verse of lyrics to the melody. Blues lyrics usually deal with everyday life. They are also quite repetitive. For example:

I got up in the morning,
I got up in the morning,
Yes, I got up in the morning,
Now I've got to face this day.

Furthermore, blues lyrics should express a personal feeling as in the example above.

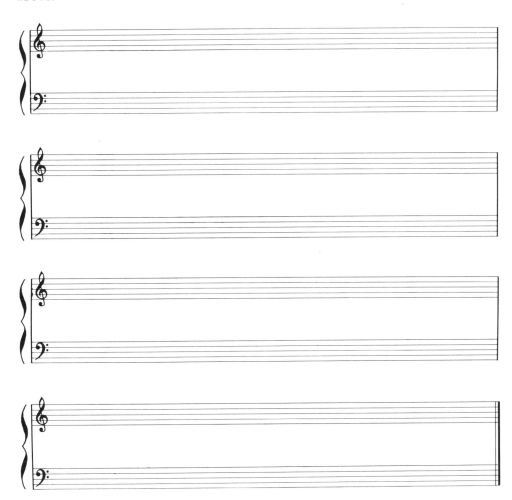

Play and sing your own blues composition.

---

**250**  Up to this point, the scales with which you have been involved are the pentatonic (five different tones), major (seven different tones), and minor (seven different tones).

The blues compositions basically used the tones of a major scale, but as you noticed, the grace notes added accidentals which considerably altered the major scale. Find the blues composition (P.M. BLUES, A.M. ROCK, or your own) which has the largest number of *altered* melody tones, including grace notes. Extract each *altered* note and arrange all of them in ascending alphabetical order (for example, A, A♯, B, C, etc.). Then add any notes necessary to include every black and white key in the octave A to A. Circle your added notes.

---

**251**    The arrangement which you have created by extracting all the melody tones from your selected blues composition, and adding some to complete the octave, is called a **chromatic scale** (twelve *different* tones). Since it includes *every* note (black and white keys on the keyboard) within an octave, the use of the chromatic scale increases the tonal possibilities available to the composer. Write this chromatic scale (starting and ending pitches are already given) in the treble clef staff:

Play the A chromatic scale in one octave (up and down) using the fingering illustrated below. Play each hand separately, then play both hands together:

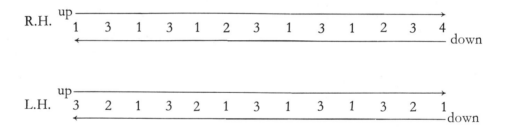

Play chromatic scales in one octave (up and down) built on the following keys: C, F♯, B♭, and E. Use the same fingerings for each scale (as illustrated above).

Now play the A, C, F♯, and B♭ chromatic scale on the ukulele. Remember—each fret represents a half step.

RESPONSE

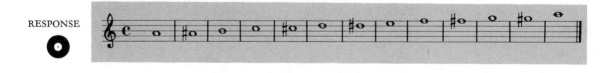

---

**252**    Chromatic scales are harmonically related to diminished chords (see frame 236, section j). Play diminished seventh chords (L.H.) built on these tones. C♯, F♯, and B. Play chromatic scales (R.H.) built on these tones as an accompaniment to each of their corresponding diminished seventh chords. Play the chord as many times as you wish in the left hand as you play the scale in the right hand. Devise comfortable fingerings for the chords. Use the scale fingerings of frame 251 for the R.H. chromatic scales.

Repeat the above procedures, but reverse the hands so that the right hand plays the chords while the left hand plays the scales.

Build *arpeggiated* diminished seventh chords on D, A, and E. Play each of these broken chords up three octaves and then down three octaves, making a smooth connection from one octave to the next (L.H., R.H., B.H.). Devise comfortable fingerings for each hand.

In silent movies, the villain and his mischievous deeds were often characterized by an abundance of diminished chords. Play some diminished chords (with the seventh) in rapid succession. This sound will give you the *villain effect*. Rock your hand back and forth on these chords as rapidly as possible. This technique creates a **tremolo** (trembling) sound.

Listen to this villain effect as played on the recording. Here is an example of a C♯ chromatic scale accompanied by C♯°7 chords. Look and listen:

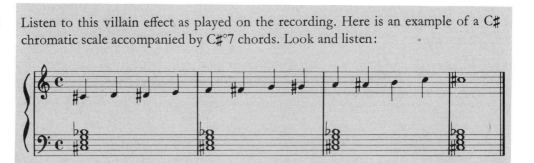

**253**

CHROMASONG

Original

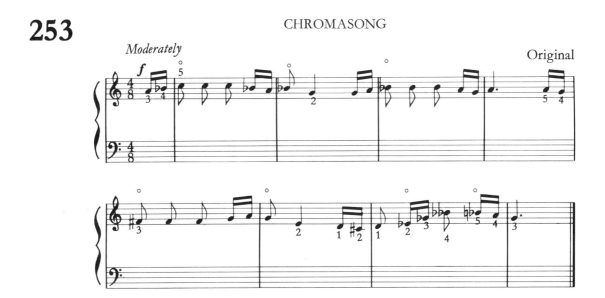

Harmonize CHROMASONG. Use diminished seventh chords only where indicated (°). Place the letter name of every chord to the left of °, and also include letter names for those chords that are not diminished. The diminished symbol ° above the melody note tells you to use that note as the root of the diminished chord.

If necessary, consult **Guidelines for Creating an Harmonic Accompaniment,** frame 235. Remember your role as a musician: let your musical ear be your guide. Add your own dynamics and pedal markings. Now play CHROMASONG on the keyboard.

RESPONSES

Analyze this arrangement of CHROMASONG. Are diminished chords used as required in frame 253? Check your own arrangement of CHROMASONG to be certain that all chords—especially the diminished seventh chords—have been correctly notated.

Listen to the recording of this arrangement of CHROMASONG as you follow the music.

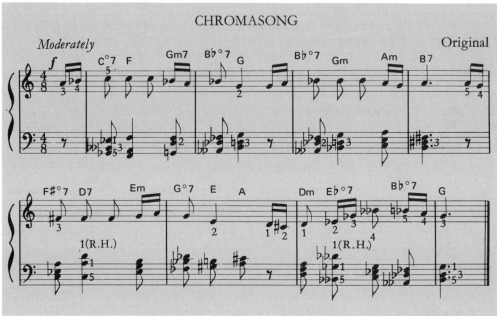

**254** An important feature of the chromatic scale is that it allows the composer to easily change from one key (scale) to another within a single composition. This device is known as **modulation.** Observe the modulations in the following composition. MOD starts in the key of E major, then modulates to C major (measure 3), then to A♭ major (measure 5), and finally back to E major (measure 7). Notice that in each key (each two-measure section), most of the tones in the scale of that key have been used. By using many different scale tones in each key, the sound of each key is more firmly established.

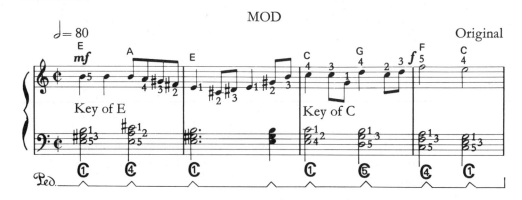

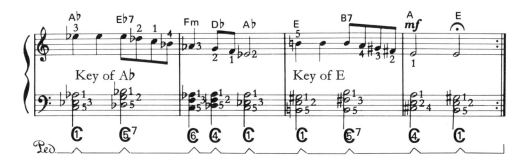

Play MOD. Are all twelve tones of the chromatic scale used in this composition? Observe that inversions are used to facilitate the smooth movement from chord to chord. Notice also that MOD has a natural crescendo because of its upward melodic movement climaxing in measure 4. From measures 5 through 8, there is a natural diminuendo because of the downward melodic movement.

**255** Using as many tones of the chromatic scale as possible, compose a short composition which starts in one key and modulates to another—then returns to the original key. A convenient form for this composition might be ABA. Indicate both letter symbols and number symbols for the chords in their respective keys, as in frame 254. Use the staffs provided in this frame to notate your composition.

**256**  You have just explored some uses of the chromatic scale. In terms of construction, the opposite of the chromatic scale is the **whole-tone scale.** What do you think this statement implies? Consider it carefully.

If you deduced that *chromatic* implies half steps between each note of a scale and *whole tone* implies whole steps between each note, you are correct. Here is a whole-tone scale, starting on middle C:

The seventh tone, logically written as B♯ (since it is a whole tone above the sixth) sounds the same as C and is therefore the enharmonic equivalent of the octave C. Thus the diagram represents the *sound* of a complete whole-tone scale from C to C. Because there are no half steps, only six different sounding tones appear in a whole-tone scale. Notate (staffs provided in this frame) and play whole-tone scales starting on F and A♭. Play these scales in one octave (up and down) using the following fingerings:

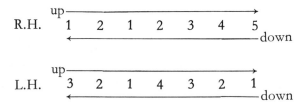

Play L.H., R.H., B.H. on the keyboard, then play the same whole-tone scales (C, F, and A♭) on the ukulele. Remember—two frets represent a whole step.

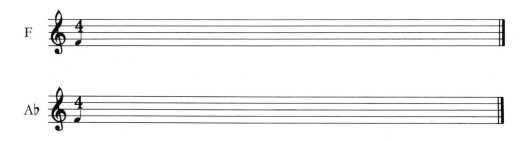

The whole-tone scale is a characteristic device of the musical style referred to as **Impressionism.** Impressionism is most closely associated with the French composers Claude Debussy (1862–1918) and Maurice Ravel (1875–1937).

Silent movies also made considerable use of the whole-tone scale and the augmented chords which are derived from this scale (see frame 236, section j). Instead of the dastardly deeds denoted by the diminished chord, the augmented chord and the whole-tone scale were used to denote suspense and the *unknown.*

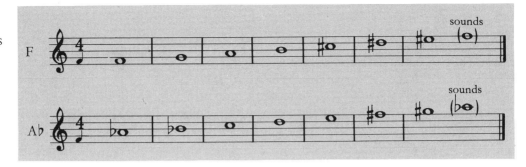

Listen to the sound of old-time movie suspense and the unknown as played on the recording.

---

**257**  Here is a short composition using a whole-tone scale and augmented chords:

Notice how the mixture of sharps and flats preserves the appropriate 1, 3, 5, 7 spelling of the C+7 chord. Sometimes triadic spelling can only be preserved by the use of a **double sharp** (meaning ♯♯ but written ✗). Here is an example:

Listen to the recording of this composition and follow the music. Pay particular attention to the sounds of the augmented chords and the whole-tone scale as compared to the sounds of the diminished chords and the chromatic scale.

---

**258**  Write your own short composition using a whole-tone scale and augmented chords. Include some augmented seventh chords, (common or major). Use the staffs provided in this frame.

**259** Now that you have become acquainted with both the chromatic and the whole-tone scales, you will be interested to learn that the chromatic scale has been used in a radically different way by many contemporary composers. This different way is referred to as the **twelve-tone** or **atonal** technique. As you learned in MOD and in your own modulation composition, it is very easy to move from one key to another through the use of chromatic scale. However, the feeling for *some* key (major or minor) was always present. In twelve-tone or atonal compositions, all sense of keys and their home tones is obscured. This disorientation and lack of tonal stability gives twelve-tone music a strange and unearthly effect, which sounds alien to the untrained ear. For this reason, it is effectively used in television and movie dramas to heighten images of strange events and psychological processes. When you watch television or go to the theatre, listen for this kind of music.

Arnold Schoenberg (1874–1951), a German composer who emigrated to America, is responsible for devising the twelve-tone system of composition. Simply stated, the basic rule for composing a twelve-tone melody (usually called a **tone row**) is that *no one tone can be repeated until each of the twelve chromatic tones has been used*. Without the repetition of tones, there is little possibility of establishing a key or a tonal center. In a *strict* tone row construction, the same interval should not be used in succession. In other words, the interval of a major third should not be followed by another major third, etc. Thus the sense of any key is further obscured. Composers today, however, *bend* this rule considerably to allow for more melodic freedom.

**260** Analyze the following tone row:

Respond to these questions and directions:

    a. Are all twelve tones of the chromatic scale included in the above tone row?

    b. Are any intervals repeated in succession? If so, circle the ones that are repeated.

    c. Play this tone row on the keyboard and sing it with letter names (devise your own fingerings).

    d. Play and sing this tone row in retrograde. Retrograde is a primary compositional technique of twelve-tone music.

RESPONSES

    a. All twelve tones of the chromatic scale are included in the tone row.

    b. One interval is repeated (in succession):

---

**261**    Examine the ways in which the tone row of frame 260 is used in the following song:

### IN THE PLANETARIUM

Music and lyrics by Alfred Balkin

Answer these questions about IN THE PLANETARIUM:

a. How many times is the complete (all twelve tones) tone row used?
b. Does the rhythm of the tone row change with each presentation of the row?
c. Does each tone in each presentation of the row always remain in the same octave?

Play and sing IN THE PLANETARIUM. Compare the keyboard fingerings written here to the ones you devised for the tone row in frame 260.

RESPONSE

a. The "complete" tone row is used four times. The fifth presentation begins on the word, PLANETARIUM, but it is not completed.
b. The rhythms of presentations one and three (starting in measures 3 and 15, respectively) are identical for the first nine tones of the row.
c. Sometimes the tones change octaves. For example, compare the D♭ in measure 4 to the D♭ in measure 10. Both are the fourth tones of the row.

---

**262**  Notate IN THE PLANETARIUM on the treble clef staffs provided in this frame and write a single line accompaniment on the base clef staffs. Also follow these guidelines:

a. Use the tone row of frame 260 as the basis for your accompaniment.
b. In the bass line, the tone row may be written in the original order—or in retrograde.
c. Use the complete row *at least* twice in the accompaniment (bass line).
d. Use mostly whole or half notes in the accompaniment when melody notes are mostly quarter and eighth notes.
e. Use quarter notes in the accompaniment if mostly whole or dotted half notes are used in the melody.

IN THE PLANETARIUM

As an example of a single-line accompaniment to IN THE PLANETARIUM, follow this music as you listen to the recording.

Notice that in that bass line the complete row has been used five times: (1) measures 1–5, (2) measures 6–10, (3) measures 11–16 (retrograde), (4) measures 16–20 (retrograde), and (5) measures 20–25. The last two measures (26–27) use the first five tones of the row.

Check your own single-line accompaniment. Be certain that you have observed guidelines a through e of frame 262.

# IN THE PLANETARIUM

Music and lyrics by Alfred Balkin

**263** Create your own twelve-tone composition, using the following guidelines:

    a. Devise an original tone row. Be certain that all twelve tones of the chromatic scale are included. Remember that F♯ is identical to G♭, A♯ is identical to B♭, etc.

    b. Your composition should be twelve measures long.

    c. Use your tone row at least three times in the melody, making certain that you exercise rhythmic variety.

    d. When harmonizing your melody in the bass clef, use any one or a combination of the following:

        (1) A single-line harmony, employing your original tone row in either forward or retrograde order.

        (2) A single-line harmony, transposing your original tone row (start on a different tone but keep all of the intervals the same distance apart).

        (3) Major, minor, augmented, diminished, common seventh, major seventh, or added sixth chords.

        (4) Vertical intervals *other than* thirds and sixths (sixths are inversions of thirds), such as seconds, fourths, fifths, and sevenths.

Twentieth-century composers commonly employ a variety of harmonic techniques such as suggested in d above. This mixture of musical styles is referred to as **musical eclecticism.** Like many other art forms today, twentieth-century music is dominated by eclecticism.

Notate your composition on the staffs provided in this frame.

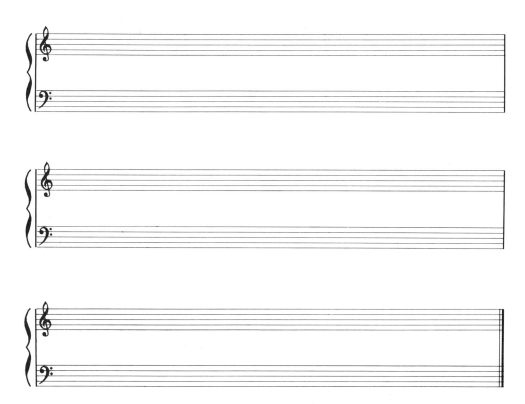

**264** Play all the white keys in succession from the D one step above middle C to the next D (up and down). Does this scale sound major? Minor? Somewhere in between?

Your answer probably was, "somewhere in between." A "somewhere in between scale" is called **modal.** This scale is neither major nor minor. You have played a modal scale from D to D (up and down). Now play scales (all white keys) from E–E, F–F, G–G, A–A, B–B, and C–C (up and down). All are modal scales. You will immediately recognize the A modal scale as identical to the A natural minor scale that you already have learned. The C modal scale is identical to the C major scale. Modal scales, like other scales, can be transposed by maintaining their intervalic relationships in the new key.

Historically modal scales are the products of Medieval Church music. But their use has been revived in both *serious* and *popular* contemporary music. Some of the most popular songs of recent years have been built on modal scales. Perhaps their unique, archaic sound (as compared to major and minor sounds) is the reason why modal scales are so popular today.

---

**265** The melody of RONDO ESPAGNOL is built upon the modal scale from E to E. This scale has a **Flamenco** sound. Flamenco music is primarily associated with dance. Although its specific roots are difficult to trace, Flamenco musical style is a striking and exotic blend of Arabian, Jewish, and Gypsy melodic patterns coupled with Spanish rhythmic and instrumental elements. Flamenco vocal and instrumental style is highly individualistic, emotional, improvisatory, and free. The guitar is its chief spokesman. (The virtuosity of some Flamenco guitarists is legendary.) Strongly accented rhythms, vigorous hand clapping and foot stamping, extraordinarily fast staccato of castanets, and free (yet controlled) body movements characterize the music and the dance of this Gypsy music of Spain.

Play RONDO ESPAGNOL on the keyboard and listen to its modal character.

RONDO ESPAGNOL

Listen to the recording of RONDO ESPAGNOL as you follow the music.
Practice RONDO ESPAGNOL until you can play it at the ♩ = 144 tempo.

**266**    The title of this particular Spanish dance is derived from its formal structure. A **rondo** is a specific form which has a main melodic theme (in this piece it is A: measures 1–4) which alternates with several different themes. In this composition, the form is ABACAD. Each theme (with the exception of D) is four measures long.

The harmonization of RONDO ESPAGNOL is mostly based on intervals of seconds, fourths, and fifths. Notice that the harmonization of the A theme is varied rhythmically with each appearance, although the same harmonies are used.

**267**    Compose your own E, F, and G themes for RONDO ESPAGNOL. Write a composition which begins with the A theme and alternates the A theme with your E, F, and G themes—vary the harmonic rhythm of the A theme each time it appears. Use the staffs below to notate your composition. Create a new rondo form: play RONDO ESPAGNOL (frame 265) and immediately follow it with your own composition (ABACADAEAFAGA).

**268** Compose your own modal melody, using one of these modal scales: D–D, F–F, G–G, or B–B. Write an harmonic accompaniment using any type of intervals, but be certain that all the harmony tones are contained in the modal scale of your melody. Your composition should be eight to twelve measures long. Devise any form you wish (e.g., ABA, ABAB, ABAC, etc.). Use the staffs provided in this frame.

**269**                    LIZA JANE

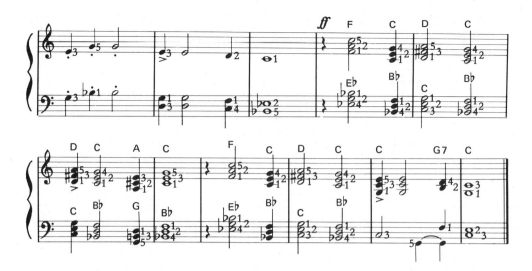

Here is a special arrangement of the traditional folk song, LIZA JANE. Play it on the keyboard. Pay particular attention to the fingerings indicated in measures 8 and 9 (bass clef). Because the thumb plays the A in measure 8 the chord in measure 9 falls comfortably under the left hand. As an experiment, substitute any other finger except the thumb playing the A and discover this fact for yourself.

Listen to the recording of LIZA JANE as you follow the music.

**270**    As you have discovered, this arrangement utilizes many of the harmonic devices which you have learned. Did you notice the form of the melody? It falls very conveniently into an A (measures 1–8), B (measures 9–16), A (measures 17–24), B (measures 25–32) form. You may have analyzed this ABAB form in four-measure phrases: AA′BB′AA′BB′. Both analyses obviously are correct. The prime (′) simply means that the parallel phrases are slightly different. Find these differences.

Knowing the form of LIZA JANE makes it easier to discuss the harmonic devices. The four-measure phrase form will be used.

A (measures 1–4) employs a chordal accompaniment. A′ (measures 5–8) uses a single-line accompaniment, mainly in contrary motion.

B (measures 9–12) has a chordal accompaniment, with some syncopation. B′ (measures 13–16) uses two-tone vertical intervals in the bass (seconds, thirds, fourths, fifths), and ends with a chord in measure 16.

A (measures 17–20) introduces a new concept to your harmonic vocabulary: **bitonality.** Bitonality refers to *music which is in two different keys at the same time.* The melody is in the key of C major. Notice that it starts on 3 of the C major scale. The accompaniment is in the key of F major. Notice that it starts on 3 of the F major scale. The two lines are in parallel motion. A′ (measures 21–24) is also bitonal and parallel: the melody is in the key of C major; the accompaniment is in the key of E♭ major. In this A and A′ of the LIZA JANE arrangement, bitonality is created because the accompaniment to the C major melody consists of the original melody played in the transposed keys of F and E♭. Bitonality means that music is being played in *two* different keys at the same time, **polytonality** means *more than two* keys are being played at the same time. In measures 23 and 24, polytonality is created by the addition of a third transposed key: B♭ (the bass line). In these two measures, the melody in *each* line is 3–3–2–1 of the particular key.

B (measures 25–28) employs a bitonal chordal accompaniment. The chords in the treble clef are different from the chords in the bass clef. B′ (measures 29–32) uses bitonal chords in the first two measures; the last two measures are in C major (𝐂, 𝐄, and 𝐂 ).

Bitonality and polytonality, along with the twelve-tone system of composition, represent significant harmonic and melodic approaches to twentieth-century "serious" music.

---

**271**  Another feature of this arrangement of LIZA JANE is the use of ninth chords (introduced in frame 236). In measures 2 and 4 of LIZA JANE, the seventh is excluded from the C9 chord. In measure 3 the third is omitted from the B♭9maj7 chord. In measures 9–12, both the third and the seventh are omitted from the C9 chord, although the third (E) briefly appears in the melody in measure 11.

Construct the following ninth chords. First notate them, then play them on the keyboard. Play each chord four times: (a) complete with all tones, (b) omitting the fifth, (c) omitting the seventh, and (d) omitting the third. Listen carefully to the sounds you are creating.

Be on the lookout for ninth chords when you are playing popular music.

RESPONSE

Your chords may look slightly different from the above, but all five tones must be present in each chord.

**272**

Original

MUL - TI MET - RIC, MUL-TI MET - RIC means more than one time sig-na-ture in the mu - sic; means more than one time sig - na - ture in the mu - sic.

Sing and play MULTI METRIC on the keyboard. Observe the changing time signatures. You will recall this device from your rhythmic experiences in Chapter Two.

Listen to the recording of MULTI METRIC as you follow the music.

**273**   **Multimetric** refers to the device of changing time signatures in the same composition. Its application is best described by the words and music of this song. Multimetric writing, and the harmonic and melodic ideas which you have studied in this chapter, are the most characteristic devices of twentieth-century music. The composer most responsible for popularizing multimetric time signatures was Igor Stravinsky (1882– 1971). His early orchestral compositions such as *The Firebird Suite* (1910), *Petrushka* (1911), and, in particular, *The Rite of Spring* (1913), have served as models of multimetric writing which many twentieth-century composers emulate.

In these compositions, Stravinsky also employed **polymetric** writing. This device refers to the simultaneous performance of *more than one time signature*. (**Bimetric** would be a more precise term when only two time signatures are used simultaneously—this would parallel the definition of bitonal as opposed to polytonal. The term, however, has not come into general usage, so polymetric continues to be used as defined above.) If the bass of MULTI METRIC were in a different time signature than the treble, would this song then be multimetric or polymetric?

Which tone has been eliminated from the B♭maj7 chord (the harmonic foundations of measures 1 through 8)? The B♭maj7 chord, because of its constant repetition, functions as an ostinato bass figure and, in so doing, it brings a strong feeling of unity to MULTI METRIC.

Discover the considerable use of bitonality in MULTI METRIC.

---

**274** Create a nine-measure multimetric melody and harmonize it in the following ways:

a. Transpose portions of your melody and use them to accompany the melody in the original key (bitonal accompaniment). You may want to use more than one transposed key in your accompaniment (such as in LIZA JANE, frame 269, measures 23–24). (polytonal accompaniment).

b. Use chords of a key different than your melody (bitonal).

c. Use vertical intervals—mostly fourths, fifths, and seconds.

Write your composition on the staffs provided.

**275**

For many experimental composers, even the twelve-tone system (with its breaking down of the traditional tonal barriers) was too restrictive for their musical tastes. They wanted to explore the world of sound beyond that of musical tones. Everything in the environment became a legitimate sound source for these composers. This movement, which broadened the musical spectrum, began in Paris in the 1930's. It was referred to as **Musique Concrète** (pronounced my′ zēk kôn kret′). In Chapter One, your manipulation of environmental sounds, although more rudimentary than the efforts of the Paris composers, was certainly akin to *Musique Concrète*. This is where *your* involvement with music began. *Musique Concrète* is where the Paris composers continued *their* involvement with music, but only after many years of musical training and thought.

*Musique Concrète* was able to flourish with the perfection of the tape recorder. With this equipment, all environmental sounds as well as any tonal materials can be manipulated by using different tape speeds, dynamic levels, layers of sounds and tones, sounds played backward, etc. All of these techniques are capable of distorting traditional sounds to the point where they are completely new and unfamiliar to the listener. These sounds often appear as *effect* music in movies, television, and theater. These specific types of sounds have been categorized as **tape recorder music.** Refer back to your best aleatory compositions in Chapter One and record them with some of the devices mentioned above. If a reel-to-reel tape recorder is available record a section of your composition at $7\frac{1}{2}$ ips (inches per second). Listen to it at $7\frac{1}{2}$ ips, then at $3\frac{3}{4}$ ips, then at $1\frac{7}{8}$ ips. Is it not a vastly different sound experience at each speed? To carry this one step further, use another tape recorder set at $7\frac{1}{2}$ ips, and record your original composition as it plays at $1\frac{7}{8}$ ips on the first tape recorder. Then, play the second tape recorder at $3\frac{3}{4}$, etc. Obviously, this technique has many possibilities.

**276**

**Electronic Music** is an extension of tape recorder music which transcends the limitations of environmental sounds. In this technique, a variety of electronic equipment (oscillators, generators, filters, amplifiers, etc.) is employed to produce sounds which cannot be manufactured any other way. **Synthesizers** (such as the Moog) can now integrate these various components into one master unit. This facilitates the composition of electronic music by making its technical apparatus easier to operate and less expensive to own. Synthesizers are also being used by elementary school students. Many rock groups employ a variety of unusual electronic sounds which add to the excitement of the musical effect, but which are difficult to classify. Universities now offer courses which are devoted exclusively to the composition of electronic music.

Electronic music should be considered as an adjunct compositional technique. It is not meant to replace tonal music in its many manifestations. As a matter of fact, a typical movie or television **score** (the notated music itself) is likely to combine *traditional* music along with *Musique Concrète* and Electronic Music. Anything goes in music today.

**277**  Match the most appropriate concept in the following list to each description (a–z). All concepts will be used, and each will be used only once.

chromatic scale
twelve-bar blues progression
modal scale
tone row
bitonal
polymetric
whole-tone scale
diminished seventh chord
musique concrète
polytonal
tape recorder music
multimetric
augmented triad

rondo
Flamenco music
modulation
atonal composition
retrograde
✘
tremolo
musical eclecticism
score
electronic music
grace note or appoggiatura
bimetric
music

_____ a. All the white keys contained in any octave.

_____ b. An F and a B♭ chord sounding simultaneously.

_____ c. No key center or home tone.

_____ d. Sophisticated manipulation of environmental sounds.

_____ e. One and one-half steps between each of its four members.

_____ f. This arrangement of chords: four measures of **₵**, two measures of **₵₄**, two measures of **₵**, one measure of **₵₅**, one measure of **₵₄**, and two measures of **₵**.

_____ g. Every tone in any octave played in order.

_____ h. More than one time signature in various musical lines sounding simultaneously.

_____ i. More than one time signature in a single musical line.

_____ j. Exciting musical amalgam of Spanish, Arabian, Jewish, and Gypsy music.

_____ k. Slides to a chord tone from one half step or one whole step above or below, and has no counted time value.

_____ l. A notated musical composition.

_____  m. Double sharp.

_____  n. Two whole steps between each of
its three members.

_____  o. A shaking tone (vocal or instrumental).

_____  p. A tone row or any other musical
theme performed in backward
motion.

_____  q. The form is ABACADAE, etc.

_____  r. Oscillators, generators, amplifiers,
synthesizers, strange sounds.

_____  s. Uses natural sounds but frequently
distorts them.

_____  t. Music which is simultaneously
played in three or more different
keys.

_____  u. All the whole steps in an octave.

_____  v. Mixture of musical styles.

_____  w. Changing keys within a composition.

_____  x. A more accurate, but rarely used,
substitute for polymetric.

_____  y. A twelve-tone melody.

_____  z. Anything and everything from a–y.

RESPONSES

| | |
|---|---|
| _modal scale_ | a. All the white keys contained in any octave. |
| _bitonal_ | b. An F and a B♮ chord sounding simultaneously. |
| _atonal composition_ | c. No key center or home tone. |
| _musique concrète_ | d. Sophisticated manipulation of environmental sounds. |
| _diminished seventh chord_ | e. One and one half steps between each of its four members. |
| _twelve-bar blues progression_ | f. This arrangement of chords: four measures of 𝄴, two measures of 𝄴, two measures of 𝄴, one measure of 𝄴, one measure of 𝄴, and two measures of 𝄴. |
| _chromatic scale_ | g. Every tone in any octave played in order. |
| _polymetric_ | h. More than one time signature in various musical lines sounding simultaneously. |

| | |
|---|---|
| *multimetric* | i. More than one time signature in a single musical line. |
| *Flamenco music* | j. Exciting musical amalgam of Spanish, Arabian, Jewish, and Gypsy music. |
| *grace note* *or* *appoggiatura* | k. Slides to a chord tone from one half step or one whole step above or below, and has no counted time value. |
| *score* | l. A notated musical composition. |
| ✕ | m. Double sharp. |
| *augmented triad* | n. Two whole steps between each of its three members. |
| *tremolo* | o. A shaking tone (vocal or instrumental). |
| *retrograde* | p. A tone row or any other musical theme performed in backward motion. |
| *rondo* | q. The form is ABACADAE, etc. |
| *electronic music* | r. Oscillators, generators, amplifiers, synthesizers, strange sounds. |
| *tape recorder music* | s. Uses natural sounds but frequently distorts them. |
| *polytonal* | t. Music which is simultaneously played in three or more different keys. |
| *whole tone scale* | u. All the whole steps in an octave. |
| *musical eclecticism* | v. Mixture of musical styles. |
| *modulation* | w. Changing keys within a composition. |
| *bimetric* | x. A more accurate, but rarely used, substitute for polymetric. |
| *tone row* | y. A twelve-tone melody. |
| *music* | z. Anything and everything from a–y. |

**278** Your involvement with music has brought you full circle—back to environmental sounds. Along the circle, you have become a composer, a performer, and a skilled listener.

If you have been sincere and conscientious in your *Involvement with Music*, you now have the fundamental skills and concepts necessary to play, compose, discuss, and listen to music. Hopefully, you have also acquired the desire to integrate the musical experience into your life and the lives of those around you.

# Appendix A Lesson Plans

The nine lesson plans in this Appendix, designed for application in an elementary school classroom, are intended to supplement and reinforce many of the concepts developed in Chapters 1 through 5. All lesson plans are structured according to goals, entry behaviors (minimum student behaviors necessary for participation in the lesson procedures), performance objectives, procedures, and materials.

Teachers can devise their own evaluative techniques based upon the performance objectives in each lesson. Achievement of each objective can be measured in terms of affective, cognitive, or psychomotor responses. Some objectives are measured with two, or perhaps all three types of response. Remember that any response can be calculated quantitatively (How much did the child accomplish in relation to the objective?) or qualitatively (How successfully did the child accomplish the objective?).

Many of the performance objectives in these nine lesson plans require qualitative responses, since they are rather general. The teacher may use these objectives as a guide for writing more specific sub-objectives, some of which will require quantitative responses. Example: *The student will be able to play three pentatonic scales on the keyboard with no more than one pitch error* (sub-objective to objective 3, Lesson Plan 5).

Special attention should be given to the structuring of classroom situations that require affective responses from students. Attitude, for example, is a basic ingredient in every situation. It is demonstrated by student interest in achieving the objectives, enthusiasm for the tasks, attention span, etc. Although these responses sometimes are difficult to measure, they must be taken into account. Cognitive and psychomotor responses can be drastically limited or enhanced by such affective items as attitude, enthusiasm, motivation, and individual values.

None of these lesson plans can be completed in a single class period. The teacher must consider each plan in terms of its performance objectives. The *number* of objectives achieved during one class meeting depends entirely upon student progress and grade level. Therefore, the teacher must pace his or her procedures according to each classroom situation.

*All complete songs used in these lesson plans are found in Appendix C. Pentatonic songs without staff notation are found in Appendix B.*

LESSON PLAN 1  (*Chapter One*)
## Environmental Sound Composition

### Goals

1. The student will become more aware of the compositional possibilities based on sounds to be found in the classroom.
2. The student will gain added confidence and security in his/her own ability to create.

### Entry Behaviors

No special requirements

### Performance Objectives

1. Each student will demonstrate awareness of the music-making possibilities of environmental sounds by creating and performing a 10- to 15-second sound composition based on three sound sources discovered in the classroom. The body may *not* be used as a sound source but can be used as an activating agent.
2. Each student will demonstrate understanding of the following concepts: sound source, sound-producing combination, activating agent, and environmental sounds by first performing the composition and then through verbalization (utilizing the foregoing terminology accurately), describing how the composition was put together.
3. Each student will demonstrate understanding of dynamics by utilizing softness and loudness in the performance of the composition and verbalizing (using the term after the performance) about how dynamics were employed.
4. Each student will gain some insight into group composition by having his/her own composition incorporated into that of the group.
5. Each student will demonstrate added confidence and security in his/her own ability to create by:

   a. creating a new composition;
   b. by taking less time to create another composition;
   c. by creating a more original or interesting composition;
   d. creating a longer composition than the required minimum.

### Procedures

1. Ask each member of the class to recall one sound heard in the classroom on the previous day. Encourage each class member to try to remember a different sound (but accept any reasonable answer as a legitimate response). Write the responses on the chalkboard or overhead projector. Answers might include: bell ringing, doors closing, buzzing in corridors, pencil being sharpened, book dropping, chalk scraping, lights being turned on, desks opening and closing, etc.
2. Explain that all these sounds may be referred to as *environmental sounds,* since the immediate environment is the classroom, and that is where the sounds are being made.
3. Inform the class that every sound will be called a *sound source.* The source is their classroom.

4. Ask the members of the class to beat on their desks with their hands. Have the class decide that the desk was the sound source.

5. Ask what actually turned the sound source into a real sound. They will likely respond, "our hands."

6. Explain that their hands became activating agents which set the sound source in motion and created a sound-producing combination. The poster or overhead transparency shown in the materials section would be helpful here.

7. Ask the class to use their desks again as a sound source, but this time, request that they strike their desks with a different activating agent (pencil, pen, ruler, book, etc.). Observe the various activating agents and record them on the chalkboard or overhead transparency.

8. Make it clear by demonstration that an activating agent is also a sound source (as is everything), but it is being used (struck) here to set another sound source in motion. If a book hits a pencil, the book is the activating agent and the pencil is the sound source. If the pencil is used to strike the book, the book becomes the sound source. In each case, the results are sound-producing combinations.

9. Announce that the class will have five minutes to discover three sound sources in the room which they will use to create a sound composition. Their sound compositions will last from 10 to 15 seconds. Make it clear that all sounds are acceptable, and that many people might well discover similar sounds. However, reinforce the idea that the same sound sources used with different activating agents create different sound-producing combinations (e.g., different kinds of drum sticks and mallets produce different sounds on the same drum). Do not mention repetition of sound. Let that idea evolve.

10. Invite each student to present his/her short environmental sound composition using dynamics as part of the presentations.

11. Ask the students how their compositions have been put together (using the new terminology).

12. Arrange the class into six groups. Group 1 will now perform *one* of their sounds at a given signal, followed by groups 2 through 6 performing one of their sounds on cue. The dynamics will be varied from soft (on 1) to loudest (on 6).

**Materials**

1. Overhead transparencies and projector, chalkboard, or posters can be used to present these concepts:
   a. environmental sounds come from many sound sources.
   b. a sound source and an activating agent create a sound-producing combination.
   c. a sound source is silent until set in motion by some activating agent.
   d. groups of sound-producing combinations put together in a meaningful way create sound compositions.

2. Tape recorder (three speeds).

LESSON PLAN 2 (*Chapter One*)
*Sound Sources and Activating Agents*

**Goals**

1. Using the body as a sound source, the student will become more aware of music-making possibilities.

2. The student will understand the use of unity and variety in composition.
3. The student will understand the use of limited materials in composition.
4. The student will understand the concept of a *round*.
5. The student will understand the concept of *distortion*.

**Entry Behaviors**
No special requirements

**Performance Objectives**
1. Each student will demonstrate awareness of the music-making possibilities inherent in the body by creating and performing a 30- to 60-second composition based on 12 different sound-producing combinations.
2. Each student will demonstrate understanding of the difference between sustained and nonsustained sounds, as produced by the body, by selecting and performing six of both types in one composition.
3. Each student will demonstrate understanding of unity and variety in a composition by isolating one of the 12 sounds and repeating it consistently throughout the composition (unity), and contrasting it each time with a "different" sound (variety).
4. Each student will demonstrate ability to compose within given limitations by being confined to sounds that can be produced by the body exclusively. This includes vocal sounds, but does not include stamping, striking objects with the hands, etc. The body must be both the sound source and activating agent.
5. Each student will demonstrate ability to participate in a group composition experience by joining with two other students to select and perform 12 overall sounds which will be presented as a group composition.
6. Each student will demonstrate understanding of a round by performing rounds in both a small and a large group.
7. Each student will demonstrate an understanding of distortion by being able to distinguish between a recording of his/her group composition being played at $7\frac{1}{2}$ ips and one being played at $3\frac{3}{4}$ or $1\frac{7}{8}$ ips.

**Procedures**
1. Using the body exclusively as the medium for both sound sources and activating agents, each member of the class will create a composition using 12 different sound-producing combinations evenly divided between sustained (vocal) and nonsustained sounds. The composition will last from 30 to 60 seconds.
2. Each student will verbally identify his/her sound-producing combinations as sustained or nonsustained.
3. Each student will demonstrate an awareness of unity and variety by consistently repeating at least one of the twelve sound-producing combinations and using it in contrast with other sounds (e.g., 1-2-1-3-1-4-1-5). Dynamics should be used to reinforce the repetition and contrast.
4. Each student will perform the composition as a solo.
5. Each student will join forces with two other students. Each of the three students will again perform his/her composition for the small group so that the members of the group can listen carefully to one another's individual efforts.

6. The small group will select the 12 sounds which most appeal to them. The sounds will be evenly distributed between sustained and nonsustained. Each member's contribution will include at least two of his/her original sounds.
7. Each group will now select and write down the order of sounds to be played.
8. Each group will play its composition for the class.
9. Each group will perform its composition as a three-part round. Each member will play all 12 sounds following this procedure:
   a. Member 1 begins alone. Each sound is played three times.
   b. Member 2 enters with the first sound when member 1 begins the fifth sound. Each sound is played three times.
   c. Member 3 enters with the first sound when member 2 begins the fifth sound. Each sound is played three times.
   d. Each member of the group plays the 12 sounds three times through, so that member three will be performing alone at the end of the composition.
10. Record each composition at $7\frac{1}{2}$ ips.
11. Discuss the various compositions as they are performed. Have the class comment on the individual sounds, and as to which compositions they especially like. Ask them for reasons why they like certain compositions.
12. Have the class select those 12 sounds which they found the most interesting.
13. Arrange these sounds in an agreed upon order to make a new composition.
14. Decide which two sounds will be repeated consistently throughout the new composition (e.g., 1-2-1-3-1-4-1-5-2 etc.). The repeated sounds do not always have to be in that order (e.g., 1-2-1-3-2-4-2-5-1 etc.). Let the class set its own repeat pattern. Try the composition with different repetition/contrast patterns.
15. Show the different sounds arrangements on the overhead projector or chalkboard.
16. Perform and record these compositions. Emphasize how varying the repeat pattern makes the composition sound quite different even though all the sounds are the same.
17. Play back some of the compositions at $3\frac{3}{4}$ ips, and help the class identify the original sounds. It may be difficult, since the compositions were recorded at $7\frac{1}{2}$ ips.
18. Discuss the concept of distortion and how playing compositions back at speeds other than those at which they were recorded disguises the sounds so that they appear to be completely different.
19. Emphasize this point further by playing the compositions back at $1\frac{7}{8}$ ips and asking the class to identify sounds which you point out on the overhead projector or chalkboard. (They will find it still harder to do this.)
20. Play back a few of the small group compositions at $1\frac{7}{8}$ ips and ask whatever group(s) created these particular compositions to stand up.
21. Play these same compositions back at the original $7\frac{1}{2}$ ips and ask the groups to stand when they hear their compositions.
22. Divide the entire class into four groups and perform the class composition (decide upon the best repetition/contrast arrangement) as a four-part round. Follow this diagram (could be a visual aid) for the procedure, which is identical to Step 9 (except for a fourth part).

## Materials
1. Overhead projector or chalkboard
2. Tape recorder (three speeds).

263

**Additional Comments**

Though the behavioral objectives are rather interdependent, this lesson plan could be the source of at least five music periods without losing the thread of the objectives from day to day. The teacher, of course, would have to reinforce the concepts being learned so that they would not be overlooked by the students. The procedures lend themselves to being broken up into shorter segments.


LESSON PLAN 3   (*Chapter Two*)

## Beat, Count, and Rhythm

### Goals

1. The student will understand the conceptual differences between beat, count, and rhythm.
2. The student will understand how tempo can affect the beat.

### Entry Behaviors

1. The students can demonstrate their understanding of time signature, beat, rhythm.
2. The students can demonstrate their understanding of tempo.
3. The students can demonstrate their understanding of compound time.
4. The students can demonstrate their understanding of all note values from the sixteenth note to the whole note.

### Performance Objectives

1. Given a specific musical example(s), the student will demonstrate understanding of the *difference* between the beat, the count, and the rhythm by verbally identifying the various time elements, counting aloud and clapping, or in some other way, sounding them out separately and/or together.
2. Given a specific musical example(s), the student will demonstrate understanding of the concept that the beat and the count can be the same by verbally explaining the relationship and clapping, or in some other way, sounding the beat while counting aloud.
3. Given a specific musical example(s), the student will demonstrate understanding of the concept that the beat and count can be different because of the designated tempo. This will be shown by students verbalizing the relationship, then clapping the rhythm while counting aloud and keeping the beat with the foot.
4. Given a specific musical example(s), the student will demonstrate understanding of the concept that the beat, count, and rhythm can be the same by verbally identifying each time element, then clapping, or otherwise sounding them while counting aloud and keeping the beat with the foot.

*Performance Objective 1*

1. Show a transparency of the song, "Playing in the Park."
2. The students will verbally identify the count, beat, and rhythm respectively: The count is 12, there are four beats to the measure; and the notes and words of the song represent the rhythm.

3. Reinforce the concept of compound meter using $\frac{12}{8}$ as an example.
4. The students will clap the count (twelve steady eighth notes in groups of three), and tap their feet on each of the four beats (at the beginning of each three, eighth-note group) while counting the beat aloud (1 2 3 4).
5. The students will say and clap the rhythm of the words.
6. The students will say the words as they keep the beat with their feet.
7. The students will hear a recording of "Playing in the Park."
8. Play the recording a second time and ask students to sing with it. As an alternative for singing with the recording, have the students discover the ups, downs, and sames of the melody tones by giving them the first tone and letting them find the rest. As they find each one, reinforce it at the piano. Advise them in their discovery process to use up, down, and same hand motions.

*Performance Objective 2*
1. Show transparency of the song, "Sunday in the City."
2. Ask students what kind of tempo the lyrics of the song suggest.
3. Students will read lyrics aloud.
4. After someone has answered that the lyrics suggest a slow tempo, play the recording of the song and ask students to confirm or deny the response to the question.
5. Play the recording again, and ask students to keep the beat with their feet.
6. Ask: "How many beats do you feel in each measure?" Someone will answer "four."
7. Ask: "How many counts are in each measure?" Someone will answer "four."
8. Students will clap the rhythm while counting aloud and keeping the beat with their feet.
9. Ask: "What is the relationship between count and beat in this song?" Someone will answer "the same."
10. Reinforce this response by telling students that in a slow tempo, the number of counts and beats will most likely be the same.
11. Play the recording again and ask students to sing with it.

*Performance Objective 3*
1. Show transparency of the song, "People Rushing."
2. Ask students what kind of tempo the lyrics of the song suggest.
3. After someone has answered "fast," say the words of the song until they are secure.
4. The class will recite the words as fast as they can while keeping the beat with their feet.
5. Ask: "How many beats did you feel in each measure?" Someone will answer "two."
6. Ask: "How many people felt two beats in each measure?" Most hands will be raised.
7. Ask: "How many counts are in each measure?" Someone will answer "four."
8. Ask: "How do you know it's four?" Someone will answer, "Because the time signature says so."

9. Ask: "Then what's the relationship between count and beat in this song—the same or different?" Someone will answer "different."
10. Reinforce this response by telling students: "In fast tempos, the count and beat are very often different. The tempo determines the beats."
11. Play the recording, and have students clap the beat while saying the words.
12. Sing "People Rushing" accompanied by the record. If desired, this song and any other in the unit may follow the same alternative procedure described earlier when students were learning to sing "Playing in the Park."
13. Set a much slower tempo for "People Rushing" and ask the students to sing it in that tempo. Have them keep the beat with their feet.
14. Ask: "Did the beat change, and if so, how many beats are now in each measure?" Someone will probably answer that the beat changed, and there are now four beats in each measure instead of two.
15. Reinforce the concept of tempo by changing the beat, and also suggest that since the tempo was changed, the lyrics don't have the same meaning. Ask them what effect the tempo change made on the whole song.
16. Sing the song in the proper tempo once again along with the record.

*Performance Objective 4*

1. Show transparencies of the following songs:
   a. "Old Hundred"
   b. "Tallis' Canon"
   c. "Green Grow the Lilacs"
   d. "Midnight Cowboy" (first four measures, rhythm only).
2. Have class clap the rhythm of a through d while counting aloud and keeping the beat with their feet. Point out any pickup notes.
3. Ask: "Did you have any difficulty doing all three things at one time?" Someone might answer "yes," but more people will say "no."
4. Ask: "Why do you think it was so easy to do all three things at one time?" Hopefully, the answer will be: "Because they are all the same."
5. Have class discover and verbalize specifically that the count, the beat, and the rhythm (with a few exceptions that should be pointed out) are all the same.
6. Class will sing each of the three songs. ("Tallis' Canon" might eventually be learned as a canon.)
7. Show transparency of "Sweet Betsy from Pike."
8. Have class clap the rhythm while counting aloud and keeping the beat with their feet. Point out pickup note. The tempo will be fairly slow.
9. Ask: "Are the rhythm, count, and beat of this song the same or different?" The likely answer will be the "same."
10. Ask: "How many beats are in each measure?" Someone will answer "three."
11. The class will sing "Sweet Betsy from Pike" in the same slow tempo.
12. Have class sing the song in a considerably faster tempo while keeping the beat with their feet.
13. Ask: "Has anything changed?" The likely answer will be: "The beat has changed."
14. Ask: "How many beats do you feel in each measure?" Answer will be "one."
15. Ask: "What made the beat change?" Answer will be "the tempo."

16. Reinforce idea once again that the tempo can change the beat—but in slower tempos, there is music written in which the beat, count, and rhythm are the same.

**Materials**

1. Transparencies of the following songs:
    a. "Playing in the Park"
    b. "Sunday in the City"
    c. "People Rushing"
    d. "Old Hundred"
    e. "Tallis' Canon"
    f. "Green Grow the Lilacs"
    g. "Sweet Betsy from Pike"
    h. "Midnight Cowboy" (Chapter 2, frame 112, example j).

2. Overhead projector
3. Recording: *We Live in the City* (Numbers 15, 13, and 3) Theodore Presser Co., Bryn Mawr, Pa. 19010.
4. Piano.


LESSON PLAN 4 *(Chapter Two)*

*Silence and the Rest*

### Goals

1. The student will understand the use and importance of silence in music.
2. The student will understand how rests are used to notate silence in time.
3. The student will understand how rests can produce syncopation.


### Entry Behaviors

1. The students can demonstrate their understanding of all time signatures.
2. The students can demonstrate their understanding of all note values from sixteenth notes to whole notes. (This includes dotted notes.)
3. The students can demonstrate their understanding of syncopation as created by accent markings.
4. The students can demonstrate their understanding that the strong accent normally occurs on the first count of a measure.


### Performance Objectives

1. The students will demonstrate their understanding of the quarter rest by counting and indicating these rests with silent gestures as a contrast to their clapping the notes out loud.
2. The students will demonstrate their understanding of quarter rests by creating and performing short examples which incorporate them.
3. The students will demonstrate their understanding of syncopation produced by quarter rests by including such syncopation in their own examples. They will also describe the syncopation verbally both in their own examples and others.

## Procedures

1. Show transparency of steady quarter notes in **4/1** time.

2. Students will clap and stamp the four quarter-note beats as they count aloud. Rhythm instruments such as bongos, maracas, cowbells, etc., can be used with or instead of clapping and stamping.

3. Play a medium tempo rock recording of your choice which has a strong beat in **4/4** time.

4. Students will clap and stamp the beat while counting aloud as in procedure 2.

5. Show transparency of these measures.

6. Students will clap and stamp the beat while counting aloud. Ask them to clap only on the notes but to count throughout. Where there is no note, the students will indicate this with any fairly quiet movement (e.g., stretching hand(s), shrugging shoulders, sliding foot, moving forward in place, bending to the side, etc.). Encourage a variety of responses. You might even place students in groups when you observe similarities in movements. (This could create interesting patterns.)

7. Explain that the beats on which the students moved silently are called rests, and that rests are used to indicate silence in time. Point out that the use of silence provides contrast and greater rhythmic interest in a musical composition.

8. Ask: "What kind of a note do you think each rest is equal to?" Most likely answer will be "a quarter note."

9. Ask: "Why?" Someone will answer, "because each rest equals one count and so does the quarter note."

10. Ask: "What do you think this rest is called?" Most likely answer will be "a quarter rest."

11. Reinforce this answer by explaining that there is an equivalent rest for every different kind of note, and whatever number of counts a note receives in a certain time signature, the equivalent rest will receive the same number of counts. Inform the class that they will have opportunities to work with eighth, half, and whole rests in the next few lessons.

12. Ask: "Did the rests fall on the strong or weak counts?" Someone will answer, "the strong counts."

13. Ask: "If the rests fall on the strong counts, what does that do to the accents?" someone will answer, "the accents fall on the weak counts."

14. Ask: "When the accent falls on the weak counts, what is this pattern called?" Someone will answer "syncopation."

15. Compare this type of syncopation produced by rests and the type produced by accent marks.

16. Play the same or a similar rock or jazz recording once again, and ask the students to keep the syncopated beat with their hands, but to move quietly on the quarter rests in any way they want.

17. Ask class members to write down all the combinations of quarter notes and quarter rests that can occur in a single **4/4** measure. Request that some of these combinations include syncopated patterns. They should discover all combinations:

18. Select all the different combinations and write them on the chalkboard or overhead transparency.
19. Have class members identify the syncopated patterns.
20. Clap and count all of them, continuously utilizing previous procedures. Rhythm instruments may be used instead.
21. Play a recording similar to those previously used (procedures 3 and 16).
22. Repeat procedure 20 along with the recording. First sound the patterns a through n from left to right, and keep repeating these patterns in that same order until the recording is over.
23. For variety, play another recording; this time, sound the patterns a through n but then reverse them—n through a. Keep repeating the patterns in the left to right, right to left order until the recording is completed.
24. Show transparencies of "Children's Prayer" and "In My Class".
25. Have the class discover what is similar and what is different from the way the quarter rest is used in each of these songs. They should learn that "Children's Prayer" uses the rest but not in a syncopated way, since the accent still falls on the strong beat. "In My Class" uses the rest to produce syncopation.
26. The students will clap the rhythm of each song.
27. Using recordings of both of these songs, the students will clap the rhythm of each song along with the record.
28. The students will sing each song along with the record or accompanied by some instrument.

### Materials and Equipment

1. Phonograph
2. Overhead projector
3. Transparencies for rhythms shown (Procedure 18)
4. Transparencies of songs, "Children's Prayer" and "In My Class."
5. Recordings: "Children's Prayer," *Discovering Music Together,* Book 6, Album S601, Record 1, Side B, Band 4. "In My Class," *We Live in the City,* Number 4.

### Additional Suggestions and Comments

The same procedures from 1 to 23 can be followed in $\frac{3}{4}$ time to produce quite different musical effects. There are many excellent jazz oriented recordings of the following popular songs to accompany rhythmic patterns in $\frac{3}{4}$ time. They include: "What the World Needs Now," "Matchmaker" (from *Fiddler on the Roof*), "I Feel Pretty" (from *West Side Story*), "My Favorite Things" (from *The Sound of Music*), "Scarborough

Fair," "Taste of Honey," "Gravy Waltz," "Bluesette." There are many others. Children's songs in a jazz waltz feeling include "The City" and "The Bus Terminal" (from *We Live in the City*).

$\frac{5}{4}$ time might be explored similarly, though the list of materials is short. It includes: "Take Five" (Dave Brubeck), "Mission Impossible" (theme from TV show), "Everything's Alright" (from *Jesus Christ, Superstar*), and the children's song "In a Department Store" (from *We Live in the City*).

There are very few folk songs which have examples of the type of syncopation explored in this lesson, but there are many popular songs which do. Some of these are: "Games People Play" (Appendix C), "This Guy's in Love with You," "Do You Know the Way to San Jose?," "Didn't We," "King of the Road," "Yesterday," (and other Beatles' songs), "The World I Used to Know" (by Rod McKuen), "Son of a Preacher Man," "Sunrise, Sunset" (from *Fiddler on the Roof*), and numerous others.

Using popular songs with elementary school students can often pose a problem as to the lyrics. The individual teacher must evaluate the lyrics as to the advisability of using a particular song in the classroom.

The type of syncopation explored in this lesson is encountered frequently in children's songs from *We Live in the City*, such as "A Big Apartment House," "Some of My Friends," "Skyscrapers," and "Have You Ever Seen?" Explore the various new elementary school music series for other examples. Like previous lessons, this lesson is a unit in conception. This means that it can easily be broken down into component parts to be the basis for a number of lessons, perhaps four or five. For instance, procedures 24 to 27 lend themselves readily to one complete lesson, providing the sequence has been taught up to that point.

LESSON PLAN 5  (*Chapter Three*)
## Black Keys and the Pentatonic Scale

### Goals

1. The student will understand the way in which the black keys are arranged on the keyboard.
2. The student will understand the concept of pentatonic scale.

### Entry Behaviors

1. The students can demonstrate their understanding of all aspects of rhythm.
2. The students can demonstrate their understanding of the difference between whole and half steps.

### Performance Objectives

1. The students will demonstrate their visual and conceptual understanding of how the black keys are arranged by verbalizing those relationships after copying from an overhead transparency of a one-octave keyboard.

2. The students will demonstrate their tactile understanding of how the black keys are arranged by playing specific black keys with specific fingers (on the cardboard keyboard and at the piano).
3. The students will demonstrate their understanding of how pentatonic scales are formed by playing any given pentatonic scale on the black keys.
4. The students will demonstrate their understanding of how the black keys can be used to accompany any pentatonic song by accompanying these songs while other students sing.

**Procedures**

*Performance Objective 1*

1. Show an overhead transparency of a one-octave keyboard. This could be more than one octave, but only one octave would be shown at first.
2. Have the students discover that the black keys are arranged in groups of twos and threes.
3. Show a transparency of a two- or three-octave keyboard.
4. Have the students discover that the same pattern continues to exist no matter how many octaves there are.
5. Pass out crayons and construction cardboard.
6. Show the one-octave keyboard again.
7. Ask the students to copy the transparency using pencil and ruler, making the white keys approximately 4 inches high by $\frac{3}{4}$ inch wide, and the black keys $2\frac{1}{2}$ inches high by $\frac{1}{2}$ inch wide.
8. Inspect all keyboards at the students' desks and give help where needed.
9. When all keyboards are conceptually correct, have the students color their black keys with any color crayon they wish. The white keys will remain white. Advise the students to take considerable care since they will be using their keyboards throughout the year.

*Performance Objective 2*

1. Ask students to place one finger of the right (and then the left) hand across the group of two black keys as shown on the transparency. (Demonstrate this on the transparency.)
2. Ask students to place one finger of the right (and then the left) hand across the group of three keys.
3. Show the larger keyboard transparency and reinforce the concept of black keys in groups of twos and threes as the consistent pattern through the entire length of a piano keyboard.
4. Ask students to hold up both hands with palms facing each other.
5. Ask them to move both thumbs, and tell them that thumbs are called finger 1 on a keyboard instrument. Follow the same procedure with both second fingers (2); both third, fourth, and fifth (3, 4, 5) fingers.
6. Ask students to place the thumb of the right hand on the first black key in the group of two.
7. Ask them to place the second finger on the second black key in the group of two.
8. Ask that the students place fingers 3, 4, and 5 on each of the three keys in the group of three.

9. Play this group of black keys from left to right and right to left. Have a student simultaneously fingering these keys on the overhead transparency.
10. Repeat procedure 9 and have class sing the finger numbers as they play them from left to right and right to left.
11. Repeat procedures 6 to 10 using the left hand fingers 5, 4, 3, 2, 1 (from left to right).

*Performance Objective 3*

1. Select groups of four students for each piano.
2. Have each student place his/her five fingers of the right hand on the black keys as each has done at the cardboard keyboards.
3. At a given signal, the students will play each key with fingers 1 through 5 from left to right and back. The students at their desks will finger their keyboards and sing the finger numbers. All fingers will be played at the same tempo.
4. Repeat procedures 2 and 3 using the appropriate fingers of the left hand. (Procedures 2 through 4 will last approximately two minutes per group.)
5. Tell students that this group of five black keys is a scale and that a scale is a group of tones (here produced by the keys) arranged in a specific order. Elaborate by telling them that this particular black-key scale is a pentatonic scale because it consists of five ("penta" in Greek means five) keys in a specific order. Let them know that five different black keys starting anywhere are pentatonic scales.
6. Ask: "How many different places on the black keys can we start a pentatonic scale?" Someone will answer, "five."
7. Continue procedures 2 through 4 until all students have the opportunity to perform once at the piano during the class period.

*Performance Objective 4*

1. Show transparency of "Goodbye, Old Paint."
2. Tell class that this song is built on the pentatonic scale even though it uses all white keys, but these white keys have the same whole and half step relationship as the black keys.
3. Show transparency of the keyboard. Point out the white keys in this song and have the students count the steps between each of the five keys.
4. Play this pentatonic scale on the white keys. It starts on C. Class will sing.
5. Play the black-key pentatonic scale which starts on D flat. Class will sing.
6. Ask the students whether the two pentatonic scales sound the same or different. Someone will probably answer, "They sound the same, but one sounds a little lower than the other."
7. Ask: "Why do you think they sound the same?"
8. Let the class discover that the whole steps and half steps in both scales are precisely the same, and that is why they sound the same. Advise them that whenever musical scales have the same whole step/half step relationships they will sound the same, even though they do not start or end in the same places. If desired, procedure 8 could be expanded with both the same and different five-tone scales being explored. Some would be pentatonic, and others wouldn't.
9. Tell students that a pentatonic scale, be it on white or black keys, can be identified in three ways: a. It has five different tones; b. It has no half steps between any two keys; c. It has one and a half steps between two specific keys.

10. Tell students that all pentatonic songs can be played exclusively on the black keys.

11. Class will learn to sing "Goodbye, Old Paint" by whatever methods you choose.

12. Invite three students to the piano, and assign each student to one or two octaves of the keyboard.

13. Assign a rhythmic pattern to each of the three students. ($\frac{3}{4}$ ♩ ♩ ♩ top octave; $\frac{3}{4}$ ♩. ♩ middle octave; $\frac{3}{4}$ ♩. lower octave) Tell students that they may play any combination of black keys with their rhythm. Let them play their rhythms for all to hear. The class will count and play the rhythms on their keyboards.

14. Give students the starting pitch so that they can be prepared to sing.

15. Set the beat for one measure and the three students will now play their black key accompaniments using the assigned rhythms. Their first four measures will be an introduction.

16. On cue, the remainder of the class will sing the first verse and chorus of "Goodbye, Old Paint" to the accompaniment of the three students. (For added experience, the students can switch parts twice so that they have a chance to play all parts.)

17. Analyze the accompaniment and ask for suggestions on how to improve it.

18. Repeat procedures 12 through 17 with remaining groups of students. Each group will accompany one verse and chorus.

19. Using "Swing Low, Sweet Chariot" as the song, repeat procedures 11 through 17. The only difference will be the $\frac{4}{4}$ time signature instead of $\frac{3}{4}$. Allow students at the piano to create their own rhythmic patterns for their accompaniments.

20. Tell students that pentatonic songs are found all over the world, particularly in Japan, China, Ireland, Eastern Europe, and in North and South America with songs of various Indian tribes, spirituals, and cowboy songs.


## Materials

1. Overhead projector
2. Transparencies
   a. Piano keyboard
   b. "Goodbye, Old Paint"
   c. "Swing Low, Sweet Chariot"
3. Piano
4. Recordings, if desired, of both songs. These can be found in amost any elementary music series record supplement.


## Additional Comments

1. This plan is a unit plan with activities and concepts that can easily be broken into two weeks of daily classroom music. Taken individually, some of the performance objectives ideally should require two or three lessons in themselves.
2. Appendix B has a number of pentatonic songs which can be substituted for the two used here, or which can be used for enrichment experiences.

3. With a little ingenuity and thought, pentatonic songs (Appendix B) can be sung together if in similar ($\frac{2}{4}$ and $\frac{4}{4}$) time signatures (e.g., "Get on Board" with "Sometimes I Feel Like a Motherless Child"; "Goodbye, Old Paint" with "There's a Hole in the Bucket," both $\frac{3}{4}$). This is because all of the songs are using the same five black keys. Doing this task creates some attractive two-line harmonies, and this opens up the concept of harmony for exploration.

LESSON PLAN 6   (*Chapter Three*)
## *The White Keys*

### Goals

1. The student will understand the pattern of the white keys on the piano.
2. The student will know the names of the white keys.

### Entry Behaviors

1. The students can demonstrate their ability to play pentatonic songs and scales.
2. The students can demonstrate their understanding of the octave concept.
3. The students can demonstrate their understanding of all aspects of rhythm.

### Performance Objectives

1. The students will demonstrate their ability to locate and name any white key on the piano by playing any given key on request and singing the letter name.
2. The students will further demonstrate their knowledge of the white keys by playing their choice of any one of a selected group of short songs when given the rhythm and the key names.

### Procedures

*Performance Objective 1*

1. Students will finger a pentatonic scale on their cardboard keyboards (starting on D flat) while a student(s) plays the scale at the piano. All students sing up and down the scale on the neutral syllable "la." If tone bells are available, some students may play their pentatonic scales on them.
2. Show an overhead transparency of a two-octave keyboard.
3. Ask students to place their right hand thumb on the white key immediately to the left of the group of two black keys.
4. Identify this key as C and mark it on the transparency.

5. Play C and have the class sing this tone on the letter C as they finger it.
6. Keep the thumb in place, and ask students to place the second finger on the next white key to the right of C.
7. Lead students to identify this key as D. Mark it on the transparency.
8. Play D and have the class sing this tone on the letter D as they finger it.
9. Ask students to move their thumbs immediately to the left of C onto the adjoining white key.
10. Ask: "What kind of a step was this—whole or half?" The likely answer will be "half."
11. Have students identify this key as B. Mark it on the transparency.
12. Play B and have the class sing this tone on the letter B as they finger it. Some may play it on the tone bells, and others may play it with or instead of the teacher at the keyboard.
13. Follow steps 9 through 11 for A.
14. Advise the students that A is the first letter of our musical alphabet, and that our musical alphabet consists of seven different letters.
15. Ask: "What is the last letter of our musical alphabet?" Someone will answer "G."
16. Ask: "What do you think comes after G?" Someone will answer "A", "A again", or possibly "H."
17. Ask all students to place their fifth finger of the left hand on A, fourth on B, third on C, and second on D.
18. On cue, all students will sing the tone A as they press their left-hand fifth fingers on their cardboard keyboards along with the piano.
19. Continue this procedure with B, C, and D with the fourth, third, and second fingers respectively. Add tone bells if available.
20. Ask students to retain the left-hand position and place the second, third, fourth, and fifth fingers of the right hand on the four remaining white keys starting with E.
21. Have students name the remaining white keys. They will probably say "E, F, G, and A."
22. Ask students to finger and sing the octave A to A. Reinforce the idea that the relationship is 1 to 8 (or 1 again).
23. Reinforce the concept that an octave is always 8 in relation to 1 no matter what the key, white or black.
24. Follow procedures 18 and 19 for learning the key names E through A.
25. Ask four students to come to the piano. Assign a specific octave to each student.
26. Each of the four students will place fingers 5, 4, 3, 2, of the left hand on A, B, C, D respectively. Fingers 2, 3, 4, 5 of the right hand will be placed on E, F, G, and A respectively.
27. The four students will play the As in the octave on a given cue, and then follow procedures 18 and 19 to play all of the keys contained in the octave from A to A.
28. The next group of four students will place their left and right hands in the same finger order as before but on the octave B to B. All students will do the same on their cardboard keyboards.
29. Follow previous procedures for singing and playing the keys in this octave both up and down. (Remember, tone bells may be used to reinforce the singing and playing.)
30. The next group of four students will follow previous procedures on the octave C to C, and each octave will be changed with each succeeding group of four students.

31. Students will play this game. Randomly select individual keys to be played (e.g., C, G, F, E) anyplace on the piano. Each team will consist of four or five members. The first person on any team who plays the correct key gets points for his/her team. After the key is played correctly, another member of that particular team shows the key on the overhead projector. This type of game might be an effective follow up to the more formal previous procedures.

*Performance Objective 2*

1. Show transparencies of all the five-finger position songs listed in the "Materials" section of this lesson and found in Appendices B and C.
2. Play each song one or two times as the students finger them at their cardboard keyboards and sing them on a neutral syllable (L.H. and R.H.).
3. Ask: "Do you notice anything different about the way the music is notated?" They will answer "yes" and they may ask about the lines and spaces as well as other symbols which they have not yet encountered.
4. Give this information about their new discoveries if they ask.
   a. The lines and spaces indicate the highness and lowness of pitches. The higher the line or space, the higher is the pitch and vice versa. Indicate that the staff will be the subject of the next music lesson.
   b. The G clef sign helps locate a particular G on the keyboard, and at the same time, knowing what it does makes it easier to locate "any" key on the keyboard when given notes on the staff.
   c. Sharps require that any key is played a half step higher. Flats require that any key be played a half step lower.
   d. The capital letters above the staff indicate certain harmonies that are to be played with the melodies. Let the class know that these symbols will be dealt with in a future lesson(s).
5. Advise the students that all of them will have a chance to play any one of the songs you have just played.
6. Tell the students that they may select their own songs, and that you would like two students at the piano for every song.
7. Show the songs in order once more, and ask two students to play the same particular songs. Compile a list of teams for each song.
8. Invite the two students to the piano to play their selection, first in the right hand then the left hand.
9. Continue this process until all students have played some song at the piano.

**Materials**

1. Piano
2. Two-octave cardboard keyboards for every class member
3. Resonator bells (optional)
4. Overhead projector
5. Transparencies of:
   a. two-octave keyboard
   b. "Jingle Bells,"* "Merrily We Roll Along," "Mary Had a Little Lamb," "Go

* Found in Appendices B and C (all others found in elementary music series texts).

Tell Aunt Rhody," "Whistle, Daughter, Whistle," "The Elephants,"* "Grandma Jones,"* "When the Saints Go Marching in," "Little Jack Horner," "Grandma Grunts," "Going Home," "Ode to Joy," "Hokey Pokey,"* "The Donkey,"* "Hole in the Bucket,"* "Get on Board."*

## Additional Comments

1. If it is desired, the class can make up appropriate, appealing, and more meaningful new words for these melodies.
2. All the procedures in this lesson lend themselves to learning the staff also.

LESSON PLAN 7 (*Chapter Four*)
## *Sharps, Flats, and Scales*

### Goals

1. The student will understand the function of sharps and flats.
2. The student will understand the differences between major, minor, and chromatic scales.

### Entry Behaviors

1. The students can demonstrate understanding of all aspects of rhythm.
2. The students can demonstrate understanding of letter notation on the treble staff.
3. The students can demonstrate ability to name and play any white key on the keyboard.

### Performance Objectives

1. The students will demonstrate their understanding of sharps and flats by playing any key that is requested and by identifying it by two different names (e.g., A♯ or B♭).
2. The students will demonstrate their understanding of the chromatic scale by playing chromatic scales built on B and C.
3. The students will demonstrate their understanding of the major scale by:
    a. playing all or part of a given major scale on the keyboard
    b. singing any given major scale with letters and/or numbers
    c. arranging a group of eight students (labeled with individual note names) in the order of a given major scale
    d. arranging a scrambled group of thirteen tone bells in the proper order of a particular major scale
    e. verbalizing how an assigned major scale is put together in terms of steps and half steps
    f. recognizing a major scale from staff notation
    g. writing a given major scale on the staff with proper accidentals

Found in Appendices B and C.

h. composing (in a group) an eight-measure melody built on a particular major scale.

4. The students will demonstrate their understanding of the pure minor scale by:
   a. following the same procedures shown in behavioral objectives 3 a to h
   b. recognizing the difference between a pure minor scale and a major scale by raising one hand or two hands for minor when scales are heard.

## Procedures

*Performance Objective 1*

1. Make a key name for every member of the class. These letter names will be about twelve inches square and include sharps and flats. All black keys will be labeled with two letter names (A♯ and B♭). The letters will start with A and progress at least two complete octaves plus starting again. There will likely be three As.

2. After all students have pinned on their letters, arrange thirteen students in the front of the room to represent a complete chromatic scale from A to A. The students representing black keys will stand on small boxes or stools behind the appropriate keys.

3. Show a transparency of a three-octave keyboard beginning on A. All the black keys will be labeled with two names.

4. Play an A on the piano. Ask the class to sing it by letter name. Tone bells may also be used to reinforce the singing along with/or instead of the piano. Ask students with the letter A to stand as you point out the A on the transparency.

5. Play an A♯ on the piano and repeat procedure 4.

6. Ask class for the difference between the first A and A♯. The likely answer will be: "The second A is higher."

7. Let class discover that the second A is a half step higher.

8. Tell class that when a tone is raised by a half step, the higher tone is called a *sharp*, which is symbolized by this sign (♯) in notation. The letter name remains the same.

9. Play a B, etc.

10. Ask class: "What is the difference between A♯ and B?" Likely answer will be "a half step."

11. Ask: "Is A♯ now lower or higher than B?" Answer will be "lower."

12. Tell class that when the sound of A♯ is referred to as some kind of a B, it is called B flat. Elaborate by telling them when a tone is lowered by a half step, the lower tone is called a *flat,* which is symbolized by this sign (♭) in notation. The letter name remains the same.

13. Point out A♯ or B♭ on the transparency, and emphasize that every black key can be called by two names, a sharp or flat, and that the one which is used depends on whether the key is raised or lowered by a half step. Tell class that all sharps, flats, and anything else that alters a particular note, are called *accidentals.*

14. Follow procedures 4 through 7 with every key up to A, an octave above the original. Be sure to emphasize that each key can be labeled with two possible letters and symbols.

15. Ask class: "How many different keys (not just letter names) are contained in one octave?" Likely answer will be "twelve." Someone might answer "thirteen."

16. Tell class that when all the half steps in any octave are played, this is called a *chromatic* scale, and that a chromatic scale has twelve different tones and number 13 is the octave of number 1.

17. The class will sing a chromatic scale from A to A both ascending and descending. Tell them to sing sharps ascending (A, A♯, B, C, C♯, etc.) and flats descending (A, A♭, G, G♭, etc.). Play each tone on the piano and have members of the scale (in front of the classroom) join hands with each succeeding tone. Those who are sitting will finger the keys on their cardboard keyboards.

18. Repeat this procedure but give each standing student a tone bell to play in conjunction with the singing.

19. Point to individual keys and ask that person who is sitting with the corresponding key letter in the chromatic scale to play that key on the piano. Advise all students sitting at their seats to finger each key on their cardboard keyboards. Tone bells can reinforce each key as it is played.

20. Continue this procedure until sufficient experience has been given.

21. Have the group which is standing go to their seats and exchange places with the group that is sitting.

22. Repeat procedures 17 to 20, but in procedure 17, perform chromatic scales built on B and C.

*Performance Objective 2*

1. Arrange a C chromatic scale with thirteen students standing in front of the classroom. All the white keys will again be in front.

2. Ask the students in the front row to sing their letters up and down as they are played on the piano and pointed out on the overhead transparency. The students at their seats will play tone bells and sing.

3. Ask students: "How many different letters are used in this scale?" Likely answer will be "seven." Ask: "What was the eighth letter?" Answer will probably be "the same as the first."

4. Ask that the scale be performed again using the 1 through 8 numbers.

5. Tell class that this is called a major scale and have them notice that, except for the octave, each letter name is different.

6. Play some other major scales on the piano to reinforce the sound.

7. Ask class to discover the whole- and half-step arrangement of the major scale. Make sure that they discover the half steps between 3 and 4; 7 and 8. Reinforce this concept verbally and with the overhead projector. Have class understand that all major scales are composed of whole steps except between 3 and 4; 7 and 8, which are half steps.

8. Have class finger the C scale as it is pointed out on the transparency.

9. Ask the D♭ to step out in front of the group and to take a tone bell which corresponds to his/her letter. Tell the class that they are going to form a D♭ major scale.

10. Ask students at their desks to pick out the next member of the scale. Let the first student who answers correctly go up to the front of the room and place the proper letter (student) next to the D♭. (This will be E♭.) The student who answered will also find the corresponding tone bell (lettered E♭ or D♯) and hand it to the student who is now standing in the scale position.

11. Have the class identify the relationship of D♭ to E♭ as a whole step.

12. Follow procedures 10 and 11 for the rest of the D♭ major scale making sure that the class identifies each set of number-letter relationships as to whole and half steps.

13. When there are eight students standing in front, ask them to play their tone bells on cue.
14. Ask class if this sounds like the other major scales they have heard. Likely answer will be "yes."
15. Have entire class sing this scale by the letters and the numbers as it is pointed out on the transparency or the keyboard.
16. Show a transparency with the notes of the D♭ major scale written out on the treble clef staff. Point out that all accidentals must be written to the left of the notes precisely on the line or space of the particular note.
17. Ask: "How many flats are in the scale?" Someone will answer "five."
18. Ask "Why?" Lead class to discover that the five flats enable the half steps between 3 and 4 and 7 and 8 to be preserved just as in the built in half steps in the C major scale between 3 and 4 (E and F) and 7 and 8 (B and C).
19. Have the class sing, play tone bells, and finger notes of the D♭ major scale.
20. Show a transparency of an E major scale in notation.
21. Follow procedures 9 to 15 in having class discover that this is an E major scale, and have them determine the formation of the entire scale.
22. Have class discover how many sharps are used in the E major scale and why.
23. Ask class to write D major and F major scales on staff paper (G clef).
24. Show the correct scales on transparencies by having class supply the notes of each scale.
25. Divide the class into groups of four. Assign each group a particular major scale with which to create an eight-measure composition. The composition will start and end with the key tone. Any combination of note values from eighth notes to whole notes may be used. If the group wants to put words to its composition, it is encouraged to do so. Each group will be given fifteen minutes to complete the composition.
26. Each group will write its composition on an overhead transparency and present it to the class, first rhythmically, then by letter names and also by scale numbers. If there are words, they will also be presented. If the group finds too much difficulty in transferring composition to written notation, the composition should be tape recorded and the music teacher will then notate it.

*Performance Objective 3*

Follow same basic procedures for learning the natural minor scale as followed in learning the major scale. Start with the A minor scale and select reinforcement materials (other minor scales) at your discretion. Stress the formation of the natural minor scale in relation to the half-steps between 2 and 3 and 5 and 6. Emphasize the difference between the half-step relationships of the major scale (3 to 4, 7 to 8) and the minor scale (2 to 3, 5 to 6).

*Performance Objective 4*

1. Advise students that they will hear five sets of scales. Both scales in a set will start and end on the same key. Each set will usually contain one major and one minor scale. Sometimes, however, the set will contain two major or two minor scales.
2. Ask students to listen carefully to each set of scales for differences between major and minor. Have students indicate which kind of scale the first one is by raising

their left hands for major, their right hands for minor, and both hands if the scales are the same. When both scales are the same, the students will verbally identify which kind.

3. As reinforcement, show transparencies of sets of major and minor scales (with the same key tone) side by side. The students will identify by the notation which one is major and which one is minor.

4. Play a number of songs, both major and minor, and ask the class to verbally identify which songs are built on major scales and which are built on minor.

5. Let class decide which of these songs they might like to sing.

### Materials

1. Piano
2. Overhead projector
3. Transparencies:
   a. three-octave keyboard
   b. D♭ major scale in notation on treble clef staff
   c. E major scale in notation on treble clef staff
   d. Clear transparencies for group compositions
4. Resonator bells
5. Enough 12 inches × 12 inches sheets of cardboard or construction paper for each member of class
6. Enough safety pins for all the 12 inches × 12 inches sheets
7. Staff paper.

## LESSON PLAN 8  (*Chapter Four*)
### *Major and Minor Chords*

### Goals

1. The student will understand the structure of major chords.
2. The student will understand the structure of minor chords.

### Entry Behaviors

1. The students can demonstrate understanding of the keyboard, key names and their note locations on the treble staff.
2. The students can demonstrate their understanding of all major and minor scales.

### Performance Objectives

1. The students will demonstrate their understanding of major chord structure (triads) by:
   a. playing selected major chords on the piano through recognition of the chord symbols and awareness of the relationships

    b.  arranging selected major chords with resonator (tone) bells

    c.  singing the three separate tones of selected major chords with proper numbers and/or letters

    d.  verbalizing letter names of chords and showing the formation of the chords on a keyboard transparency

    e.  playing any major chord on the autoharp or chromaharp

    f.  accompanying selected songs on the piano, and/or autoharp/chromaharp, and/or tone bells

2.  All objectives are the same as 1, but every major chord now becomes minor (e.g., "Playing selected minor chords on the piano, etc.").

**Procedures**

*Performance Objective 1*

1.  Arrange thirteen students in a chromatic scale (as in previous lesson) from middle C to the octave above.

2.  Have the eight students with the letters of the C major scale step forward. Each student will have a corresponding tone bell.

3.  Have students play the C major scale by the numbers. The students at their desks will finger the C major scale.

4.  Ask the numbers 1 (C), 3 (E), and 5 (G) to step forward. Have them play their respective tone bells separately, then together.

5.  Divide the class into three groups and repeat procedure 4 with each group singing one of the three tones.

6.  Tell students that these three tones form a *major chord,* and that a three-tone chord is usually referred to as a *triad.* Let them know that all major triads include the 1, 3, and 5 of a major scale, and that the symbol for a major triad is the letter name itself (in this case, C).

7.  Have the three students step back into the major scale arrangement and let the class discover that there are two steps between tones 1 and 3 and one and a half steps between tones 3 and 5. Reinforce this concept with a transparency of the keyboard.

8.  Class will repeat the C major triad, singing, playing tone bells, and fingering C, E, and G on their keyboards.

9.  Invite four students at a time to play the C major triad on the piano until the entire class has had a chance to play.

10.  Tell class that they are going to form a D major triad. Let them discover that the three tones are D, F♯, and A. Follow the basic performance procedures of 4, 5, 8, and 9.

11.  Select two other major triads and follow procedure 10 throughout.

12.  Divide class into groups of three. Assign a major triad to each group. Each group will point out the three keys on a keyboard diagram, select the proper tone bells, and play the triad (each playing all three tones) on the piano.

13.  Place an autoharp or chromaharp on a table in front of the classroom. Select major chords to be played (e.g., F, G, etc.). The first student to identify all three members of the particular chord will go to the instrument and strum that chord a few times. Don't select chords that cannot be played on the instrument.

14.  Pass the instrument around so that every student ultimately gets an opportunity to choose and play a major chord.

15. Select familiar one- and two-chord songs from Appendixes B and C and have students accompany them on the autoharp/chromaharp, and/or tone bells, and/or piano.

*Performance Objective 2*

Follow the precise procedures of Performance Objective 1 (Procedures 1–15) in the learning of minor chords. Emphasize that tones 1, 3, and 5 of the minor scale make up the minor triad, and the step formation of the minor triad is the exact opposite of the major triad (one and a half steps between tones 1 and 3, and two steps between tones 3 and 5. Advise students that the minor chord symbol has a small m after the capital letter (e.g., Fm is F minor.)

## Materials

1. Overhead projector
2. Transparency of a two-octave keyboard
3. Transparencies of selected songs (major and minor) from Appendix C
4. Piano
5. Autoharp/Chromaharp
6. Resonator bells.

## LESSON PLAN 9 (*Chapter Five*)
### *Twelve-Tone Composition*

### Goals

The students will become acquainted with twelve-tone composition.

### Performance Objectives

1. The students will demonstrate their basic understanding of twelve-tone composition by creating and performing original tone rows.
2. The students will further demonstrate their understanding of twelve-tone composition by incorporating and describing at least three compositional devices learned in this lesson (e.g., retrograde, vertical use of notes in row) into their compositions.

### Procedures

1. Show class a large poster made of construction paper on which are found all the twelve different members of the chromatic scale from C to B. This poster will include a keyboard with letters underneath as well as on the keys.
2. Ask class: "What does this poster represent?" Likely answer will be "a chromatic scale."
3. With scissors, cut out each of the twelve scale members in front of the class. Drop these papers into a bag.
4. Ask individual students to pick one letter out of the bag. Have each letter placed from left to right on a table.

5. When all twelve letters have been selected, write them in order on a transparency.
6. Ask twelve other students to select the corresponding tone bell and have them play those tones (using quarter notes) in that order. The rest of the class will sing them on a neutral syllable.
7. Tell class that this represents a tone row, and that a tone row:
   a. consists of all twelve tones of the chromatic scale
   b. avoids, if possible, too much repetition of the same interval
   c. does not repeat the same tone until all twelve tones have been sounded once
   d. avoids the feeling of a home tone such as found in major and minor scales and songs—sounds "far out"
   e. can present the twelve tones horizontally, vertically, or any combination of both
   f. makes no difference what octave a tone is played in—as long as it complies with rules b and c
   g. can use any rhythms
   h. can be played backwards (in retrograde).
8. Have group play the tone row again and analyze it for some of the criteria mentioned in 7.
9. Have class answer the question: "Does it sound 'far out' enough?" If not, what might be done to make it more so.
10. Have it played on the piano and bells—some tones being played by piano and others by bells (vary the octaves placement).
11. Have it played backwards and forwards at the same time, but the backward portion will be played in half notes while the forward remains in quarter notes.
12. Experiment with the piano playing the row in vertical movement while the tone bells and voices perform in horizontal movement (the vertical movement will be in whole notes while the tone bells and voices are in quarter notes).
13. Have class devise words for the tone row (once sounded, the row may be repeated to make a more satisfactory composition).
14. Add rhythm instruments or rhythmic sounds using the voice or body.
15. Tell class that tone-row composition at a more advanced level is one of the most important approaches to music in the twentieth century, and that it was first developed by the composer Arnold Schoenberg.
16. Shuffle the tone row and repeat procedures 1 to 14.
17. Divide class into groups which will create their own twelve-tone compositions and present them to the class. (Each group will receive twelve minutes to devise their row and ten minutes to practice their composition; students will be advised that the most important thing is not to repeat the same tone twice before all others have been sounded.)
18. After row compositions have been presented, some of them will be combined.


### Materials

1. Tone bells
2. Piano
3. Poster with chromatic scale
4. Clear transparency
5. Rhythm instruments.

## Additional Comments

There is an infinite amount of twelve-tone recorded music by such composers as Arnold Schoenberg (the originator), Alban Berg, Anton Webern, Ernst Krenek, Milton Babbitt, Roger Sessions, Pierre Boulez, Elliot Carter, Luigi Dallapiccola, and others. Playing some of this music could prove quite fascinating to the student.

# Appendix B  Pentatonic Songs

Each of the songs in Appendix B is based on a pentatonic scale, which means that they can be played on the black keys exclusively. Each song is notated rhythmically, includes finger numbers, and can be played without any knowledge of the musical staff. Words are also included so that these songs can be sung as well as played on the keyboard. *Bracketed titles indicate songs that can be played by either hand separately.*

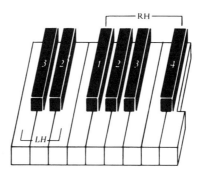

AMAZING GRACE!

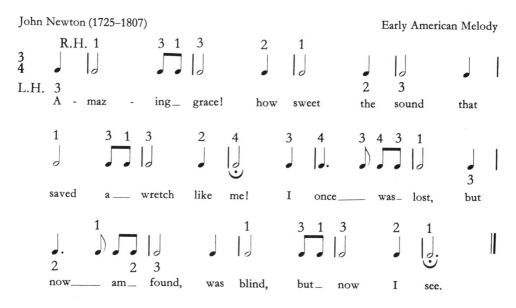

John Newton (1725–1807)                    Early American Melody

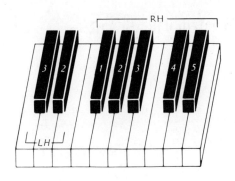

## AULD LANG SYNE

Robert Burns                                                                 Scottish

R.H. 1       3  2   1 2  3  1    3   4  5

L.H. 3

Should auld ac-quaint-ance be    for-got, And nev - er brought to   mind?  Should

4    3     1  2   1 2 3  1        1      5

                                    2  3

auld  ac-quaint-ance be    for-got, And  days   of auld lang syne?    For

4    3     1  2   1 2 5  4    3   4  5

auld___ lang___ syne,  my dear, For  auld___   lang___   syne;    We'll

4    3     1  2   1 2 3  1        1

                                    2  3

take   a cup of   kind - ness yet for  auld___  lang___  syne.

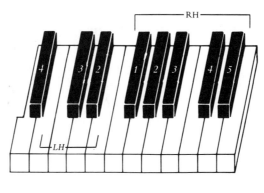

## CINDY

Appalachian

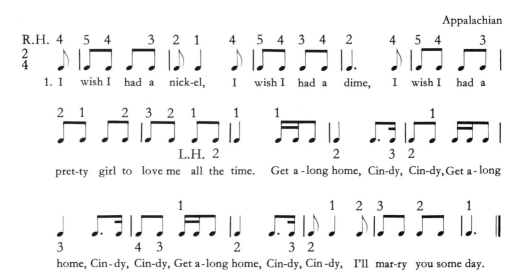

R.H.   4   5   4    3   2   1    4   5   4   3   4   2    4   5   4    3

1. I wish I had a nick-el, I wish I had a dime, I wish I had a

2 1   2 3 2 1   1   1

L.H. 2    2    3 2

pret-ty girl to love me all the time. Get a-long home, Cin-dy, Cin-dy, Get a-long

1    1 2 3   2    1

3    4 3    2    3 2

home, Cin-dy, Cin-dy, Get a-long home, Cin-dy, Cin-dy, I'll mar-ry you some day.

2. I wish I were an apple,
   A-hanging on a tree,
   And every time my Cindy passed,
   She'd take a bite of me.

3. I wish I had a needle,
   As fine as I could sew,
   I'd sew that gal to my coat tail,
   And down the road I'd go.

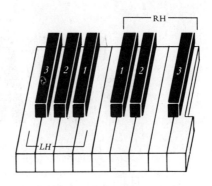

## EVERY TIME I FEEL THE SPIRIT

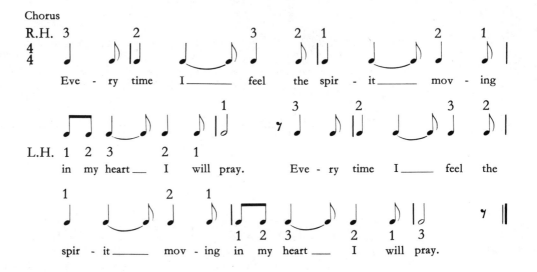

Chorus

R.H.

Eve - ry time I___ feel the spir - it___ mov - ing

L.H.

in my heart___ I will pray. Eve - ry time I___ feel the

spir - it___ mov - ing in my heart___ I will pray.

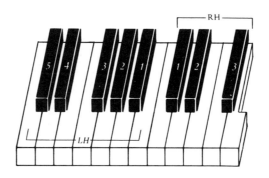

## FROG WENT A-COURTING

English

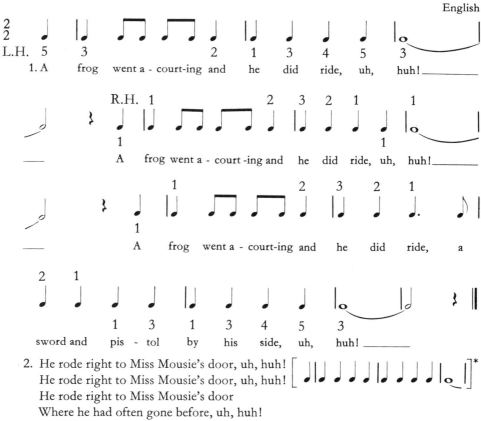

2. He rode right to Miss Mousie's door, uh, huh!
   He rode right to Miss Mousie's door, uh, huh!
   He rode right to Miss Mousie's door
   Where he had often gone before, uh, huh!

3. He took Miss Mousie on his knee, uh, huh! (repeat twice)
   Said, "Miss Mousie, will you marry me?" uh, huh! etc.

4. "Without my Uncle Rat's consent, uh, huh! (repeat twice)
   I couldn't marry the president!" uh, huh! etc.

5. Uncle Rat gave his consent, uh, huh! (repeat twice)
   So they got married and off they went, uh, huh! etc.

* Though there are rhythmic changes from verse to verse (such as in verse 2), the basic melody remains the same.

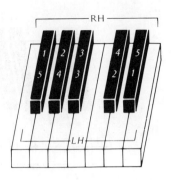

# [GAMES PEOPLE PLAY]

Words and Music by Joe South

R.H. 3      2 1              3      2  1 2

L.H. 3      4 5              3      4  5 4

Oh, the games peo-ple play    now,      ev-'ry night and ev-'ry  day,    now.

3      4 3  5              3      2  1 2
3      2 3  1              3      4  5

Ne-ver mean-in' what they  say,    now.   Nev-er say-in' what they mean.

3      2 1              3      2 1 2
3      4 5              3      4 5 4

And they while a - way the ho  - urs      in their i - vo-ry  tow - ers,

3      4 3  5      3 4 5  3 4 5  3 2 1
3      2 3  1      3 2 1  3 2 1  3 4 5

'Til they're cov-ered up with flow - ers,  in the back of  a  black lim-ou-sine.

# [GET ON BOARD]

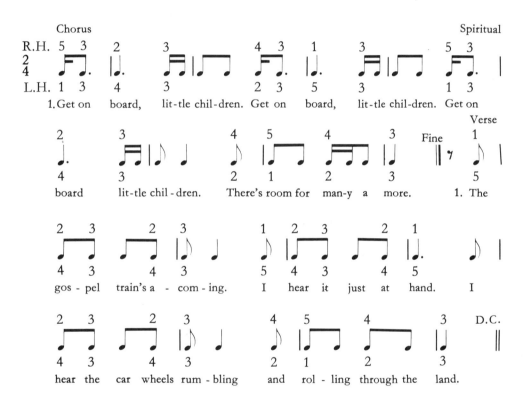

Chorus ... Spiritual

R.H. 5 3 / 2 / 3 / 4 3 1 / 3 / 5 3

L.H. 1 3 / 4 / 3 / 2 3 5 / 3 / 1 3

1. Get on board, lit-tle chil-dren. Get on board, lit-tle chil-dren. Get on

2 / 3 / 4 5 4 3 Fine / Verse 1

4 / 3 / 2 1 2 3 / 5

board lit-tle chil-dren. There's room for man-y a more. 1. The

2 3 / 2 3 / 1 2 3 2 1

4 3 / 4 3 / 5 4 3 4 5

gos - pel train's a - com - ing. I hear it just at hand. I

2 3 / 2 3 / 4 5 4 3 D.C.

4 3 / 4 3 / 2 1 2 3

hear the car wheels rum - bling and rol - ling through the land.

2. I hear the train a-coming, a-coming round the curve.
   She loosened all her steam and brakes, she's straining every nerve.

3. The fare is cheap and all can go, the rich and poor are there.
   No second class aboard this train, no difference in the fare.

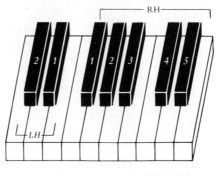

## GOODBYE OLD PAINT

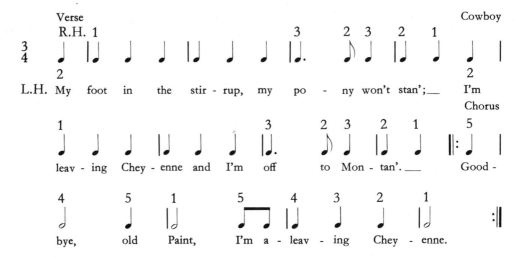

Verse
R.H. 1                            3       2   3   2   1          Cowboy

2
L.H. My   foot   in   the   stir - rup,   my   po  -   ny   won't   stan';___   I'm

Chorus

1                        3       2   3   2   1      5

leav - ing   Chey - enne   and   I'm   off      to   Mon - tan'. ___     Good -

4      5      1        5      4      3      2      1

bye,      old      Paint,     I'm a - leav - ing   Chey - enne.

* In Appendix A, Lesson 5, Performance Objective 4, Procedures 1–4, use the white key pentatonic scale which is shown by the finger numbers on the front edge of the white keys.

294

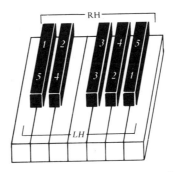

[HOLE IN THE BUCKET]

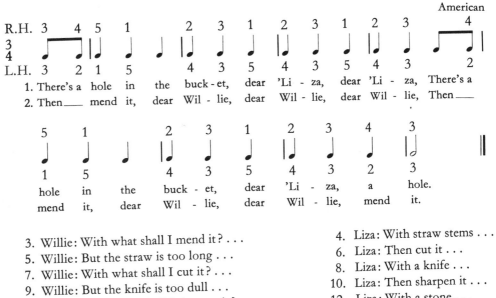

American

1. There's a hole in the buck-et, dear 'Li - za, dear 'Li - za, There's a
2. Then___ mend it, dear Wil - lie, dear Wil - lie, dear Wil - lie, Then___

hole in the buck-et, dear 'Li - za, a hole.
mend it, dear Wil - lie, dear Wil - lie, mend it.

3. Willie: With what shall I mend it? . . .
5. Willie: But the straw is too long . . .
7. Willie: With what shall I cut it? . . .
9. Willie: But the knife is too dull . . .
11. Willie: With what shall I sharpen it? . . .
13. Willie: But the stone is too dry . . .
15. Willie: With what shall I wet it? . . .
17. Willie: In what shall I carry it? . . .
19. Willie: There's a hole in the bucket . . .

4. Liza: With straw stems . . .
6. Liza: Then cut it . . .
8. Liza: With a knife . . .
10. Liza: Then sharpen it . . .
12. Liza: With a stone . . .
14. Liza: Then wet it . . .
16. Liza: With water . . .
18. Liza: In a bucket . . .

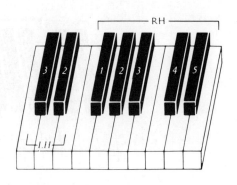

# LITTLE DAVID, PLAY ON YOUR HARP

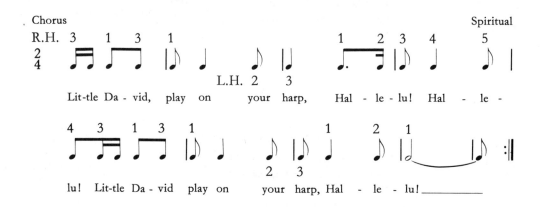

Chorus

Spiritual

R.H. 3  1  3  1            1  2  3  4    5

L.H. 2   3

Lit-tle Da - vid,  play  on    your harp,    Hal - le - lu!  Hal - le -

4  3  1  3  1            1  2  1

2  3

lu!  Lit-tle Da - vid  play  on    your harp, Hal - le - lu!_____

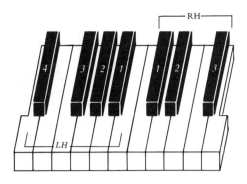

## LITTLE WHEEL A-TURNING

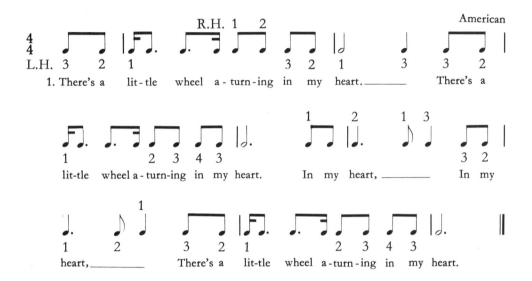

American

R.H. 1 2

4/4

L.H. 3 2 1    3 2 1    3    3 2

1. There's a lit-tle wheel a-turn-ing in my heart._____ There's a

1    2 3 4 3    1 2    1 3    3 2

lit-tle wheel a-turn-ing in my heart. In my heart,_____ In my

1    1 2    3 2 1    2 3 4 3

heart,_____ There's a lit-tle wheel a-turn-ing in my heart.

2. There's a little song a-singing in my heart . . . etc.
3. There's a happy feeling beating in my heart . . . etc.
4. Oh, I feel just like a-shouting in my heart . . . etc.

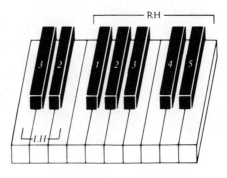

## LONESOME VALLEY

Spiritual

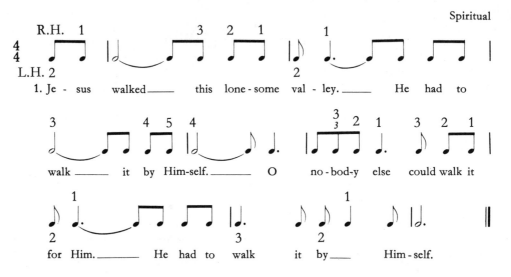

1. Je - sus walked—— this lone - some val - ley.—— He had to walk—— it by Him-self.—— O no-bod-y else could walk it for Him.—— He had to walk it by—— Him - self.

2. We must walk this lonesome valley, we have to walk it by ourselves.
   O nobody else can walk it for us. We have to walk it by ourselves.

3. You must go and stand your trial; you have to stand it by yourself.
   O nobody else can stand it for you; you have to stand it by yourself.

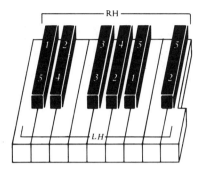 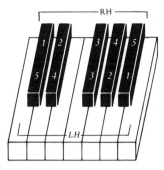

[NOBODY KNOWS THE TROUBLE I'VE SEEN]

Chorus                                                                                    Spiritual

R.H. 5  1   2  3    4  5
4
4
L.H. 1  5   4  3    2  1

No-bod - y  knows  the trou - ble I've  seen,

1   2  3    2  1

5   4  3    4  5

No-bod - y  knows but Je - sus.

5  1   2  3    4  5

1  5   4  3    2  1

No-bod - y  knows  the trou - ble I've  seen,

⑤   5  4  5  3

①   1  2  1  3

glo - ry  hal - le - lu - jah!

* Circled numbers represent the higher set of fingerings (see diagram above).

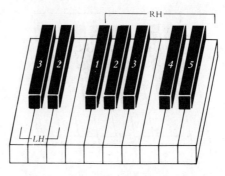

## SWING LOW, SWEET CHARIOT

Spiritual

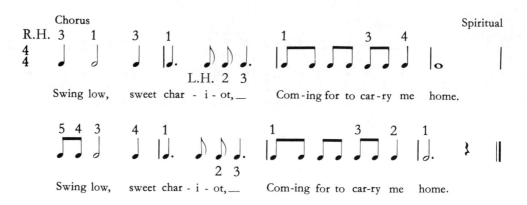

Swing low, sweet char - i - ot, __ Com-ing for to car -ry me home.

Swing low, sweet char - i - ot, __ Com-ing for to car -ry me home.

# Appendix C  Songs

This song repertoire combines familiar popular songs and contemporary children's songs with more traditional folk songs, spirituals, hymns, fun and game songs, seasonal songs, nursery songs, and rounds. Primary considerations in selecting the songs included musical and lyrical appeal, ease of performance (many songs need only one or two chords for harmonization), adaptability for use with the lesson plans of Appendix A, and practical application to the elementary school classroom. Though supplementary song texts are useful and have been recommended, the number and variety of song materials in Appendix C are more than sufficient to provide consistent activity and enjoyment for the student of music.

## AMAZING GRACE!

I Chronicles 17:16–17
John Newton, 1723–1807

Early American Melody

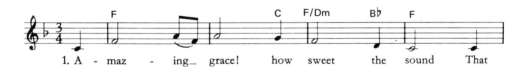

1. A - maz - ing_ grace! how sweet the sound That

saved a_ wretch like me! I once___ was_ lost, but

now___ am_ found, Was blind, but_ now I see.

2. 'Twas grace that taught my heart to fear,
   And grace my fears relieved;
   How precious did that grace appear
   The hour I first believed!

3. Through many dangers, toils, and snares,
   I have already come;
   'Tis grace hath brought me safe thus far,
   And grace will lead me home.

4. The Lord has promised good to me,
   His word my hope secures;
   He will my shield and portion be
   As long as life endures.

5. Yea, when this flesh and heart shall fail,
   And mortal life shall cease,
   I shall possess, within the veil,
   A life of joy and peace.

# THE ANIMAL FAIR

Traditional

I went to the an-i-mal fair, _____ The birds and the beasts were
The fun-ni-est was ___ the monk, ___ He climbed up the el-e-phant's

there, _____ The old ra-coon, by the light of the moon, Was
trunk, _____

comb-ing her au-burn hair. _____ The el-e-phant sneezed and

fell on his knees, And what be-came of the monk? _____

# ARE YOU SLEEPING?

French Round

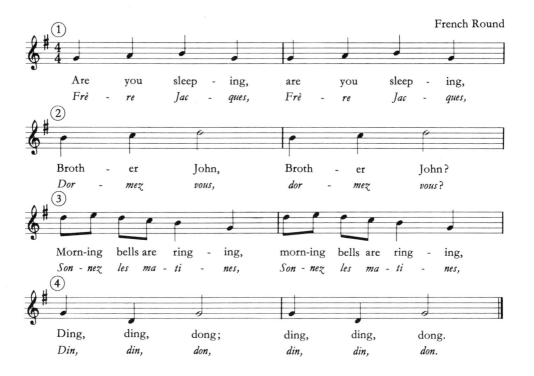

① Are you sleep - ing, are you sleep - ing,
*Frè - re Jac - ques, Frè - re Jac - ques,*

② Broth - er John, Broth - er John?
*Dor - mez vous, dor - mez vous?*

③ Morn-ing bells are ring - ing, morn-ing bells are ring - ing,
*Son - nez les ma - ti - nes, Son - nez les ma - ti - nes,*

④ Ding, ding, dong; ding, ding, dong.
*Din, din, don, din, din, don.*

# BARNYARD SONG

Kentucky Mountain Song

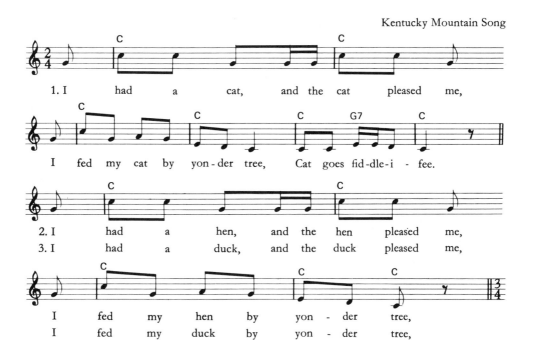

1. I had a cat, and the cat pleased me,
I fed my cat by yon-der tree, Cat goes fid-dle-i - fee.

2. I had a hen, and the hen pleased me,
3. I had a duck, and the duck pleased me,

I fed my hen by yon - der tree,
I fed my duck by yon - der tree,

Hen goes chim-my chuck, chim-my chuck, Cat goes fid-dle-i-fee.
Duck goes quack,____ quack,____

4. Goose goes swishy, swashy. Duck goes quack, quack. Hen goes chimmy chuck, etc.
5. Sheep goes baa, baa. Goose goes swishy, swashy. Duck goes quack, quack, etc.
6. Add other animals (e.g. dog goes bow, wow. Sheep goes baa, baa. Goose goes, etc).

## BOW, BOW, O BELINDA

American Singing Game

1. Bow, bow, O Be-lin-da, Bow, bow, O Be-lin-da,

Bow, bow, O Be-lin-da, Won't you be my dar-ling?

2. Smile, smile, O Belinda, etc.
3. Say yes, O Belinda, etc.
4. From now on, Belinda, etc.
5. Add other verses.

## CHILDREN'S PRAYER

Engelbert Humperdinck (1854–1921)
Words by Ardelheid Wette

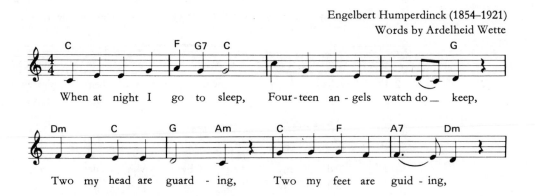

When at night I go to sleep, Four-teen an-gels watch do__ keep,

Two my head are guard-ing, Two my feet are guid-ing,

Two are on my right hand, Two are on my left hand,

Two who warm-ly cov - er, Two who o'er me hov - er,

Two to whom 'tis giv - en to guide my steps to hea - - ven.

## DEAF WOMAN'S COURTSHIP

American

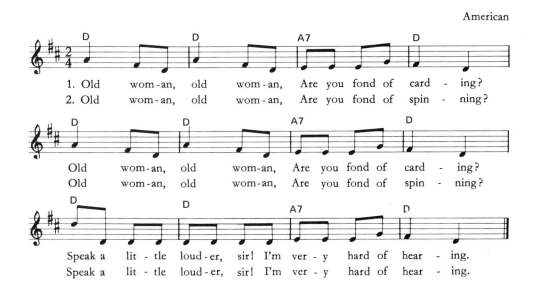

1. Old wom-an, old wom-an, Are you fond of card - ing?
2. Old wom-an, old wom-an, Are you fond of spin - ning?

Old wom-an, old wom-an, Are you fond of card - ing?
Old wom-an, old wom-an, Are you fond of spin - ning?

Speak a lit - tle loud - er, sir! I'm ver - y hard of hear - ing.
Speak a lit - tle loud - er, sir! I'm ver - y hard of hear - ing.

3. Old woman, old woman, Will you darn my stocking? (*twice*)
   Speak a little louder, sir! I'm very hard of hearing.

4. Old woman, old woman, Will you let me court you? (*twice*)
   Speak a little louder, sir! I just begin to hear you.

5. Old woman, old woman, Don't you want to marry me? (*twice*)
   Oh, my goodness gracious me! I think that now I hear you!

# DONA NOBIS PACEM
## (Give Us Peace)

Traditional Round

# DOWN BY THE STATION

Traditional Round

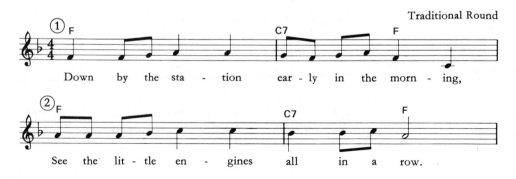

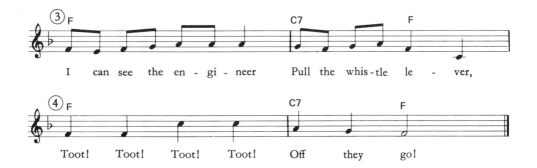

I can see the en - gi - neer Pull the whis-tle le - ver,

Toot! Toot! Toot! Toot! Off they go!

## THE ELEPHANTS

Traditional

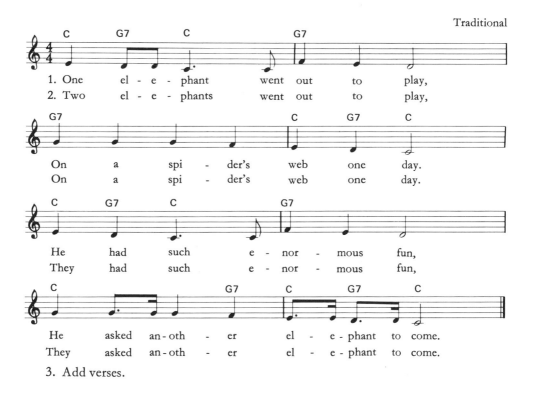

1. One el - e - phant went out to play,
2. Two el - e - phants went out to play,

On a spi - der's web one day.
On a spi - der's web one day.

He had such e - nor - mous fun,
They had such e - nor - mous fun,

He asked an - oth - er el - e - phant to come.
They asked an - oth - er el - e - phant to come.

3. Add verses.

## THE FARMER IN THE DELL

English

1. The far - mer in the dell,____ The far - mer in the dell,

Hi! ho! the der - ry oh, The far - mer in the dell. ____

2. The farmer takes a wife . . .
3. The wife takes the child . . .
4. The child takes the nurse . . .
5. The nurse takes the dog . . .

6. The dog takes the cat . . .
7. The cat takes the rat . . .
8. The rat takes the cheese . . .
9. The cheese stands alone . . .

## GAMES PEOPLE PLAY

Words and Music by Joe South

Oh, the games peo-ple play now, ev-'ry night and ev-'ry
oth - er cry; Break a heart then we
to you, Sing-in' Glo-ry Hal-le-
what you see What's hap-pen-in' to

day, now. Nev - er mean-in' what they say, now.
say good-bye; Cross our hearts and we hope to die.
lu - jah! and they're try'n' to sock it to you.
you and me. God grant me the se - ren - i - ty,

Nev-er say-in' what they mean. And they while a - way the
That the oth - er was to blame. Nei - ther one will ev - er
In the name of the Lord. They gon - na teach you how to
To re - mem-ber who I am. 'Cause you're giv - in' up your

ho - urs In their i - vo - ry tow - ers,
give in. So, we gaze at an eight by ten,
me - di - tate; Read your hor - o - scope, cheat your fate,
san - i - ty For your pride and your van - i - ty,

'Til they're cov - ered up with flow - - ers, In the
Think-in' 'bout the things that might have been ____
And fur - ther - more to hell with hate ____
Turn your back on hu - man - i - ty. ____

308

back of a black lim-ou-sine.
____ it's a dir-ty rot-ten shame.
____ Come__ on__ get on board.
____ And you don't give a da, da, da, da, da.
} La, da, da, da,

**Chorus**

da, da, da. La, da, da, da, da, da, dee.

Talk-in' 'bout you and me. And the games peo-ple play.

1.2.3.
2. Oh, we make one an-
3. Peo-ple walk-in' up
4. Look a-round, tell me

4.
La, da, da, da.

D. S. and fade out

# GOD BLESS ALL

Two Part Round

① God bless all Good friends here, A

② mer - ry mer - ry Christ-mas and a Hap - py New Year!

# GRANDMA JONES

North Carolina Mountain Song

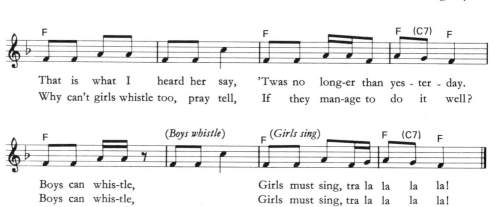

1. Grand-ma Jones said a cu-ri-ous thing, "Boys can whis-tle, but girls must sing."
2. Boys can whis-tle, of course they may, They can whis-tle the live long day.

That is what I heard her say, 'Twas no long-er than yes-ter-day.
Why can't girls whistle too, pray tell, If they man-age to do it well?

*(Boys whistle)* *(Girls sing)*

Boys can whis-tle, Girls must sing, tra la la la la!
Boys can whis-tle, Girls must sing, tra la la la la!

# GREEN GROW THE LILACS

Texas Folk Song

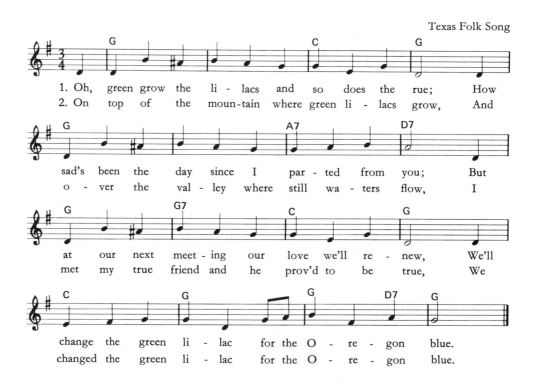

1. Oh, green grow the li-lacs and so does the rue; How
2. On top of the moun-tain where green li-lacs grow, And

sad's been the day since I par-ted from you; But
o-ver the val-ley where still wa-ters flow, I

at our next meet-ing our love we'll re-new, We'll
met my true friend and he prov'd to be true, We

change the green li-lac for the O-re-gon blue.
changed the green li-lac for the O-re-gon blue.

# GREENSLEEVES

English

1. A-las   my love_ you do   me wrong, To cast   me off__ dis-court-eous-ly;   And

I   have loved you for   so long, De-light-ing in__ your com-pan-y.

**Chorus**

Green - sleeves was all   my joy, ____ Green - sleeves was my   de - light,

Green - sleeves was my heart of gold, And who but my lad - y Green - sleeves.

2. I long have waited at your hand
   To do your bidding as your slave,
   And waged, have I, both life and land
   Your love and affection for to have.

3. If you intend thus to disdain
   It does the more enrapture me,
   And even so, I will remain
   Your lover in captivity.

4. Alas, my love, that yours should be
   A heart of faithless vanity,
   So here I meditate alone
   Upon your insincerity.

5. Ah, Greensleeves, now farewell, adieu,
   To God I pray to prosper thee,
   For I remain thy lover true,
   Come once again and be with me.

# HE'S GOT THE WHOLE WORLD IN HIS HANDS

Spiritual

1. He's got the whole world in His hands, He's got the whole world in His hands, He's got the whole world in His hands, He's got the whole world in His hands.

2. He's got the wind and rain in His hands . . .
3. He's got every little baby in His hands . . .
4. He's got you and me, brother, in His hands . . .
   He's got you and me, sister, in His hands . . .
5. He's got everybody in His hands . . .
6. He's got the whole world in His hands . . .

# HI, HO! ANYBODY HOME?

English Round

Hi, ho! An - y - bod - y home?

Meat and drink and mon - ey have I none;

Still I will be mer - ry!

# HOKEY POKEY

American Play Party Song

1. You put your right foot in,— You take your right foot out,— You put your right foot in— And shake it all a-bout, And then you do the hok-ey pok-ey And you turn your-self a-bout, And that's what it's all a-bout.

2. left foot, etc.
3. right hand, etc.
4. left hand, etc.
5. right shoulder, etc.
6. left shoulder, etc.
7. whole self, etc.

# HUSH, LITTLE BABY

Traditional

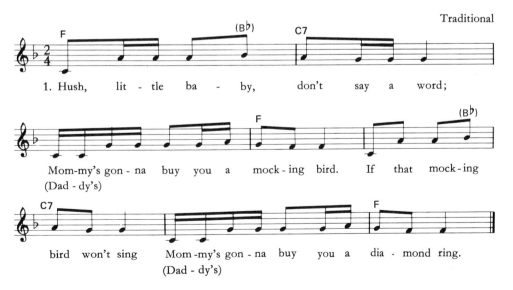

1. Hush, lit-tle ba-by, don't say a word;
(Dad-dy's)
Mom-my's gon-na buy you a mock-ing bird. If that mock-ing
(Dad-dy's)
bird won't sing Mom-my's gon-na buy you a dia-mond ring.

2. If that diamond ring turns brass
   Mommy's gonna buy you a looking glass;
   If that looking glass gets broke
   Mommy's gonna buy you a billy goat.

3. If that billy goat's too smart,
   Mommy's gonna buy you a horse and cart;
   If that horse and cart break down,
   Mommy's gonna buy you a long nightgown.

## I LEFT MY HEART IN SAN FRANCISCO

Words by Douglass Cross
Music by George Cory

## IF I SING AHEAD OF YOU

Hungarian Round

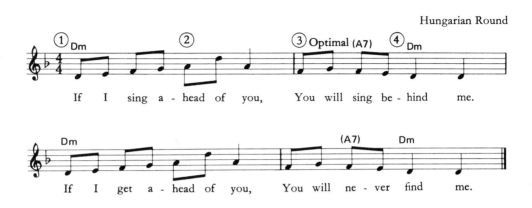

If I sing a - head of you, You will sing be - hind me.

If I get a - head of you, You will ne - ver find me.

## I'M GONNA SING

Spiritual

1. I'm gon-na sing when the spir-it says, "sing," I'm gon-na sing when the spir-it says, "sing,"_____ I'm gon-na sing when the spir-it says, "sing," And o - bey the spir-it of the Lord.

2. I'm gonna shout, etc.
3. I'm gonna preach, etc.
4. I'm gonna pray, etc.
5. I'm gonna jump, etc.
6. I'm gonna cry, etc.
7. Add verses.

# IN MY CLASS

Music and Lyrics by Alfred Balkin

In my class there are chil - dren much tall - er than I am.

In my class there are chil - dren much small - er than I am.

There are chil - dren whose skin's not the col - or of

my skin. There are chil - dren who come from far off

plac - es where I've nev - er been. In my class man - y

chil - dren use words I can - not say.

In my class there are chil - dren who don't pray like I pray.

In my class I have fun with ev - 'ry - one,

In my class ev - 'ry day.

* Alternative ending.

From "We Live in the City" by Al Balkin. © copyright 1970 Theodore Presser Company. Used by permission.

# IT'S UP TO YOU AND ME

Words by Jill Jackson

Music by Sy Miller

Coda

rit.
Peace on earth It's up to you _____ and

me. It's up to you and me. It's up to you and me. It's up to you and

## JINGLE BELLS

James Pierpont

Jin - gle bells, Jin - gle bells, Jin - gle all the

way, Oh, what fun it is to ride in a

one horse o - pen sleigh! Oh! one horse o - pen sleigh!

## JOHNNY HAS GONE FOR A SOLDIER

American

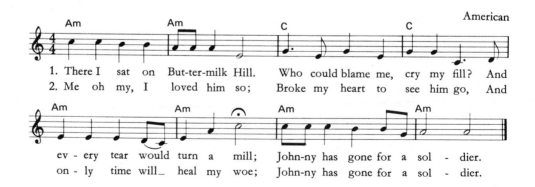

1. There I sat on But-ter-milk Hill. Who could blame me, cry my fill? And
2. Me oh my, I loved him so; Broke my heart to see him go, And

ev - ery tear would turn a mill; John-ny has gone for a sol - dier.
on - ly time will_ heal my woe; John-ny has gone for a sol - dier.

318

# KOOKABURRA

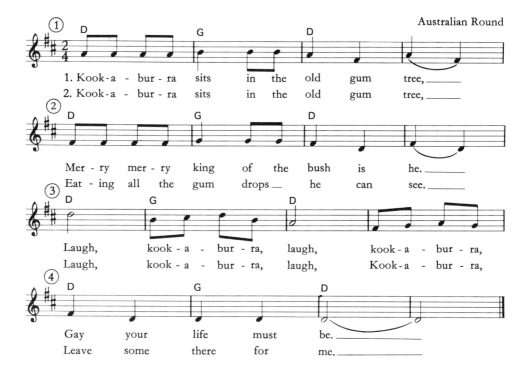

Australian Round

1. Kook-a-bur-ra sits in the old gum tree,_____
2. Kook-a-bur-ra sits in the old gum tree,_____

Mer-ry mer-ry king of the bush is he._____
Eat-ing all the gum drops he can see.

Laugh, kook-a-bur-ra, laugh, kook-a-bur-ra,
Laugh, kook-a-bur-ra, laugh, Kook-a-bur-ra,

Gay your life must be._____
Leave some there for me._____

# LET THERE BE PEACE ON EARTH
## (Let It Begin With Me)

Slowly

Sy Miller and Jill Jackson

Let there be peace on earth And let it be-gin with

me;_____ Let there be peace on earth, The

peace that was meant to be._____ With God as our

Fa-ther,_____ Broth-ers all are we._____

Let me walk with my broth-er_____ In per-fect har-mo-

ny. ____ Let peace be - gin with me, Let

this be the mo - ment now. ____ With ev - 'ry

step I take, Let this be my sol - emn vow: ____ To

take each mo - ment and live each mo - ment In peace e - ter - nal -

ly. ____ Let there be peace on earth And

1. let it be - gin with me. 2. Let it be - gin with me. ____

## LITTLE DUCKS

Traditional

1. Six lit - tle ducks that I once knew,
2. Down to the riv - er they would go,

Fat ones, skin - ny ones, fair ones too,
Wibble, wobble, wib - ble, wobble to and fro,

But the

one lit - tle duck with a feath - er in his back,

He led the oth-ers with a quack, quack, quack, quack, quack, quack.

He led the oth-ers with a quack, quack, quack, quack, quack, quack.

## LITTLE RED CABOOSE

Camp Song

Lit-tle red ca - boose, chug, chug, chug; Lit-tle red ca - boose, chug, chug, chug,

Lit-tle red ca - boose be - hind the train, train, train, train,

Smoke-stack on its back, back, back, back, Com-in' down the track, track, track, track,

Lit-tle red ca - boose be - hind the train, chug, chug.

## LOOBY LOO

English

Here we go loo - by loo, Here we go loo - by light,

Here we go loo - by loo, All on a Sat - ur - day night.____

1. I put my right hand in, ___ I take my right hand out, ___ I

give my hand a shake, shake, shake, And turn my-self a - bout. Oh,

2. left hand
3. right foot
4. left foot
5. big head
6. whole self

## LOVELY EVENING

Traditional Round

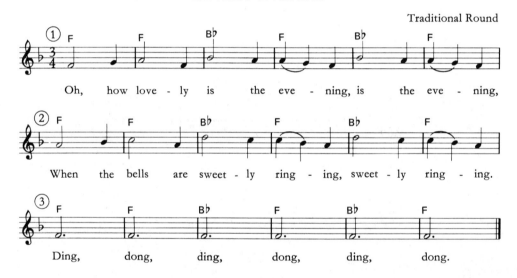

Oh, how love - ly is the eve - ning, is the eve - ning,

When the bells are sweet - ly ring - ing, sweet - ly ring - ing.

Ding, dong, ding, dong, ding, dong.

## MARY AND MARTHA

Spiritual

Ma-ry and a Mar - tha's just gone 'long,

Ma-ry and a Mar - tha's just gone 'long, Ma-ry and a Mar - tha's

322

just gone 'long, To ring those charm-ing bells; Cry - ing

1. Free grace, un - dy - ing love, Free grace, un -
2. Way o - ver Jor - dan, Lord, Way o - ver

dy - ing love, Free grace, un - dy - ing love, To
Jor - dan, Lord, Way o - ver Jor - dan, Lord, to

ring those charm - ing bells, Oh! bells!

## THE MORE WE GET TOGETHER

German

The more we get to - geth - er, to - geth - er, to - geth - er, The

more we get to - geth - er, the hap - pier we'll be. For

your friends are my friends and my friends are your friends, The

more we get to - geth - er, the hap - pier we'll be.

323

# MORNING HAS BROKEN

Words by E. Farjeon

Music adapted by Cat Stevens

rit. _ _ _ _

Morn-ing has
bro - ken    Like the first_ morn - ing,    Black-bird has
new    fall    Sun - lit from    hea - - ven,    Like the first
spo - ken    Like the first_ bird.    Praise for the
dew    fall    On the first_ grass.    Praise for the
sing - ing!    Praise for the morn - - ing!    Praise for them
sweet - ness    Of the wet gar - - den,    Sprung in com -
spring - ing    Fresh from the word.
plete - ness    Where his feet pass.

1.
Sweet the rain's

2.
Mine is the
sun - light!    Mine is the morn - ing    Born of the
one    light    E - den saw play!    Praise with e -

la - tion     Praise ev -'ry morn - - ing,     God's re - cre -

a - tion     Of the new     day!

Morn-ing has

## O HANUKAH

Jewish Folk Song
Translated by Judith Eisenstein

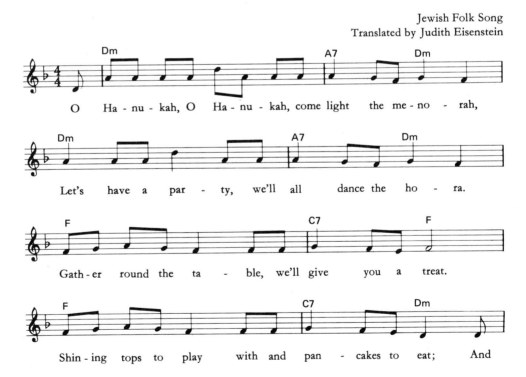

O Ha - nu - kah, O Ha - nu - kah, come light the me - no - rah,

Let's have a par - ty, we'll all dance the ho - ra.

Gath - er round the ta - ble, we'll give you a treat.

Shin - ing tops to play with and pan - cakes to eat;     And

while we are play-ing the can-dles are burn-ing low.

One for each night, they___ shed a sweet light To re-

1. mind us of days long a-go.    2. mind us of days long a-go.

## OLD HUNDRED

Words by William Kethe, 1561
Music by Louis Bourgeois, 1551

1. All peo - ple that on earth do dwell,
2. The Lord, ye know, is God in - deed;

Sing to the Lord with cheer - ful voice;
With - out our aid He did us make;

Him serve with fear, His praise forth - tell;
We are His flock, He doth us feed,

Come ye be - fore Him and re - joice.
And for His sheep He doth us take.

3. Oh, enter then His gates with praise,
   Approach with joy His courts unto:
   Praise, laud, and bless His name always,
   For it is seemly so to do.

326

# THIS OLD MAN

English Action Song

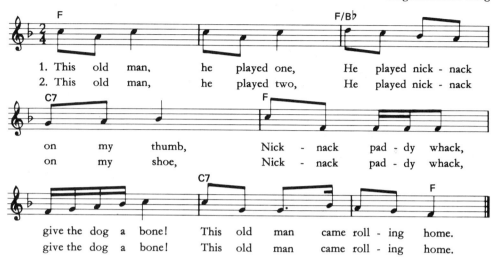

3. This old man, he played three,
   He played nick-nack on my knee, etc.
4. This old man, he played four,
   He played nick-nack on my door, etc.
5. This old man, he played five,
   He played nick-nack on my side, etc.
6. This old man, he played six,
   He played nick-nack on my sticks, etc.
7. This old man, he played sev'n
   He played nick-nack up in heav'n, etc.
8. This old man, he played eight,
   He played nick-nack on my gate, etc.
9. This old man, he played nine,
   He played nick-nack on my spine, etc.
10. This old man, he played ten,
    He played nick-nack once again, etc.

# PEOPLE RUSHING

Music and Lyrics by Alfred Balkin

327

Here, there, Ev-'ry-where. Peo-ple rush-ing to, Peo-ple rush-ing fro.

To and fro, To and fro, Peo-ple on the go. Where are those peo - ple

rush - ing? _____ I don't know!

*p molto cresc.*      *ff*      *f*

From "We Live in the City" by Al Balkin. © copyright 1970 Theodore Presser Company. Used by permission.

## PLAYING IN THE PARK

Music and Lyrics by Alfred Balkin

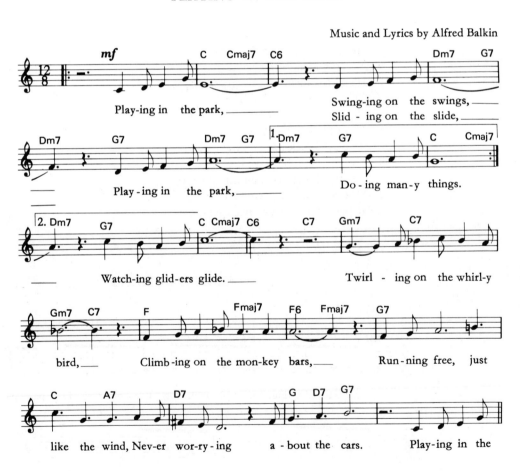

Play-ing in the park, _____ Swing-ing on the swings, _____
Slid - ing on the slide, _____

_____ Play-ing in the park, _____ Do-ing man-y things.

_____ Watch-ing glid-ers glide. _____ Twirl - ing on the whirl-y

bird, _____ Climb-ing on the mon-key bars, _____ Run-ning free, just

like the wind, Nev-er wor-ry-ing a - bout the cars. Play-ing in the

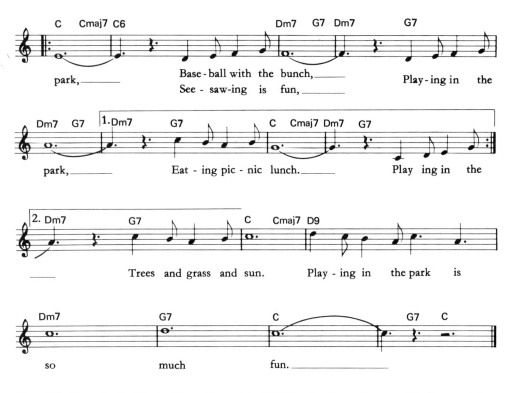

park,_____ Base-ball with the bunch,_____ Play-ing in the
See-saw-ing is fun,_____

park,_____ Eat-ing pic-nic lunch._____ Play ing in the

Trees and grass and sun. Play-ing in the park is

so much fun._____

From "We Live in the City" by Al Balkin. © copyright 1970 Theodore Presser Company. Used by permission.

## ROCKA MY SOUL

Spiritual

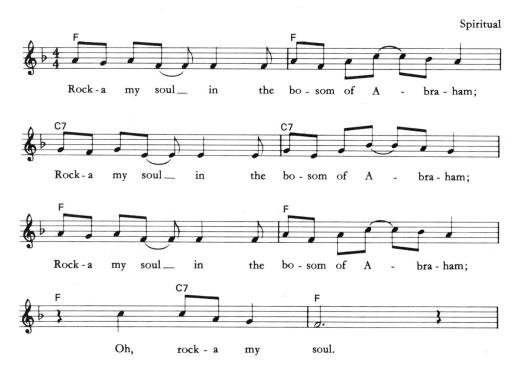

Rock-a my soul__ in the bo-som of A - bra-ham;

Rock-a my soul__ in the bo-som of A - bra-ham;

Rock-a my soul__ in the bo-som of A - bra-ham;

Oh, rock-a my soul.

So high you can't get o-ver it; So low you can't get un-der it;

So wide you can't get a-round it; You must go in at the door.

\* After singing the song once through, the last eight measures ("So high", etc.) may be sung at the same time as the first eight to make a two part song.

## SARASPONDA

Dutch Spinning Song

Sa - ra - spon-da, Sa - ra - spon-da, Sa - ra - spon-da, Ret-set-set! Sa - ra -

spon-da, Sa - ra - spon-da, Sa - ra - spon-da, Ret-set-set! Ah -

do - ray - oh! Ah - do - ray - boom-day - oh! Ah -

do - ray - boom-day ret - set - set! Aw - say - paw - say - oh!

# SCARBOROUGH FAIR

Adaptation by Albert Gamse

1. Are you go - ing to Scar - bo - rough Fair?
2. Have him make me a cam - bric shirt,
3. Have him wash it in yon - der dry well,

Pars - ley, sage, _____ rose-ma - ry and thyme. Re -
Pars - ley, sage, _____ rose-ma - ry and thyme. With -
Pars - ley, sage, _____ rose-ma - ry and thyme. Where

mem ber me to one who lives there, _____ For
out a seam or fine need - le work, _____ And
ne'er a drop of wa - ter e'er fell, _____ And

once he was a true love of mine.
then he'll be a true love of mine.
then he'll be a true love of mine.

4. Have him find me an acre of land,
   Parsley, sage, rosemary and thyme,
   Between the sea and over the sand,
   And then he'll be a true love of mine.

5. Plow the land with the horn of a lamb,
   Parsley, sage, rosemary and thyme,
   Then sow some seeds from north of the dam,
   And then he'll be a true love of mine.

6. If he tells me he can't, I'll reply:
   "Parsley, sage, rosemary and thyme."
   Let me know that at least he will try,
   And then he'll be a true love of mine.

7. Love imposes impossible tasks,
   Parsley, sage, rosemary and thyme,
   Though not more than any heart asks,
   And I must know he's a true love of mine.

8. Dear, when thou hast finished thy task,
   Parsley, sage, rosemary and thyme.
   Come to me, my hand for to ask,
   For thou then art a true love of mine.

Words and rhythm used by permission of Lewis Music Publishing Co., Inc.

## SIMPLE GIFTS

Shaker Hymn

'Tis the gift to be sim - ple, 'Tis the gift to be free, 'Tis the

gift to come down where we ought to be, And

when we find our - selves— in the place just— right, 'Twill—

be in the val - ley of love and de - light.

When true sim - pli - ci - ty is gained, To bow and to bend we—

shan't be a - shamed, To turn, turn will

be our de - light, Till by turn - ing, turn - ing we come round right.

# STREETS OF LAREDO

Cowboy Song

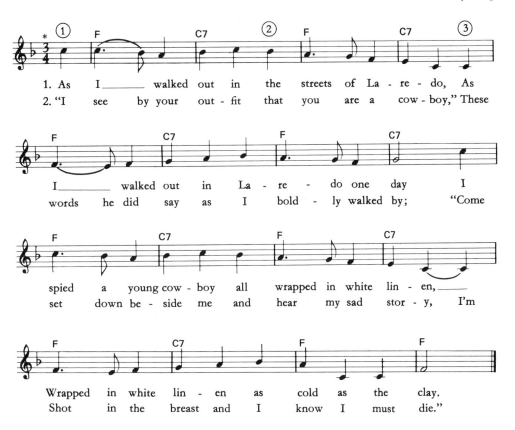

1. As I_____ walked out in the streets of La - re - do, As
2. "I see by your out - fit that you are a cow - boy," These

I_____ walked out in La - re - do one day I
words he did say as I bold - ly walked by; "Come

spied a young cow - boy all wrapped in white lin - en,_____
set down be - side me and hear my sad stor - y, I'm

Wrapped in white lin - en as cold as the clay.
Shot in the breast and I know I must die."

3. "It was once in the saddle I used to go dashing,
   Once in the saddle I used to go gay;
   First down to Rosie's and then to the card-house;
   Got shot in the breast and I'm dyin' today.

4. "Get sixteen gamblers to handle my coffin,
   Let six jolly cowboys come sing me a song,
   Take me to the graveyard and lay the sod o'er me,
   For I'm a young cowboy, I know I've done wrong.

5. "Oh, beat the drum slowly and play the fife lowly,
   Play the dead march as they carry me along,
   Put bunches of roses all over my coffin,
   Roses to deaden the clods as they fall."

6. Repeat Verse 1.

* Not a round but can be harmonized by following round procedure every two measures as shown at ①,
② and ③.

333

## SHALOM, CHAVERIM
### (Farewell, Good Friends)

Israeli Round

Sha - lom, cha-ve - rim! Sha - lom, cha-ve - rim! Sha - lom, sha - lom! Le -
Fare-well, good friends, Fare-well, good friends, Fare-well, fare - well! Till we

hit - ra - ot, le - hit - ra - ot, Sha - lom, sha - lom!
meet a - gain, till we meet a - gain, Fare - well, fare - well!

## SING TOGETHER

English Round

Sing, sing to - geth - er, Mer - ri - ly, mer - ri - ly sing;

Sing, sing to - geth - er, Mer - ri - ly, mer - ri - ly sing;

Sing, sing, sing, sing!

## SUNDAY IN THE CITY

Music and Lyrics by Alfred Balkin

Sun - day in the cit - y is qui - et and slow, Not much

rush - ing or push - ing, to get where you want to go.

334

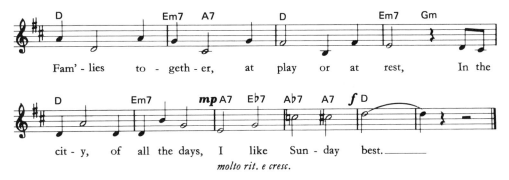

Fam' - lies to - geth - er, at play or at rest, In the

cit - y, of all the days, I like Sun - day best._____

*molto rit. e cresc.*

## SWEET BETSY FROM PIKE

Forty-niners' Song

1. Did you e - ver hear of sweet Bet - sy from Pike, Who
2. One eve - ning, quite ear - ly, they camp'd on the Platte, Up
3. 'Twas out on the de - sert that Bet - sy gave out, And

cross'd the wide prai - ries with her hus - band Ike, With
close to the road on a green gras - sy flat. Poor
down in the sand she lay rol - ling a - bout, Poor

two yoke of ox - en, a big yel - low dog, A___
Bet - sy, sore - foot - ed lay down to re - pose, And_
Ike, half dis - tract - ed, looked down in sur - prise, Say-ing

tall Shang - hai roost - er and one spot - ted hog. Sing-ing
Ike sat and gazed at his Pike Coun - ty rose.
"Bet - sy, get up, you'll get sand in your eyes!"

too - ra - lee, oo - ra - lee, too - ra - lee - ay.

4. They swam the wide rivers and crossed the high peaks,
   They camped on the prairie for weeks upon weeks,
   They fought with the Indians with musket and ball,
   And they reached California in spite of it all.
   Singing too-ra-lee, oo-ra-lee, too-ra-lee-ay.

335

## TALLIS' CANON

Words by Thomas Ken
Music by Thomas Tallis (1505–1585)
English

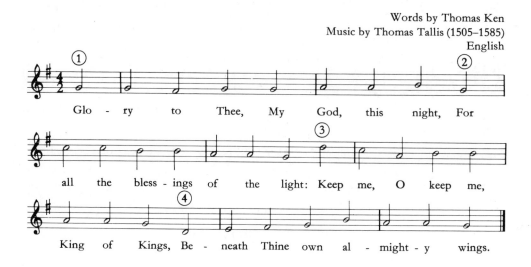

Glo - ry to Thee, My God, this night, For

all the bless - ings of the light: Keep me, O keep me,

King of Kings, Be - neath Thine own al - might - y wings.

## THANKSGIVING CANON

Traditional Canon

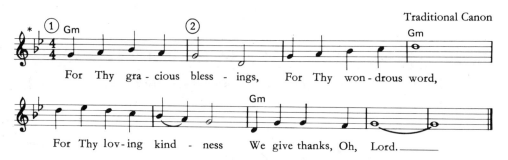

For Thy gra - cious bless - ings, For Thy won - drous word,

For Thy lov - ing kind - ness We give thanks, Oh, Lord._____

* In this two-part canon, repetition is immediate after each measure and continues throughout.

## WE WISH YOU A MERRY CHRISTMAS

Old English Carol

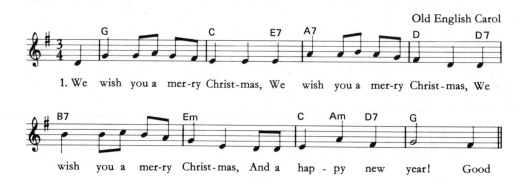

1. We wish you a mer-ry Christ-mas, We wish you a mer-ry Christ-mas, We

wish you a mer-ry Christ-mas, And a hap - py new year! Good

ti - dings to you! And all of your kin, Good

ti - dings for Christ - mas And a hap - py new year.

2. Oh, bring us some figgy pudding,
   Oh, bring us some figgy pudding,
   Oh, bring us some figgy pudding,
   And bring it out here!

3. We won't go until we got some,
   We won't go until we got some,
   We won't go until we got some,
   So bring some out here!

## WHAT SHALL WE DO ON A RAINY DAY?

1. What shall we do on a rain - y day,

rain - y day, rain - y day? What shall we do on a

rain - y day When we can't go out to play?

1. We can play games on a rainy day, etc.
2. We can sing songs on a rainy day, etc.
3. Create additional verses.

# WINDY

By Ruthann Friedman

1. Who's peek-in' out from un - der a stair - way call - ing a name that's
2. Who's trip - pin' down the streets of the ci - ty smil - in' at ev - 'ry -

light-er than air?  Who's bend-in' down to give me a rain - bow?
bod - y she sees?  Who's reach-ing out to cap-ture a mo - ment?

Ev - 'ry-one knows it's Wind - y.  Wind - y.  Wind - y.
Ev - 'ry-one knows it's

And Wind - y has storm - y eyes____ that flash_ at the

sound of lies.____ And Wind - y has wings to fly____

____ up a - bove clouds, up a - bove

clouds, up a - bove clouds, up a - bove clouds.

# Index of Musical Concepts

All terms have been indexed by frame numbers.

# Index of Vocabularies, Guidelines, and Rules

All references are to be frame numbers.

341

# Index of Songs

All songs in this index are listed by frame numbers, except for those songs found in Appendix B or C. Those songs are listed by page numbers.